CONTENTS

The Canterbury and York Society

GENERAL EDITOR: PROFESSOR R.L. STOREY

ISSN 0262-995X

DIOCESE OF NORWICH

CANTERBURY AND YORK SOCIETY VOL. XC

The Register of

William Bateman

BISHOP OF NORWICH

1344–1355

VOLUME II

EDITED BY

PHYLLIS E. POBST

ASSOCIATE PROFESSOR OF HISTORY
ARKANSAS STATE UNIVERSITY

The Canterbury and York Society

The Boydell Press
2000

First published 2000

A Canterbury and York Society publication
published by The Boydell Press
an imprint of Boydell & Brewer Ltd
PO Box 9, Woodbridge, Suffolk IP12 3DF, UK
and of Boydell & Brewer Inc.
PO Box 41026, Rochester, NY 14604–4126, USA
website: http://www.boydell.co.uk

ISBN 0 907239 60 9

A catalogue record for this book is available
from the British Library

Details of previous volumes available from Boydell & Brewer Ltd

This publication is printed on acid-free paper

Typeset by Joshua Associates Ltd, Oxford
Printed in Great Britain by
St Edmundsbury Press Ltd, Bury St Edmunds, Suffolk

ACKNOWLEDGMENTS

The Right Reverend P. J. Nott, Bishop of Norwich, gave permission to publish this register of his predecessor, William Bateman, for which I am grateful. To the extent that this edition meets the needs and standards of scholars, credit should be given those who were mentioned in the first volume, and especially Robin L. Storey, whose contribution is immeasurable.

ADDENDA ET CORRIGENDA

Vol. I

p.xi, *n.3, for* "another four were peculiars of the rector of Castle Rising, Norfolk, and eleven parishes . . ." *read* "another was the peculiar of the rector of Castle Rising, Norfolk, and seven parishes . . ."

p.16, **26**, *for* St George of Colegate *read* St George in Tombland

p.28, **53**, *for* Ryston *read* East Ruston

p.43, **147**, *for* Burgh St Peter [N] *read* Burgh Castle [S]; *add note*, John de Garboldisham of St Edmund was inst. 1339 (Reg. Bek fo.27).

p.64, **325**, *add note on Great Melton*, There were two parishes in this village, All Saints and St Mary; in 1338, Hugh Peverel was patron of All Saints (Reg. Bek fo.17^v). It is not clear which parish is indicated in **325**.

p.70, **375**, *n.72, for* **1779** *read* **1779***

p.71, **385-6**, *for* Denennys *read* Devennys

p.75, **419***, *n.4, for* **381** *read* **378***

p.79, **446-7**, *for* Campsey *read* Campsea

p.86, **496**, *n.36, for* **1615** *read* **1614**

p.93, **563**, *n.62, for* **636** *read* **637**

p.127, **912**, *n.87, for* Wyneton *read* Wyveton

THE REGISTER OF WILLIAM BATEMAN

1001 Inst. of William de Ludtheburgh, priest, to the rectory of Sall (*Salle*) [N]; patron, John de Brewese, knight. Blofield, 17 Aug. 1349.

1002 [fo.104ᵛ] HELMYNGHAM. Inst. of Nicholas Attebek of Hockering (*Hokering*) [N], priest, to the rectory of Moreton-on-Hill [N]; patron, John de Weston. Blofield, 17 Aug. 1349.

1003 Inst. of John de Mondham, acolyte, to a moiety of Hillington (*Illyngton*) [N]; patron, Robert de Ufford, earl of Suffolk. Blofield, 17 Aug. 1349.

1004* PREFECTIO PRIORIS DE LETHERYNGHAM. Confirmation of the unanimous election of Brother Roger de Huntyngfeld, OSA, priest and canon of Ss Peter and Paul Priory, Ipswich [S], as prior of Letheringham [S] by the canons there, following the resignation of Ralph de Framelyngham, the previous prior. South Elmham, 16 Aug. 1349.

1005* PREFECTIO PRIORIS DE PENTENEYE. Translation of Brother Ralph de Framelyngham, OSA, priest and canon of Ss Peter and Paul Priory, Ipswich [S], and recently prior of Letheringham Priory [S], by the bishop to Pentney Priory [N]. Pentney was destitute of its prior and of canons suitable to be elected prior, and the bishop acted by his own authority. South Elmham, 16 Aug. 1349.

1006 Inst.[1] of James Beek, subdeacon, to the rectory of Banningham [N]; patron, Mary [Roos], countess of Norfolk and marshal of England. South Elmham, 16 Aug. 1349.

1007 Inst. of Adam de Westwyk, priest, to the rectory of St Martin's, Shotesham [N]; patron in this turn, Edward III, because of the vacancy of the abbacy of St Benet's, Hulme [N]. Blofield, 18 Aug. 1349.

1008 Inst. of Thomas Coyn of Westwick [N], priest, to the rectory of Lamas (*Lammesse*) [N]; patron, Lady Joanna, widow of Roger le Strange, knight. Blofield, 18 Aug. 1349.

1009 Inst. of John de Wolterton, priest, to the rectory of Wickhampton (*Wykhampton*) [N]; patron, Edward Gerberge, knight. Blofield, 18 Aug. 1349.

1010 Inst. of Simon de Byntr', priest, to the rectory of Keswick [N]; patrons, John de Ufford, knight, and Hugh Curson. Blofield, 18 Aug. 1349.

1011 Inst. of William Ernald of Palgrave[2] to the vicarage of Stow Bedon [N]; [fo.105] patrons, the abbess and convent of Marham [N]. Blofield, 18 Aug. 1349.

---

[1] Cf. **1487**.
[2] There were three Palgraves in the diocese: Great and Little Palgrave [N], now in Sporle, and Palgrave [S].

1012 [Cancelled] Inst. of Simon Wytherich, priest, to the rectory of Mundford [N]; patron, Gerard del Islde, knight. Dated 'as above.'[3]

1013 Inst. of Thomas Boteler of Freston [S], priest, to the vicarage of Snape [S]; patrons, the prior and convent of Snape [S]. Blofield, 18 Aug. 1349.

1014 Inst. of John de Geselyngham, priest, to the vicarage of Rendham [S]; patrons, the abbot and convent of Sibton [S]. Blofield, 18 Aug. 1349.

1015 Inst. of Alan de Boxham, acolyte, to the rectory of Yelverton [N]; patron, Oliver Wygh, knight. Blofield, 18 Aug. 1349.

1016 Inst. of Thomas Straunge of East Walton (*Estwalton*) [N], subdeacon, to the rectory of Barnham Broom with the chapel of Riskes (*Ryskes*) [N]; patron, Constantine de Mortuo Mari, knight. Blofield, 18 Aug. 1349.

1017 Inst. of Peter le Masoun of Peasenhall [S], priest, to the vicarage of Bruisyard (*Bueresyerd, Buresyerd*) [S]; patrons, the prioress and convent of Campsey Ash [S]. Blofield, 18 Aug. 1349.

1018 Inst. of Roger Wardebene, priest, to the free chapel of St Margaret, Hilborough [N]; patron, Adam de Clyfton, knight. South Elmham, 19 Aug. 1349.

1019 Inst. of Edmund de Brunesleye, acolyte, to the rectory of Bridgham (*Brigham*) [N]; patron, Bishop Thomas [de Lisle] of Ely. South Elmham, 19 Aug. 1349.

1020 Inst. of John Scacher of Eye [S], priest, to the vicarage[4] of Hacheston [S]; patrons, the prior and convent of Hickling [N]. South Elmham, 19 Aug. 1349.

1021 Inst. of John de Bury, priest, to the vicarage of Sporle [N]; Bury gave oath of residence according to the constitutions; patron in this turn, Edward III, the temporalities of Sporle Priory [N] being in his hand. South Elmham, 19 Aug. 1349.

1022 [fo.105ᵛ] Inst. of Adam de Wygh, priest, to the rectory of Chelsworth [S]; patron, the abbot of Bury St Edmunds [S]. South Elmham, 20 Aug. 1349.

1023 Inst. of Harvey (*Horveus*) de Pakenham, priest, to the rectory of Bardwell [S]; patrons, the prior and convent of Bromholm [N]. South Elmham, 21 Aug. 1349.

---

[3] This entry was added in the lower margin of fo.104ᵛ but cancelled with a note: *vacat hic quia alibi videlicet iij*ᵃ *die mensis Julii hoc anno* (i.e., **714**).
[4] Vacant by resignation (**529, 940**).

1024 Inst. of Richard de Thoresby, priest, to the rectory of Stalham [N]; patron in this turn, Edward III, because of the vacancy of the abbacy of St Benet's, Hulme [N]. South Elmham, 21 Aug. 1349.

1025 [Cancelled] Inst. of John son of Geoffrey Payn of Halesworth [S], priest, to the rectory of Saxmundham [S]; patron, John de Wynkefeld, [knight]. South Elmham, 21 Aug. 1349.[5]

1026 Inst. of William Hulle of Ketteringham [N], priest, to the rectory of Griston [N]; patron, Dns Robert Bysshop, rector of a moiety of Hethersett [N]. South Elmham, 22 Aug. 1349.

1027 Inst. of Walter son of William Bytheye of Downham Market[6] (*Dounham Hythe*) [N], priest, to the vicarage of Leziate (*Leseyate*) [N]; patrons, the prior and convent of West Acre [N]. South Elmham, 22 Aug. 1349.

1028 Inst. of Richard Broun of *Saundreston*, clerk with first tonsure, to the rectory of Earl Soham (*Sohambarres*) [S]; patron, Mary [Roos], countess of Norfolk and marshal of England. South Elmham, 22 Aug. 1349.

1029 Inst. of Robert Gardener, clerk with first tonsure, to the rectory of [St Peter's[7]], Cockley Cley (*Cokeleye*) [N]; patron in this turn, Edward III, because William de Huntyngfeld, the son and heir of Sir Roger de Huntyngfeld, is his ward. South Elmham, 22 Aug. 1349.

1030 Inst. of Roger Squyer of Deopham [N], priest, to the rectory of Stratton Hall[8] (*Stratton*) [S]; patron, Sir Oliver de Stratton. South Elmham, 22 Aug. 1349.

1031 Inst. of Ralph Burgeys of Ingworth [N], priest, to a moiety of Ingworth [N]; patron, Edward III. South Elmham, 22 Aug. 1349.

1032 Inst. of Andrew de Huntyngfeld, priest, to the rectory of Hemley (*Helmele*) [S]; patron, Mary [Roos], countess of Norfolk and marshal of England. South Elmham, 23 Aug. 1349.

1033 Collation of the deanery of Humbleyard (*Humylierd*) [N] to Robert de Hardeshull, clerk with first tonsure. [fo.106] South Elmham, 23 Aug. 1349.

1034 Inst. of Richard de Bernardeston, deacon, to the rectory of Hargrave [S]; patron, the abbot of Bury St Edmunds [S]. South Elmham, 23 Aug. 1349.

---

[5] Cancelled with reference to 10 November (i.e., **1230**).
[6] *Alias* Downham Market at Hythe (Rye, *Norfolk Names*, 20).
[7] There were two parishes at 'Cleye', All Saints and St Peter's (*Taxatio*, 88); this is St Peter's (Reg. Bek fo.66ᵛ), at the east end of the village, which burned down in the reign of Elizabeth I (White, *Norfolk*, 374; *Ruined Churches*, 53).
[8] For the identification, see Reg. Bek fo.28; Stratton Hall was later depopulated and the church allowed to decay (White, *Suffolk*, 124; Dymond and Martin, *Atlas*, 73).

1035   Inst. of William de Lymborn, priest, to the rectory of Hemingstone (*Hemmyngeston*) [S]; patron, John de Brewese, knight. South Elmham, 23 Aug. 1349.

1036   Inst. of Peter son of John Cretyngg of Ipswich [S], priest, to the vicarage of Thurlston[9] (*Thurleston*) [S]; patrons, the prior and convent of St Peter, Ipswich [S]. South Elmham, 23 Aug. 1349.

1037   Inst. of John Cook of Hedenham [N], priest, to the vicarage[10] of Bedingham [N]. The bishop had nomination; patrons, the prior and convent of Walsingham [N]. South Elmham, 23 Aug. 1349.

1038   Inst. of John Wrottyng, priest, to the rectory of Milden [S]; patron, Guy de Sancto Claro, [knight]. South Elmham, 24 Aug. 1349.

1039   Inst. of John [le Clerc[11]] of Cove, priest, to the rectory of Wangford[12] (*Waunford*) [S]; patron in this turn, the abbot of Bury St Edmunds [S], because Thomas de Icword is his ward. South Elmham, 24 Aug. 1349.

1040   Inst. of John Hatfeld of Guist [N], priest, to the vicarage of Guist [N]; patrons, the abbot and convent of Holy Cross, Waltham, London diocese. South Elmham, 24 Aug. 1349.

1041   Inst. of Thomas son of Alexander de Kenford, priest, to the vicarage of Preston [S]; patrons, the prior and convent of the Holy Trinity, Ipswich [S]. South Elmham, 24 Aug. 1349.

1042   Inst. of Roger Norman of Erpingham [N], priest, to the vicarage[13] of Felmingham [N]; patron in this turn, Edward III, because of the vacancy of the abbacy of St Benet's, Hulme [N]. South Elmham, 25 Aug. 1349.

1043   Inst. of Robert de Wyngreworth, priest, [fo.106[v]] in the person of his proctor, M. William Wascelyn, to the rectory of Shipden[14] (*Shypedene*) [N]; patron in this turn, Edward III, because John, the son and heir of Hugh Broun, is his ward. South Elmham, 25 Aug. 1349.

---

[9] *Phillimore Atlas*: 'Whitton-cum-Thurlston' (231). White notes that 'the ancient hamlet of Thurlston' was consolidated to Whitton in the 16th century (*Suffolk*, 86).
[10] Vacant by resignation (**249, 967**). It is not clear which of the two churches at Bedingham this is, St Andrew or St Mary; they shared a churchyard and may have been united by this point (*Ruined Churches*, 53; *Taxatio*, 84).
[11] See **1897-8**.
[12] Near Brandon in Fordham deanery; Wangford near Southwold in Dunwich deanery was appropriated to Wangford priory (*Taxatio* 119; White, *Suffolk*, 401).
[13] See **670**, note.
[14] This village was seaward from Cromer [N], and often identified with it (**1781**). Shipden was engulfed by the sea in the early 15th century; in the 19th century some ruins were still visible at very low tides (White, *Norfolk*, 752).

1044 Inst. of Richard Alwold, clerk with first tonsure, to the rectory of [St Peter,[15]] Ringstead Magna [N]; patron in this turn, Edward III,[16] because of the vacancy of the abbacy of Ramsey. South Elmham, 25 Aug. 1349.

1045 Inst. of John de Wilton, to the rectory of Alby (*Aleby*) [N]; patron, Edward de Monte Acuto, knight. South Elmham, 26 Aug. 1349.

1046 Inst. of Gilbert de Holkham Holmes, priest, to the vicarage of Shernborne [N]; patrons, the prior and convent of Pentney [N]. South Elmham, 26 Aug. 1349.

1047 Inst. of William Wyger of Eriswell [S], priest, to the rectory of Felthorpe [N]; patrons, the prior and brothers of Weybridge [N]. South Elmham, 26 Aug. 1349.

1048 Inst. of Roger atte Spence of *Flete*, priest, to the rectory of Hawkedon (*Haukedon*) [S]; presentation was by William Hode of *Flete*, attorney (*generalis attornati*) of the patron, Walter de Bernyngham, knight. South Elmham, 27 Aug. 1349.

1049 Collation of the deanery of Hoxne [S] to Eustace de Myddelton, clerk with first tonsure. South Elmham, 27 Aug. 1349.

1050 Collation of the archdeaconry of Sudbury [S], vac. by resig. of M. Richard de Lyng, to M. Walter de Elveden DCnCL, saving anyone else's rights. South Elmham, 27 Aug. 1349.

1051 Collation of the archdeaconry of Norwich [N], to M. Richard de Lyng STD.[17] South Elmham, 27 Aug. 1349.

1052 Inst. of John Duk, priest, to the rectory of Troston (*Thurston*) [S]; patron, John de Thurston. Hoxne, 27 Aug. 1349.

1053 Inst. of John le Smyth of Hainford (*Haynford*) [N], priest, to the rectory of Moulton St Michael[18] (*Molton Maior*) [N], vac. by resig. of John Malyor; patron, John Verdon, knight. South Elmham, 29 Aug. 1349.

1054 Inst. of William de Atherston, priest, to a moiety[19] of Brome (*Brom*) [S]; patron [in this turn[20]], Mary [Roos], countess of Norfolk and marshal of England. South Elmham, 29 Aug. 1349.

---

[15] See **1826**.
[16] The king presented Alwold on 5 Aug. 1349, but he had presented Alan Mareschal only days before (28 July: *CPR 1348–1350*, 352, 356).
[17] See **300** and *CPL III*, 335–6.
[18] See **790** and note.
[19] For the moieties of Brome [S], see Augustine Page, *A topographical and genealogical history of the county of Suffolk* (Ipswich 1847), 452; and Copinger, *County of Suffolk* vol.1, 318.
[20] Usually St Mary priory, Thetford (Reg. Salmon fo.101, Reg. Ayremynne fo.42[v]).

1055 [fo.107] Inst. of Richard Parleman of Elsing [N], priest, to a moiety of North Tuddenham [N]; patron, Robert de Morle, knight. South Elmham, 29 Aug. 1349.

1056 Inst. of John de Totyngton, priest, to the vicarage of Stradsett (*Stradesete*) [N]; patrons, the abbot and convent of West Dereham [N]. South Elmham, 30 Aug. 1349.

1057 Inst. of Ralph Brome of Icklingham [S], priest, to the rectory of St John's, Beechamwell (*Bychamwell Sancti Johannis*[21]) [N]; patron, John de Benstede. South Elmham, 30 Aug. 1349.

1058 Inst. of Andrew Godyn of West Acre [N], priest, to the rectory of Godwick[22] (*Godwyk*) [N]; patrons, the prior and convent of West Acre [N]. South Elmham, 31 Aug. 1349.

1059 Collation of the rectory of St Nicholas, South Elmham [S], to Henry Wafr' of *Wyndel*, chaplain. South Elmham, 31 Aug. 1349.

1060 Inst. of Thomas de Calkhill of Larling (*Lyrlyng*) [N], priest, to the rectory of Elmswell [S]; patron, the abbot of Bury St Edmunds [S]. South Elmham, 1 Sep. 1349.

1061 Inst. of John de Stemworth, priest, to the rectory of Dunningworth[23] (*Donyngworth*) [S]; patron, Mary [Roos], countess of Norfolk and marshal of England. South Elmham, 2 Sep. 1349.

1062 Inst. of John Snod of Creeting [S], priest, to the vicarage of Attlebridge (*Attylbrigge*) [N]; patrons, the prior and convent of Holy Trinity, Norwich cathedral. South Elmham, 2 Sep. 1349.

1063 Inst. of Richard de Geyst, priest, to the vicarage of Hellington (*Helghton*, *Helgheton*) [N]; patron, William de Kerdeston, knight. South Elmham, 2 Sep. 1349.

1064 Inst. of Adam de Melles, priest, to the rectory of Cockfield (*Cokefeld*) [S]; patron, the abbot of Bury St Edmunds [S]. South Elmham, 2 Sep. 1349.

1065 Inst. of Roger de Geyst, priest, to the vicarage of Surlingham [N]. The bishop had nomination; patrons, the prioress and convent of Carrow [N]. South Elmham, 2 Sep. 1349.

[21] *Alias* Beechamwell Parva, according to Thomas Tanner (indexes of the episcopal registers, NRO Reg.30/1 and Reg.31/2, vol. 1, 557); see also **263**, note.
[22] Godwick church was a ruin by 1602, and the rectory united with Tittleshall [N] and Wellingham [N] in 1630 ('Lost Villages', 148; White, *Norfolk*, 341; see also B. Cushion *et al.*, 'Some Deserted Village Sites in Norfolk', *East Anglian Archaeology* 14 (1982), 63–5).
[23] Consolidated with Tunstall [S] in the late 16th century, its church having fallen to ruin (White, *Suffolk*, 177).

1066 [fo.107ᵛ] Inst. of John Baret of Framlingham [S], priest, to a moiety of Wetherden [S]; patron, the abbot of Bury St Edmunds [S]. South Elmham, 3 Sep. 1349.

1067 Inst. of Simon de Salle, priest, to the rectory of Nedging (*Neddyngg*) [S]; patron, John de Insula, lord of *Rougemont*.[24] South Elmham, 3 Sep. 1349.

1068 Inst. of Edmund Barker of Saxthorpe [N], priest, to the vicarage of Hemblington (*Hemelyngton*) [N]; patrons, the prior and convent of Norwich cathedral. South Elmham, 4 Sep. 1349.

1069 Inst. of Geoffrey de Weston, priest, to the rectory of Marlesford [S]; patron, Matilda, the widow of Robert de Saukevill. South Elmham, 4 Sep. 1349.

1070 Inst. of Robert son of Henry Purchas, clerk with first tonsure, in the person of his proctor, Dns Robert Edrych, to the rectory of Somersham [S]; patron, William Bohoun, earl of Northampton. South Elmham, 4 Sep. 1349.

1071 SOUTH BYRLYNGHAM.[25] Inst. of John de Beghton, clerk with first tonsure, to the rectory of North Burlingham [N]; patrons, Dni William de Bergh, Solomon [de Swaffham], rector of Caston [N], William de Felmyngham, William de Letton, and John de Swathyngg. South Elmham, 6 Sep. 1349.

1072 Inst. of James de Berneford, priest, to the rectory of Hasketon [S]; patron, John de Brewese, knight. South Elmham, 6 Sep. 1349.

1073 ECCLESIE SANCTE MARGE DE WAXTON PARVA.[26] Inst. of John Aylmer of Kimberley [N], priest, to the rectory of Little Waxham (*parva Waxtonesham sancte Margarete*[27]) [N]; patron, Lady Elizabeth, widow of Oliver de Ingham, knight. South Elmham, 6 Sep. 1349.

1074 Inst. of Roger de Chalfhunte, priest, to the rectory of Little Dunham (*Dunham parva*) [N]; patron, Thomas de Batesford. South Elmham, 6 Sep. 1349.

1075 WHELNETHAM PARVA.[28] Inst. of Thomas de Bodewell, priest, to the rectory of Little Whelnetham (*parva Whelnetham*) [S]; patron, Bartholomew de Burgherssh *le filz*, knight. South Elmham, 7 Sep. 1349.

1076 SCHYRFORD. Inst. of M. Thomas de Schirford, clerk with first tonsure, to the rectory of Shereford (*Shyrford*) [N]; patrons, the prior and convent of St Pancras, Lewes. South Elmham, 8 Sep. 1349.

---

[24] *Complete Peerage* VIII, 76.
[25] A contemporary hand corrected *North* to *South*; cf. **384**, note.
[26] MS. *Ecclesie*; a contemporary hand added *parva* and corrected *Marie* to *Margᵉ*.
[27] See **939**.
[28] A contemporary hand added *parva*.

1077   BAKETON EPISCOPI.[29] Collation to John Stanlak,[30] subdeacon, of the rectory of Bacton [S]. South Elmham, 7 Sep. 1349.

1078   Inst. of Henry Baffer' of Gooderstone [N], priest, to the vicarage of [fo.108] South Lynn (*Omnium Sanctorum Lenn'*) [N]; patrons, the prior and convent of West Acre [N]. South Elmham, 8 Sep. 1349.

1079   Inst. of Hugh Skyner of Wilton (*Wylton*) [N], priest, to the rectory of Bowthorpe (*Bouthorp*) [N]; patron, Avice (*Hawis*) de Wysham. South Elmham, 9 Sep. 1349.

1080   Inst. of Walter atte Oke of Great Bardfield (*Berdefeld magna*), clerk with first tonsure, to the rectory of Little Ellingham[31] (*Elyngham parva*) [N]; patron, Avice de Wysham. South Elmham, 9 Sep. 1349.

1081   Inst. of Robert Kydewyne, priest, to the vicarage of St Andrew's, Ilketshall (*Illeketeshal*) [S]; patrons, the prioress and convent of Bungay [S]. South Elmham, 9 Sep. 1349.

1082   Inst. of Clement Tyllok of Colby [N], priest, to the vicarage of Tuttington (*Tudyngton*) [N]; patrons, the prior and convent of Bromholm [N]. South Elmham, 10 Sep. 1349.

1083   Inst. of John de Barlyng, clerk with first tonsure, to the rectory of St Andrew's,[32] Tatterset [N]; patrons, the prior and convent of Castle Acre [N]. South Elmham, 10 Sep. 1349.

1084   Inst. of Richard Rande, priest, to the rectory of Bodney [N]; patrons, the prior and convent of West Acre [N]. South Elmham, 10 Sep. 1349.

1085   Inst. of Adam de Steynburgh, priest, to the vicarage of [a moiety[33] of] Scarning [N] (*Skernyng*); patrons, the abbot and convent of Waltham, London diocese. South Elmham, 10 Sep. 1349.

1086   PREFECTIO PRIORISSE DE BLAKEBERGH. The election of Isabella de Stanton, professed Augustinian[34] nun of Blackborough [N], to the priorate of that house was quashed by the bishop for defect of matter and form. The bishop then provided the elect as prioress, of his special grace. South Elmham, 10 Sep. 1349.

---

[29] Added in the lower margin in another contemporary hand; cf. **1644**.
[30] A notary (**17**).
[31] Later consolidated with the vicarage of Great Ellingham, several miles to the southeast (White, *Norfolk*, 364f, 416f; *Taxatio* 83, 87).
[32] See **835**, note; this church was abandoned in the early 16th century (*Ruined Churches*, 53).
[33] The other moiety was a rectory in the advowson of Geoffrey de Fransham in 1334 (*Taxatio*, 79, and Reg. Ayremynne fo.69).
[34] It was a Benedictine house: Knowles and Hadcock, 256.

1087 Inst. of Henry son of John Fleye of South Lynn [N], priest, to the vicarage of East Winch [N]; patrons, the prioress and convent of Carrow [N]. South Elmham, 11 Sep. 1349.

1088 [fo.108ᵛ] Inst. of Nigel Shyrreve, priest, to the rectory of St Andrew's,[35] Wicklewood (*Wykelwode Sancti Andree*) [N]; patrons, the prioress and convent of Campsey Ash [S]. South Elmham, 12 Sep. 1349.

1089 Inst. of John Lovell of Cresswell (*Creswell*), priest, to the rectory of Gresham [N]; patrons, the prior and convent of canons of Thetford [S]. South Elmham, 12 Sep. 1349.

1090 Inst. of John Baxtere of Dunkirk[36] (*Duncherch*) [N], priest, to the vicarage of Necton [N]; patron, Thomas de Bello Campo [Beauchamp], earl of Warwick. South Elmham, 14 Sep. 1349.

1091 Inst. of Robert de Wyrlyngworth,[37] clerk with first tonsure, to the rectory of Coney Weston (*Conghweston*) [S]; patron, the abbot of Bury St Edmunds [S]. South Elmham, 15 Sep. 1349.

1092 The election of Brother William de Hadesco, priest and professed Benedictine monk of St Benet's Abbey, Hulme [N], following the death of the previous abbot, Brother Robert de Aylesham, was quashed by the bishop for defect of matter and form. The bishop then provided the elect of his special grace, in consideration of his suitability. South Elmham manor chapel, 15 Sep. 1349.

1093 Inst. of Alexander Berwer, priest, to the vicarage of Horsey (*Horseye*) [N]; patrons, the prior and convent of Hickling [N]. South Elmham, 15 Sep. 1349.

1094 RENGETON CUM CAPELLA. Inst. of Geoffrey de Hundon, clerk with first tonsure, to the rectory of Runcton Holme[38] (*Rongeton*) [N]; patron, the abbot of Bury St Edmunds [S]. South Elmham, 18 Sep. 1349.

1095 Inst. of Ralph Bygot, priest, to the rectory of Trunch [N]; patrons, the prior and convent of Castle Acre [N]. South Elmham, 18 Sep. 1349.

---

[35] The two parishes at Wicklewood, St Andrew and All Saints (**1653**), were united and appropriated to the almoner of Norwich priory in 1365 (Reg. Percy fo.7ᵛ), when the monks claimed that St Andrew's church was falling to ruin.

[36] A hamlet in Aylsham parish (White, *Norfolk*, 452; Rye, *Norfolk Names*, 21).

[37] He held this benefice until his death in 1396 (*Calendar of Pre-Reformation Wills, Testaments, Probates, Administrations Registered at the Probate Office, Bury St Edmunds*, ed. Vincent B. Redstone, Ipswich 1907, 9).

[38] Runcton Holme with chapel (*Taxatio*, 88, note a), comprised Holme (just north of Thorpland) and Runcton (now South Runcton) less than a mile to the east. The chapel was at Runcton, the church at Holme (Faden, sheet 4). North Runcton was in Lynn deanery, with dependent chapels at Hardwick and Setchey; this was sometimes called Runcton Bardolf, after its patron (Reg. Salmon fo.92ᵛ, Reg. Ayremynne fo.8, Reg. Bek fo.23ᵛ).

1096   Inst. of Robert de Hunstanston, priest, to the vicarage of Hunstanton (*Hunstanston*) [N]. [fo.109] The bishop had nomination; patrons, the abbot and convent of Haughmond (*Haghman*). South Elmham, 18 Sep. 1349.

1097   Inst. of Roger Parleman, deacon, to the rectory of All Saints, Wacton Magna[39] (*Omnium Sanctorum de Waketon*) [N]; patron, John, lord of Segrave, knight. South Elmham, 18 Sep. 1349.

1098   Inst. of Robert Man of Goudhurst (*Gothirst*), priest, to the vicarage of Appleton[40] (*Appelton*) [N]; patrons, the prior and convent of West Acre [N]. South Elmham, 18 Sep. 1349.

1099   Inst. of William Waryn of Haslingfield (*Haselyngfeld*), priest, to the rectory of Clenchwarton with its dependent chapel[41] (*Northclenchewarton cum capella eidem annexa*) [N]; patron, Robert de Skales, knight. South Elmham, 18 Sep. 1349.

1100   Inst. of M. Roger de Bungeye, priest, to the rectory of Whepstead (*Whepested*) [S]; patron, the abbot of Bury St Edmunds [S]. South Elmham, 18 Sep. 1349.

1101   Inst. of Richard son of William the cook of Fleet in Holland (*Flete in Helond*), priest, to the vicarage of Methwold [N]; patrons, the prior and convent of Castle Acre [N]. South Elmham, 21 Sep. 1349.

1102   Inst. of Geoffrey Len of Ipswich [S], clerk with first tonsure, to the rectory of Braydeston with the chapel of Brundall[1] (*Brondale*) [N]; patron, John de Caston, knight. South Elmham, 21 Sep. 1349.

1103   Inst. of William de Felton, clerk with first tonsure, to the rectory of Warham[2] St Mary (*beate Marie de Warham*) [N]; patron, John de Norwico, knight. South Elmham, 21 Sep. 1349.

1104   Inst. of Thomas de Rede, deacon, to the vicarage of Rede [S]; patron in this turn, Edward III, the temporalities of Stoke-by-Clare Priory [S] being in his hand. South Elmham, 21 Sep. 1349.

---

[39] There were three parishes here: Wacton Magna, Wacton Parva (**1120**), and Wacton Market, the last in the advowson of St Mary's priory, Thetford (Reg. Ayremynne fo.77).
[40] Appleton dwindled in the 15th century and by 1602 all the lands were owned by Edward Paston ('Lost Villages', 142). The church was abandoned in the late 17th century (*Ruined Churches*, 51), and in White's time the rectory was a sinecure (*Norfolk*, 585); see *Phillimore Atlas*, 'Flitcham cum Appleton', 191.
[41] St Margaret church was in North Clenchwarton, and its chapel was in South Clenchwarton (Reg. Ayremynne fo.66ᵛ); the chapel was 'destroyed by the sea *c.* 1360' (*Ruined Churches*, 53).
[1] St Clement chapel was suppressed in 1547, demolished in 1820 (*Ruined Churches*, 53). Brundall had also a rectory (**1269**).
[2] There were three parishes at Warham: St Mary the Virgin, St Mary Magdalene, and All Saints (*Taxatio*, 81; Reg. Bek ff.66ᵛ, 72ᵛ); the first was abandoned in the 16th century (*Ruined Churches*, 55).

1105   Inst. of John de Methelwold, acolyte, to the rectory of Stanhoe (*Stanhowe*) [N]; patron, Adam de Clyfton, knight. South Elmham, 22 Sep. 1349.

1106   Inst. of William Chapman of Topcroft [N], priest, to a moiety of [fo.109ᵛ] Fishley [N]; patrons,[3] Roger Hardegrey, John de Berneye, Thomas de Bumpstede, and John Zimme. South Elmham, 22 Sep. 1349.

1107   Collation of the rectory of Belton [S] to Stephen Nally of Great Cressingham [N], chaplain. South Elmham, 22 Sep. 1349.

1108   Collation of the rectory of Brinton [N] to John de Thefford, acolyte. South Elmham, 22 Sep. 1349.

1109   Inst. of Robert Wylymet, priest, to the rectory of Little Barningham [N]; patron,[4] Robert[5] [de Stafford], baron of Stafford and lord of Tonbridge (*Tunbrygg*). South Elmham, 22 Sep. 1349.

1110   Inst. of John Frend of Tunstall, priest, to the rectory of Ridlington [N]; patrons, the prior and convent of Bromholm [N]. South Elmham, 23 Sep. 1349.

1111   Inst. of John atte Grene,[6] priest, to the vicarage of South Creake [N]; patrons, the prior and convent of Castle Acre [N]. South Elmham, 23 Sep. 1349.

1112   Inst. of Alexander Baron of Dennington (*Dynyngton*) [S], priest, to the rectory of Stradbroke (*Stradebrok*) [S]; patron, Richard de Breuse, knight. South Elmham, 23 Sep. 1349.

1113   Inst. of Robert Lunnkyn of Bramford [S], priest, in the person of Dns Alexander Baroun of Dennington [S], his proctor, to the rectory of Horham [S]; patron, John Jernegan. South Elmham, 23 Sep. 1349.

1114   Inst. of Richard Fransham of Methwold [N], acolyte, to a moiety of St John the Baptist, Aylmerton [N]; patron, Joan de Bars,[7] countess Warenne. South Elmham, 23 Sep. 1349.

1115   Inst. of Thomas Dorrente, clerk with first tonsure, to the rectory of Snailwell (*Snaylwell*) [Cambs.]; presentation was by M. John de Oo, vicar-general of the patron, Bishop Thomas [de Lisle] of Ely. South Elmham, 23 Sep. 1349.

1116   STYBERDE. Inst. of Thomas de Lacy, priest, to the rectory of Stibbard (*Styburd*) [N]; patron, Henry Lucy. South Elmham, 23 Sep. 1349.

---

[3] See **724**, note.
[4] Cf. **352**.
[5] *Recte* Ralph (see *Complete Peerage* XII, part 1, 174ff).
[6] *Alias* atte Grove (*CPR 1348–1350*, 574).
[7] Daughter of Henry, count of Bar, and granddaughter of Edward I; she married John, earl Warenne, and survived him until 1361 (*Complete Peerage* XII, part 1, 508, 511).

1117 Inst. of Robert dyl Moor of Eye [S], priest, to the vicarage of Gissing [N]; patrons, the prior and convent of Butley [S]. South Elmham, 23 Sep. 1349.

1118 [fo.110] Inst. of Richard Galyen of Sandringham [N], priest, to the rectory of Fritton (*Freton*) [S⁸]; patron, Robert de Mauteby, knight. South Elmham, 23 Sep. 1349.

1119 Inst. of Robert son of Thomas Baxter of West Lexham (*Westlexham*) [N], priest, to a moiety of Beeston St Andrew (*Beston*) [N]; patrons, the prior and convent of Peterstone (*Petreston*) [N]. South Elmham, 24 Sep. 1349.

1120 Inst. of John atte Assh of Bintree [N], priest, to the rectory of Wacton Parva⁹ (*Waketon parva*) [N]; patron, John Verdoun,¹⁰ lord of Brixworth (*Brykles-worth*), knight. South Elmham, 24 Sep. 1349.

1121 Inst. of Edmund Segor of Happisburgh (*Hapesburgh*) [N], priest, to the vicarage of Bacton [N] near Bromholm; patrons, the prior and convent of Bromholm [N]. South Elmham, 26 Sep. 1349.

1122 Inst. of Nicholas atte Gappe of Blofield [N], priest, to the rectory of Strumpshaw [N]; patron, John de Caston, knight. South Elmham, 26 Sep. 1349.

1123 Inst. of John de Manthorp,¹¹ clerk with first tonsure, to the rectory of Pettaugh (*Pethawe*) [S]; patron, Thomas de Gyppewico. South Elmham, 26 Sep. 1349.

1124 Inst. of John Akewra, priest, to a moiety of Great Wreningham [N]; patrons, the prioress and convent of Carrow [N]. South Elmham, 27 Sep. 1349.

1125 BERNYNGHAM MAGNA. Inst. of Thomas Dod of *Bernyngton*, priest, to the rectory of Great Barningham¹² [N]; patron, Lady Elizabeth, widow of John de Hedersete, knight. South Elmham, 27 Sep. 1349.

1126 Inst. of Simon Cary of Mundsley [N], priest, to the rectory of Overstrand [N]; patron, Geoffrey son of Alan de Shipeden. South Elmham, 27 Sep. 1349.

1127 Inst. of Walter Mauneysyn, priest, to the rectory of Frenze¹³ (*Frense*) [N]; patron, John de Ludham, knight. South Elmham, 28 Sep. 1349.

⁸ Morley identified the county ('Catalogue', 52); he dates this institution to 1359.

⁹ St Mary church at Wacton Parva was dilapidated in the 15th century and the rectory consolidated to Wacton Magna in 1522 (White, *Norfolk*, 710; *Ruined Churches*, 55). There was still a village at Wacton Parva in 1428, but Allison says that the site was abandoned in the 16th century ('Lost Villages', 159; but cf. Faden, sheet 5).

¹⁰ See *Complete Peerage* XII, part 2, 244f; and see John Verdon in the index.

¹¹ Manthorp was later killed by Edmund de Gippeswicz, who was pardoned by the king in 1352 (*CPR 1350–1354*, 327).

¹² See **351n**.

¹³ About a mile northeast of Diss, it was independent until the 19th century ('Lost Villages', 147; *Ruined Churches*, 50; White, *Norfolk*, 718).

1128 Inst. of William Chapman of Tostock (*Tostok*) [S], priest, to the vicarage of Ashwicken (*Wyken*) [N]; patrons, the prior and convent of West Acre [N]. South Elmham, 28 Sep. 1349.

1129 Inst. of Henry Cok, priest, in the person of his proctor, John Suldern, clerk, to the rectory of Little Thurlow [S]; patron in this turn, Edward III, the temporalities of Stoke-by-Clare [S] being in his hand. South Elmham, 28 Sep. 1349.

1130 [fo.110ᵛ] Inst. of Adam le Clerk of Worlingham [S], priest, to the rectory of Barnby (*Barneby*) [S]; patrons, the prior and convent of Butley [S]. South Elmham, 29 Sep. 1349.

1131 Inst. of Robert Brokedysh, priest, to the rectory of Marlingford [N]; patron, Robert de Wachesham, knight. South Elmham, 30 Sep. 1349.

1132 Inst. of James Beauchamp, priest, to the vicarage of Great Cornard (*Cornerth magna*) [S]; patrons, the abbess and convent of Malling (*Mallyng*). South Elmham, 2 Oct. 1349.

1133 Inst. of William Dun, priest, to the rectory of Witton [in Blofield deanery] [N]; patrons,[14] Solomon [de Swaffham], rector of Caston [N], William de Bergh, William de Letton, John de Swatthing, and William Felmyngham. South Elmham, 2 Oct. 1349.

1134 Inst. of Robert de Hardeshull, priest, to the rectory of Heydon [N]; patron, John de Brewese, knight. South Elmham, 2 Oct. 1349.

1135 VICARIA DE THRESTON. Inst. of Stephen de Bouthorp, priest, to the vicarage of Tharston (*Troston*) [N]; patrons, the prior and convent of Pentney [N]. South Elmham, 2 Oct. 1349.

1136 Inst. of Walter de Metton, clerk with first tonsure, to the rectory of Chevely (*Chevele*) [Cambs.]; patron, Lady Margaret, widow of John de Pulteneye, knight. South Elmham, 3 Oct. 1349.

1137 Inst. of Simon de Bernyngton, priest, to the rectory of Saxlingham Thorpe (*Saxlyngham Thorp*) [N]; patron, Lady Elizabeth, widow of William de Monte Acuto, knight. South Elmham, 3 Oct. 1349.

1138 Inst. of John Southgate of Stockton [N], deacon, to the rectory of Geldeston [N]; patron, John Bygot, knight. South Elmham, 4 Oct. 1349.

1139 Inst. of Richard le Irreys of Fladbury (*Fladebury*), priest, to the rectory of Chattisham (*Chatesham*) [S]; patrons, the prioress and convent of Wix. South Elmham, 4 Oct. 1349.

---

¹⁴ As in **1071**.

1140   Inst. of John Trayly, clerk with first tonsure, to the rectory of Swanton Morley (*Swanton Morle*) [N]; patron, Robert de Morle, knight. South Elmham, 5 Oct. 1349.

1141   Inst. of John Baxter of *Hakewold*, priest, to the rectory of Kelling (*Kellyngg*) [N]; [fo.111] patron, John Avenel. South Elmham, 5 Oct. 1349.

1142   Inst. of Peter Wrayl of Elveden [S], priest, to the rectory of Little Fakenham [S]; patrons, the prior and convent of St Denys outside Southampton (*Suthampton*). South Elmham, 5 Oct. 1349.

1143   Inst. of William Knythocle, priest, to the rectory of Litcham [N]; patron, Sybil de Felton. South Elmham, 6 Oct. 1349.

1144   Inst. of John de Hardleston, priest, to the rectory of Blaxhall (*Blakeshale*) [S]; patron, Mary [Roos], countess of Norfolk and marshal of England. South Elmham, 6 Oct. 1349.

1145   Inst. of William Galpyn of Cretingham [S], priest, to the free chantry in the parish church of Dennington [S]; patron, Adam de Skakelthorp, rector of Dennington [S]. South Elmham, 6 Oct. 1349.

1146   Inst. of John Oldman of Aylmerton [N], priest, to a moiety of Aylmerton [N]; patron, Simon Bygot of Felbrigg (*Felbrigge*) [N]. South Elmham, 6 Oct. 1349.

1147   RYDONE.[15] Inst. of Walter Kolville, priest, to the rectory of Roydon[16] [N]; patron, Robert de Ufford, knight, earl of Suffolk. South Elmham, 6 Oct. 1349.

1148   Inst. of William Bataylle of Ringstead Magna [N], priest, to the rectory of Ridlington (*Wrydelyngton*) [N]; patron,[17] Richard Talbot, knight. South Elmham, 7 Oct. 1349.

1149   Inst. of Thomas Wryghte of Ketteringham [N], priest, to the rectory of Garveston [N]; patron, John Bardolf, knight, lord of Wormegay [N]. South Elmham, 7 Oct. 1349.

1150   Inst. of M. Edmund de Myldenhale, acolyte, to the rectory of East Bradenham (*Estbradenham*) [N]; patron, the abbot of Bury St Edmunds [S]. [n.p.], 7 Oct. 1349.

1151   Inst. of Thomas Godknap of Redenhall [N], priest, to the vicarage of Roughton [N]; patrons, the prioress and convent of Bungay [S]. South Elmham, 7 Oct. 1349.

[15] A hand, pointing at the heading, was drawn in brown ink, not used elsewhere on the folio; the drawing is unlike that at **749**.
[16] See Watkin, *Inventory* 2, xiv, 135.
[17] But cf. **506**, **1110**.

1152 Inst. of John de Melles of Brampton, priest, to the rectory of Gasthorpe (*Gasthorp*) [N]; patron,[18] Mary [Roos], countess of Norfolk and marshal of England. South Elmham, 7 Oct. 1349.

1153 Inst. of Simon Hod of Swanton, priest, to the rectory of St Botolph's in Norwich; patron, John Aylmer[19] of Erpingham [N]. South Elmham, 8 Oct. 1349.

1154 [fo.111ᵛ] Inst. of John Davy of Cirencester (*Cirsestr'*), priest, to [a moiety] of Sidestrand (*Sydestronde*) [N]; patron, Michael de Ponynges, knight. South Elmham, 8 Oct. 1349.

1155* Collation of the mastership of the grammar schools of Norwich to M. Peter Petyt of Herringfleet [S]. South Elmham, 8 Oct. 1349.

1156 Inst. of William son of John Walter of New Buckenham (*nova Bokenham*) [N], priest, to the rectory of Griston [N]; patrons, the prior and convent of Buckenham [N]. South Elmham, 8 Oct. 1349.

1157 Inst. of Richard de Tathewell, priest, to the rectory of Knapton (*Knapeton*) [N]; patron, Richard Playz, knight. South Elmham, 9 Oct. 1349.

1158 Inst. of Roger de Southgate of Swainsthorpe, priest, to the rectory of St Mary,[20] Swainsthorpe [N]; patron, John Gasselyn of Swainsthorpe. South Elmham, 9 Oct. 1349.

1159 Inst. of Roger Pylleberghe of Flowton (*Flogeton*) [S], priest, to the vicarage of Edwardstone [S]; patrons, the prior and convent of Earls Colne. South Elmham, 11 Oct. 1349.

1160 Collation of the rectory of Rollesby [N] to Dns Simon de Rykynghale, chaplain. South Elmham, 11 Oct. 1349.

1161 Inst. of Robert atte Brigge of Buxton [N], priest, to the rectory of Hockering (*Hokeryngg*) [N]. Robert de Morle, knight, had nomination; patrons, the prior and convent of St Mary's church, Southwark, Winchester diocese. South Elmham, 11 Oct. 1349.

1162 Inst. of William Langham of Wighton [N], priest, to a third part of St Mary's, Itteringham [N]; patrons,[21] Walter Walcote, knight, Thomas de Swathyng, Alexander de Wolterton, rector of Field Dalling (*Dallyngg*) [N], John de Wolterton, Edward de Swathyng, and Ralph Copsy. South Elmham, 12 Oct. 1349.

---

[18] Usually St Mary priory, Thetford (Reg. Ayremynne fo.16).
[19] *Alias* John son of Aylmer de Sygate of Erpingham in 1333, 1335 (Reg. Ayremynne ff.57ᵛ, 76).
[20] Here were two parishes, St Peter and St Mary; St Mary church was demolished in the 16th century (White, *Norfolk*, 698; *Ruined Churches*, 54).
[21] Cf. **652**.

1163   Inst. of Nicholas Moyse, priest, to the vicarage of Haughley (*Haughele*) [S]; patrons, the abbot and convent of Hailes. South Elmham, 10 Oct. 1349.

1164   Inst. of Nicholas de Colney, clerk with first tonsure, to the rectory of Fring [N]; patron,[22] William de Colneye. South Elmham, 14 Oct. 1349.

1165   Inst. of John de Pender of *Sonyngdon*, [fo.112] priest, to the rectory of Little Blakenham (*Blakenham super Montem*) [S]; patron, John Typpetot,[23] lord of Langar, knight. South Elmham, 14 Oct. 1349.

1166   Inst. of M. Peter Darran, priest, ([margin] in the person of Francis Saier, his proctor,) to the rectory of Bebington (*Bebyngton*) in Coventry and Lichfield diocese, in exchange[24] for Icklingham All Saints [S]; patrons, the abbot and convent of Warburton (*Werburgg*). South Elmham, 14 Oct. 1349.

1167   Inst. of John Manca, priest, in the person of Francis Sarezyn, his proctor, to the rectory of Icklingham All Saints [S], vac. by resig. of Dns Peter Darran, in exchange for Manca's rectory of Bebington in Coventry and Lichfield diocese, as above; patron, John [de Woodstock[25]], earl of Kent. South Elmham, 14 Oct. 1349.

1168   Inst. of Richard Seyne of Holkham (*Hokham*) [N], priest, to the vicarage of Watton [N]; patron in this turn,[26] by gift of the king, Mary [Roos], countess of Norfolk and marshal of England. South Elmham, 15 Oct. 1349.

1169   Inst. of Peter de Baldeswell, priest, to the vicarage of Neateshead (*Neteshirde*) [N]; patron in this turn, Edward III, because of the vacancy of the abbacy of St Benet's, Hulme [N]. South Elmham, 15 Oct. 1349.

1170   Inst. of Thomas Orger, priest, to the rectory of Woolverstone (*Wolferston*) [S]; patron, William de Lopham. South Elmham, 16 Oct. 1349.

1171   PORTIO IN ECCLESIA DE TOFTES MON^ACHORUM. Inst. of Geoffrey Purchas, priest, to the portion which John Ked of Moulton [N] recently obtained[27] in the rectory of Toft Monks (*Monkestoftes*) [N]; patron in this turn, Edward III, the temporalities of Toft Monks Priory[28] (*Toftes*) [N] being in his hand. South Elmham, 16 Oct. 1349.

---

[22] Cf. **55**.

[23] See *Complete Peerage* XII, part 2, 95f.

[24] No commission is mentioned.

[25] See *Complete Peerage* VII, 148–150.

[26] Usually St Mary priory, Thetford (Reg. Salmon fo.20).

[27] Inst. 2 June 1327 (Reg. Ayremynne fo.14^v); the rector's portion was one-third and the priory kept the other two-thirds of the incomes (*Taxatio*, 83).

[28] Toft Monks was a dependent of Préaux abbey, Lisieux diocese, which usually exercised this advowson through the prior as its proctor (Reg. Ayremynne fo.14^v; Knowles & Hadcock 85, 93).

1172 Inst. of Robert de Alby, priest, to the vicarage of Hanworth (*Haneworth*) [N]; patrons, the prior and convent of Hickling [N]. South Elmham, 16 Oct. 1349.

1173 Inst. of John [Larke[29]] of Waterden, priest, [fo.112^v] to the rectory of Bawsey (*Bauseye*) [N]; patron in this turn, Edward III, the temporalities of Eye Priory [S] being in his hand. South Elmham, 16 Oct. 1349.

1174 Inst. of Roger Melcheborn, priest, to the vicarage of Assington (*Asington*) [S]; patrons, the prior and convent of Hatfield Peverel (*Hatfeld Peverel*). South Elmham, 17 Oct. 1349.

1175 Inst. of Richard Kiffold of Sandringham [N], priest, to the rectory of St Andrew's, Congham [N]; patron, Thomas de Baldeswell. South Elmham, 18 Oct. 1349.

1176 Inst. of Bartholomew son of William de Aula of Wighton [N], priest, to the vicarage of West Lexham [N]; patrons, the prior and convent of Peterstone [N]. South Elmham, 18 Oct. 1349.

1177 Inst. of William de Dokkyng, priest, to the rectory of Wilby (*Wylbeygh*) [S]; patron, Dns John Swan,[30] priest. South Elmham, 19 Oct. 1349.

1178 Inst. of John, son (*natus*) of Robert de Lay of Brundish (*Brundysch*) [S], priest, to St Andrew's chapel, Stradbroke (*Stradebrok*) [S]; patron, Thomas de Wynkefeld. South Elmham, 19 Oct. 1349.

1179 Inst. of Hugh Martyn, priest, to the rectory of Withersfield (*Wetheresfeld*) [S]; patron, Lady Margaret de Pulton. South Elmham, 19 Oct. 1349.

1180 Inst. of Robert de Belton, priest, to the vicarage of Chippenham (*Chipenham*) [Cambs.]; patrons, the abbot and convent of Walden. South Elmham, 20 Oct. 1349.

1181 Inst. of Thomas Dubel of Melles [S], priest, to the vicarage of Offton (*Ofton*) [S]; patron [in this turn[31]], Mary [Roos], countess of Norfolk and marshal of England. Poringland [N] (*Poringlond*), 22 Oct. 1349.

1182 Inst. of Paul atte Wode of Middleton[32] (*Middelton*), subdeacon, to the rectory of West Winch (*Westwynch*) [N]; patron, John atte Wode. Thorpe next Norwich, 23 Oct. 1349.

[29] See **1841**.
[30] A John Swan was rector from 1310 (Morley, 'Catalogue', 78) until at least 1342 (Reg. Bek fo.59^v).
[31] Usually St Mary priory, Thetford (Reg. Ayremynne fo.62^v).
[32] Probably Middleton [N], less than a mile from West Winch.

1183   Inst. of Robert Lawes, priest, to the rectory of Beeston Regis[33] (*Beston*) [N]; presentation was by Dns Henry de Walton, attorney general[34] of Henry [of Grosmont], earl of [fo.113] Lancaster. Thorpe next Norwich, 23 Oct. 1349.

1184   Inst. of Thomas de Blofeld of Saxlingham [N], priest, to the rectory of Bayfield (*Bayfeld*) [N]; patrons, Thomas de Walcote, rector of Felbrigg [N], and Simon de Walcote,[35] rector of Walcott [N]. Thorpe next Norwich, 23 Oct. 1349.

1185   Inst. of Thomas Burchard, priest, to the rectory of Brettenham [N]; presentation was by Alan [de Walsyngham], prior of Ely cathedral, vicar-general of Bishop Thomas [de Lisle], the patron. Thorpe next Norwich, 23 Oct. 1349.

1186   Inst. of Robert de Walesham, acolyte, to the rectory of Stansfield [S]; patron, Lady Elizabeth [de Burgh], Lady of Clare. Thorpe next Norwich, 23 Oct. 1349.

1187   Inst. of John Balle of Thrandeston [S], priest, to the vicarage of Yoxford [S]; patron in this turn, Mary [Roos], countess of Norfolk and marshal of England, the advowsons of the monks of Thetford [N] being in her hand. Thorpe next Norwich, 24 Oct. 1349.

1188   Inst. of William Robyn of Swaffham [N], priest, to the chantry of the chapel in the manor of Queen Philippa at Swaffham; patron, Queen Philippa. Thorpe next Norwich, 24 Oct. 1349.

1189   Inst. of Richard de Burton, clerk with first tonsure, to the rectory of South Cove [S]; patrons, the abbot and convent of St Mary's church, York. Thorpe next Norwich, 24 Oct. 1349.

1190   Inst. of Robert [Dauns[36]] of Grundisburgh (*Grundesburgh*) [S], priest, to the rectory of North Cove (*Northcove*) [S]; patron, Edward III. Thorpe next Norwich, 24 Oct. 1349.

1191   Inst. of Robert Waryn of Mautby (*Malteby*) [N], priest, to a moiety of [St Mary's[37] in] Burnham Westgate [N]; patron, John son of Alexander Fastolf of Great Yarmouth [N]. Thorpe next Norwich, 25 Oct. 1349.

1192   Inst. of Edmund de Welholm, clerk with first tonsure, to the rectory of Snetterton St Andrew[38] (*Snyterton Sancti Andree*) [N]; patron, Lady Alice, widow of Sir Hugh de Bokenham. Thorpe next Norwich, 26 Oct. 1349.

---

[33] The union of the duchy of Lancaster with the crown in the 15th century brought this parish into the king's advowson.

[34] See R. Somerville, *History of the Duchy of Lancaster* vol. 1 (1953), 358, 360.

[35] He held this benefice until his death in 1383 (*Norwich Wills* 2, 380).

[36] See **1897–8**.

[37] See **427**, note.

[38] Not in *Taxatio*; St Andrew's was abandoned in the 16th century (*Ruined Churches*, 54). For All Saints, see **719**.

1193 Inst. of Robert de Binhale, priest, to the rectory of St Laurence in Norwich; patron, the abbot of Bury St Edmunds [S]. Thorpe next Norwich, 26 Oct. 1349.

1194 Inst. of Nicholas de Messyngg, subdeacon, to the rectory of Freston [S]; patron, Sir Thomas de Holbrok. Thorpe next Norwich, 26 Oct. 1349.

1195 PREFECTIO PRIORIS DE SNAPES. Brother John de Colne, [fo.113ᵛ] priest and professed Benedictine monk of St John's Abbey, Colchester, London diocese, was admitted by the bishop to the priorate of Snape [S], at the presentation of the abbot and convent of St John's. Thorpe next Norwich, 27 Oct. 1349.

1196 Collation of the deanery of Hitcham (*Hecham*) [N] to John, clerk with first tonsure, the son of Robert de Norwico, goldsmith in London. Thorpe next Norwich, 27 Oct. 1349.

1197 Inst. of Thomas de Hoyton, priest, to the rectory of St Peter of Wood Norton (*Wodenorton*) [N]; patron, Vincent de Norton. Thorpe next Norwich, 27 Oct. 1349.

1198 VICARIA DE WESTBEKHAM. Inst. of Peter de Wadgate, priest, to the vicarage of West Beckham (*Westbecham*) [N]; patrons, the prior and convent of Holy Trinity, Norwich cathedral. Thorpe next Norwich, 27 Oct. 1349.

1199 TREMELEY MARTINI.[39] Inst. of James le Bray, priest, to the rectory of Trimley [St Martin[40]] [S] (*Tremeley*); patron, John Peverel. Thorpe next Norwich, 28 Oct. 1349.

1200 Inst. of Adam de Skakelthorp,[1] priest, in the person of Dns John de Lenn, his proctor, to the rectory of Cawston (*Causton*) [N]; patron, Robert de Ufford, earl of Suffolk. Thorpe next Norwich, 28 Oct. 1349.

1201 Inst. of William Hulle of Ketteringham [N], priest, to the rectory of Cranwich [N]; patron, Adam Clyfton, knight. Thorpe next Norwich, 28 Oct. 1349.

1202 Inst. of John le Veylde of Bodney [N], priest, to the rectory of Rockland St Andrew[2] (*Sancti Andree de Rokelond*) [N]; patron, Matilda, daughter of Henry Carbonel. Thorpe next Norwich, 29 Oct. 1349.

---

[39] *Martini* is a contemporary addition.

[40] See **1308**, note.

[1] A clerk of the earl of Suffolk (*CPP* I, 73), he held this benefice until his death in 1370 (*Norwich Wills* 2, 334).

[2] St Andrew's church was abandoned by 1700, and the rectory consolidated with Rockland All Saints (White, *Norfolk*, 418); Rockland St Peter (**21**) was in the same village (*Ruined Churches*, 52).

1203 Inst. of Robert de Fouldon, priest, to a portion[3] of Dickleburgh (*Dyckelburgh*) [N] called 'in the field' (*in Campo*); patron, the abbot of Bury St Edmunds [S]. Thorpe next Norwich, 29 Oct. 1349.

1204 Inst. of John de Bek[4] of Banham [N], priest, to a moiety of Shelfanger [N]; patron, John Verdon, knight. Thorpe next Norwich, 30 Oct. 1349.

1205 Collation of the prebend of the dawn mass in the College of St Mary in the Fields in Norwich to Robert de Eton, priest. Thorpe next Norwich, 30 Oct. 1349.

1206 Inst. of John de Walsham, priest, to the rectory of St Margaret [of Westwick], Norwich; patron, John de Norwico of Yoxford [S]. Thorpe next Norwich, 31 Oct. 1349.

1207 [fo.114] Inst. of Richard Stak of Wood Rising (*Woderysing*) [N], priest, to the vicarage[5] of Thrigby (*Trykkeby*) [N]; patrons, the abbot and convent of Langley [N]. Thorpe next Norwich, 2 Nov. 1349.

1208 Inst. of Geoffrey de Wymondale, priest, to the rectory of Athelington (*Alyngton*) [S]; patrons, the prior and convent of Butley [S]. Thorpe next Norwich, 3 Nov. 1349.

1209 Inst. of John de Redyngg of Barningham,[6] priest, to the vicarage of Hockham[7] (*Hokham*) [N]; patron in this turn,[8] Mary [Roos], countess of Norfolk and marshal of England. Thorpe next Norwich, 3 Nov. 1349.

1210 Collation of the rectory of Hevingham [N] to John Kenston, priest. Thorpe next Norwich, 4 Nov. 1349.

1211 Inst. of John Grym of Bramerton [N], priest, to the vicarage of Bodham [N]; patrons, the abbot and convent of Langley [N]. Thorpe next Norwich, 4 Nov. 1349.

---

[3] There were five portions in Dickleburgh parish: one for the prior of Butley, one for the prior of Horsham St Faith, and those of Henry, Alexander, and Richard (*Taxatio*, 84, 'Dyttleburg'). At least two of these last three were in the advowson of the abbot of Bury St Edmunds (see **1214**). On this division see T. Williamson, *The Origins of Norfolk* (Manchester 1993), 151.

[4] *Alias* Atte Bek; he held the neighbouring vicarage of Winfarthing [N] from 1338 until 1354 (Reg. Bek fo.14; **1884**).

[5] Vacant by resignation (**499, 1009**).

[6] He held this benefice until his death in 1372 (*Norwich Wills* 2, 304).

[7] The registers and *Taxatio* (87) show only one Hockham, appropriated to the monks of Thetford; this could be Hockham Magna (Holy Trinity) or Parva (St Mary). St Mary church 'was demolished after the reign of Richard II' (White, *Norfolk* 417; see also *Ruined Churches* 54, and Faden sheet 5).

[8] Usually St Mary Priory, Thetford (Reg. Salmon fo.63).

1212   Inst. of John Gilbert, priest, to the vicarage of Little Melton [N]; patrons, the prior and convent of Ixworth [S]. Thorpe next Norwich, 4 Nov. 1349.

1213   Inst. of John de Brathweyth, acolyte, to the rectory of Mellis [S]; patron, Robert de Ufford, earl of Suffolk. Thorpe next Norwich, 4 Nov. 1349.

1214   Inst. of William de Melford, priest, to the portion [called Semerhall[9]] of Dickleburgh [N] which was held by the late Dns John de Hemenhale; patron, the abbot of Bury St Edmunds [S]. Thorpe next Norwich, 4 Nov. 1349

1215   Inst. of Thomas Bee of Hardley (*Hardelee*) [N], priest, to the vicarage[10] of Heckingham [N]; patrons, the abbot and convent of Langley [N]. Thorpe next Norwich, 4 Nov. 1349.

1216   Collation of the vicarage of Beighton (*Beyghton*) [N] to William de Ersham, priest. [fo.114[v]] Thorpe next Norwich, 5 Nov. 1349.

1217   Inst. of John Hubert of Dickleburgh [N], acolyte, to a third part of Itteringham [N]; patron, John de Garrenn.[11] Thorpe next Norwich, 5 Nov. 1349.

1218   Inst. of William de Thornton, Lincoln diocese, priest, to the vicarage of Loudham[12] (*Ludham iuxta Campesse*) [S]; patrons, the prioress and convent of Campsey Ash [S]. Thorpe next Norwich, 5 Nov. 1349.

1219   Inst. of Robert de Condry, priest, to the rectory of Bramerton [N]; patron, William de Leye, knight. Thorpe next Norwich, 6 Nov. 1349.

1220   Inst. of Thomas [Chyld[13]] of Debenham, acolyte, to the rectory[14] of Dennington [S]; patron, William son of Richard de Wyngefeld. Thorpe next Norwich, 6 Nov. 1349.

1221   Inst. of Thomas de Calkhill, priest, to the rectory of Palgrave [S]; patron, the abbot of Bury St Edmunds [S]. Thorpe next Norwich, 6 Nov. 1349.

1222   Inst. of John Aylmer, priest, to the rectory of Lessingham [N]; presentation was by the prior of Ogbourne St George, proctor-general in England of the abbot of Bec-Hellouin. Thorpe next Norwich, 6 Nov. 1349.

1223   Inst. of Walter Hert of Debenham [S], priest, to the rectory of Little Wenham [S]; patron,[15] Mary de Holbrok. Thorpe next Norwich, 6 Nov. 1349.

---

[9]   Reg. Percy, ff.63[v]–64; and see note, **1203**.
[10]   Vacant by resignation (**452**, **1211**).
[11]   *Alias* Warren (cf. **468**).
[12]   Loudham village may have disappeared by emparking; the parish was absorbed into Pettistree, its neighbour to the west (*Taxatio*, 116; White, *Suffolk*, 147).
[13]   See **587**.
[14]   Vacant by resignation: **1145**, **1200**.
[15]   See **1231**.

1224 Inst. of Clement de Knapeton, priest, to the rectory of Great Livermere [S]; patron, Thomas Geneys, knight. Thorpe next Norwich, 6 Nov. 1349.

1225 Inst. of Thomas Mabylion, deacon, to the rectory of Weeting Saint Mary [N]; patron, Richard Playz, knight. Thorpe next Norwich, 9 Nov. 1349.

1226 Inst. of John de Baldeswell, priest, to the rectory of Gunthorpe [N]; patron, John Avenel. Thorpe next Norwich, 11 Nov. 1349.

1227 Inst. of Hugh atte Brok of Hacheston (*Heggeston*) [S], priest, to the rectory of St Mary's, Congham [N]; patron, John de Orreby, knight. Thorpe next Norwich, 11 Nov. 1349.

1228 Inst. of Edmund Cotenham of Coveney, priest, to a moiety of St Edmund's church, Taverham [N]; patron, John Peverel. Thorpe next Norwich, 11 Nov. 1349.

1229 Inst. of Robert de Wode of Akenham [S], priest, ([margin] in the person of his proctor, Dns Robert [Lunnkyn[16]] of Bramford [S], the rector of Horham [S],) to the rectory of Sproughton [S]; patron, John Aspale, knight. Thorpe next Norwich, 11 Nov. 1349.

1230 Inst.[17] of John son of Geoffrey Payn of Halesworth [S], priest, to the rectory of Saxmundham [S]; patron, John de Wyngefeld, knight. Thorpe next Norwich, 10 Nov. 1349.

1231 [Common Pleas] writ[18] *admittatis non obstante reclamacione* ordering the bishop to admit a suitable presentee of Gilbert de Debenham and his wife Mary[19] to the church of Little Wenham [S] because they have recovered the presentation against John de Moundeville, William de Moundevill, John de Sancrost and John de Neketon by default. Tested by J[ohn] de Stonore. Westminster, 1 Dec. 1349. Rot. Cxxix San' . . .

1232 [fo.115] Inst. of William Briton of East Walton [N], priest, to the free chapel of St James the Apostle, Terrington [N]; patrons, John Bardolf of Mapledurham (*Mapelderham*), knight, William [son of?] Alexander[20] senior, and Thomas and John, sons of William Howard of Wiggenhall [N]. Thorpe next Norwich, 13 Nov. 1349.

1233 Inst. of Richard Benetict, priest, to the vicarage of Arminghall [N]; patrons, the prior and convent of Holy Trinity, Norwich cathedral. Thorpe next Norwich, 14 Nov. 1349.

---

[16] See **1113**.
[17] Added by another contemporary hand in the lower margin; cf. **1025**.
[18] Actual writ, measuring 25.5 by 5 cms, between ff.114–15 and sewn to fo.113, directly beside **1223** (*q.v.*). It has a filing hole at its left end.
[19] See **1223** and **1405**.
[20] MS. *militis Willelmi* (inserted from margin) *Alexandri*.

1234 Inst. of William Casp, acolyte, in the person of his proctor, Dns John [Casp[21]], the rector of St Mary,[22] Creeting [S], to the rectory of St Olave's, Creeting [S]; patron, Tydemaunn de Lymbergh. Thorpe next Norwich, 14 Nov. 1349.

1235 Inst. of Adam de Cheston, clerk with first tonsure, to the rectory of Spexhall [S]; patrons, the abbot and convent of St Mary's, York. Thorpe next Norwich, 14 Nov. 1349.

1236 Inst. of William de Snyterton, priest, to the rectory of Thurington (*Thorington*) [S]; patrons, the prior and convent of Blythburgh (*Bliburgh*) [S]. Thorpe next Norwich, 14 Nov. 1349.

1237 Inst. of Bartholomew de Salle, priest, in the person of his proctor, Dns John [Nudde[23]] of Shotesham, rector of Fordley[24] (*Fordele*) [S], to the rectory of Theberton [S]; patron, Sir John de Segrave. Thorpe next Norwich, 14 Nov. 1349.

1238 Inst. of Hamo Gerard of Bawburgh [N], priest, to the [manor] chapel of St Andrew of Hales,[25] Loddon [N]; patron, John de Hales, knight. Thorpe next Norwich, 16 Nov. 1349.

1239 Inst. of Thomas son of John Glover of East Walton [N], priest, to a third part of Narburgh [N]; patron, William de Narburgh. Thorpe next Norwich, 17 Nov. 1349.

1240 Inst. of John Thebaud of Rishangles (*Rysangles*) [S], clerk with first tonsure, to the rectory of Elmswell [S]; patron, the abbot of Bury St Edmunds [S]. Thorpe next Norwich, 17 Nov. 1349.

1241 Inst. of Richard Olyver, acolyte, to the rectory of Groton (*Groten*) [S]; patron, the abbot of Bury St Edmunds [S]. Thorpe next Norwich, 17 Nov. 1349.

1242 Inst. of Adam Keme of Stoke, priest, to the vicarage of Stoke Nayland [S]. [fo.115ᵛ] The bishop had nomination; patron in this turn, Edward III, the temporalities of Prittlewell Priory being in his hand. Thorpe next Norwich, 18 Nov. 1349.

---

[21] Instituted 1334; patrons were St Mary priory at Creeting, a cell of Bernay (Reg. Ayremynne fo.64ᵛ, Knowles & Hadcock 83).
[22] Creeting had three parishes, All Saints, St Mary and St Olave. St Olave church fell to ruin in the 17th century; All Saints was demolished in the early 19th century (*Taxatio* 115, 123; White, *Suffolk*, 232).
[23] See Reg. Ayremynne fo.72ᵛ.
[24] Fordley and Middleton [S] shared a churchyard; the parish was absorbed into Middleton, probably in the 17th century (*Taxatio*, 118; White, *Suffolk*, 384).
[25] This chapel was subject to the vicar of Holy Trinity parish in Loddon.

1243   Inst. of William de Griston, priest, to the rectory of Larling [N]; patrons, the Master and brothers of the College of St John the Evangelist at Rushworth[26] (*Russheworth*) [N]. Thorpe next Norwich, 18 Nov. 1349.

1244   Preferment by the bishop of Nicholas de Wrotham, priest and brother of the College of St John the Evangelist at Rushworth [N], to the mastership of that college, vac. by resig. of Dns John Godwyk, in accordance with the election held by the brothers there, and the presentation of the patron, Dns Edmund Gonevill. Thorpe next Norwich, 18 Nov. 1349.

1245   Inst.[27] of John Auncel, clerk with first tonsure, to the rectory of Beeston Regis [N]; patron, Henry [of Grosmont], earl of Lancaster. Thorpe next Norwich, 18 Nov. 1349.

1246   Inst. of Simon de Dullyngham, priest, to the rectory of Wolferton [N]; patron, Robert de Ufford, earl of Suffolk. Thorpe next Norwich, 18 Nov. 1349.

1247   Preferment by the bishop of Brother Hugh de Pardines, priest and professed Benedictine monk of Conches Abbey (*Conch*), Rouen diocese,[28] to the priorate of St Faith Priory, Horsham [N], in accordance with his canonical election and at the presentation of Robert de Benhale, knight, the patron of Horsham. Thorpe next Norwich, 19 Nov. 1349.

1248   Inst. of Nicholas de Ollerker, clerk with first tonsure, to the rectory of Little Waxham [N]; patron, Lady Elizabeth, widow of Oliver de Ingham, knight. Thorpe next Norwich, 19 Nov. 1349.

1249   Collation of the vicarage of [a moiety[29] of] St Peter's, Wiggenhall [N], to Roger Colman of *Hecham*, priest. Thorpe next Norwich, 19 Nov. 1349.

1250   Inst. of Henry Pollard of Didlington (*Dedelington*) [N], priest, to the vicarage of Rougham [N]. The bishop had nomination; patrons, the prior and convent of West Acre [N]. Thorpe next Norwich, 20 Nov. 1349.

1251   Preferment by the bishop of Brother John de Holkham, priest and professed Augustinian canon of Peterstone Priory (*Sancti Petri de Petra*) [N], to the priorate of that house.[30] The bishop committed to him all administration, saving in all things the episcopal rights. Thorpe next Norwich, 20 Nov. 1349.

---

[26] Founded by John de Gonevill, who endowed it with this advowson (Knowles & Hadcock 417, 436; see also **88**, **1559***).

[27] Beside the marginal heading a contemporary hand noted 'app° W. de Elveden'. The meaning is not clear.

[28] *Recte* Evreux diocese, Rouen archdiocese.

[29] St Peter was in moieties, one appropriated to Shouldham priory and the other in the bishop's collation (Reg. Ayremynne fo.73, *Taxatio*, 80).

[30] No election is mentioned.

1252 [fo.116] Inst. of John de Framesden, priest, to the rectory of Claydon [S]; patron, John de Brewes, knight. Thorpe next Norwich, 21 Nov. 1349.

1253 Inst. of Clement de Paston, priest, to the rectory of Wattisfield [S]; patron, the abbot of Bury St Edmunds [S]. Thorpe next Norwich, 23 Nov. 1349.

1254 Inst. of Hugh Cane of Chacombe (*Chaucombe*), deacon, to the rectory of Alburgh [N]; patron, John, Lord of Segrave, knight. Thorpe next Norwich, 21 Nov. 1349.

1255 Inst. of William de Baxgrave, acolyte, to the rectory of Edingthorpe (*Edythorp*) [N]; patron, Joan de Barre, countess Warenne. Thorpe next Norwich, 26 Nov. 1349.

1256* (i) The bishop dispensed Thomas de Mor of *Saham*, deacon, to hold a benefice despite his defect of age, by papal authority[31] for 60 clerks of the diocese aged 21. Mor was not yet 23 but older than 20. He was next instituted to the rectory of Great Poringland [N] (*Poringlond magna*[32]); patron [in this turn[33]], Mary [Roos], countess of Norfolk and marshal of England.

(ii) PRIMUS IN GRATIA. Letter of institution. Thorpe next Norwich, 26 Nov. 1349.

1257 Collation of the deanery of Thetford[34] [N] to Richard Rothe, subdeacon. Thorpe next Norwich, 26 Nov. 1349.

1258 SECUNDUS IN GRATIA.[35] Dispensation (as in **1256***) of Eudes de Mauteby, clerk with first tonsure, over 20 but under 23, followed by his institution to the rectory of Mautby [N]; patron, Robert de Mauteby, knight. Thorpe next Norwich, 27 Nov. 1349.

1259 Inst. of Ralph son of Roger Carlef of Hethersett (*Hetersete*) [N], priest, to the vicarage[36] of Flixton [St Mary] [S]; patrons, the prioress and convent of Flixton [S]. Thorpe next Norwich, 27 Nov. 1349.

1260 Inst. of Nicholas Westgate of Thurston (*Threston*) [S], priest, to the vicarage of Ketteringham [N]; [fo.116ᵛ] patrons, the prior and convent of Pentney [N]. Thorpe next Norwich, 29 Nov. 1349.

1261 Inst. of Robert atte Cros of Thurlow [S], priest, to the rectory of Little Bradley [S]; patron in this turn, Edward III, the temporalities of Stoke-by-Clare Priory [S] being in his hand. Thorpe next Norwich, 29 Nov. 1349.

---

[31] See **1296**.
[32] Great Poringland (All Saints, East Poringland) is now simply 'Poringland' (*Phillimore Atlas*, 194).
[33] Usually St Mary priory, Thetford (Reg. Ayremynne fo.71ᵛ).
[34] Vacant by resignation (**277**, **1267**).
[35] Noted by contemporary hand in inner margin.
[36] Vacant by resignation (**673**, **1208**).

1262   Inst. of William de la Chambr', priest, to the rectory of Thompson [N]; patrons, Thomas de Shardelowe, knight, and his brother John. Thorpe next Norwich, 5 Dec. 1349.

1263   Collation of the archdeaconry of Sudbury [S], vac. by resig. of [M.] Thomas de Wynchestr',[37] to M. Thomas de Methelwold DCnCL. Thorpe next Norwich, 8 Dec. 1349.

1264   Collation of the deanery of Orford [S] to Robert de Hardeshull,[38] clerk with first tonsure. Thorpe next Norwich, 8 Dec. 1349.

1265   Inst. of Thomas Calwer of Holkham [N], priest, to the vicarage[39] of Stradsett [N]; patrons, the abbot and convent of West Dereham [N]. Thorpe next Norwich, 11 Dec. 1349.

1266   Collation of the deanery of Humbleyard [N] to Thomas de Thornham, clerk with first tonsure. Thorpe next Norwich, 11 Dec. 1349.

1267*   (i) TERTIUS IN GRATIA.[40] Dispensation (as in **1256***) of Robert de Walton, acolyte, of Norwich diocese, under 24 but over 20, followed by his collation to the rectory of Thornage [N]. Thorpe next Norwich, 13 Dec. 1349.
  (ii) Text of the dispensation.

1268   Inst. of John son of Robert de Toynton, acolyte, to the rectory of St Mary Unbrent (*Sancte Marie Combusta*) in Norwich; patrons, the dean and canons of the College of St Mary in the Fields, Norwich. Thorpe next Norwich, 14 Dec. 1349.

1269   Inst. of Remy de Dunston, clerk with first tonsure, to the rectory of Brundall[41] (*Brundale*) [N]; patron, Sir Thomas de Sancto Omere.[42] Thorpe next Norwich, 14 Dec. 1349.

1270   [fo.117] Collation of the deanery of Cranwich[43] [N] to Robert de Hardreshull, clerk with first tonsure. Thorpe next Norwich, 14 Dec. 1349.

1271   Collation of the deanery of Orford [S] to John de Hardeshull, clerk with first tonsure. Thorpe next Norwich, 14 Dec. 1349.

---

[37] For his exchange with Elveden (see **1050**), not recorded in this register, see *Fasti* 4, 30. See also Appendix III.
[38] For his circulation of deaneries, see **1033, 1266, 1270–1**.
[39] Vacant by resignation (**1056, 1361**).
[40] Contemporary note in inner margin.
[41] St Lawrence of Brundall was consolidated with Little Plumstead and Witton by the 19th century (White, *Norfolk*, 503f).
[42] See Millican, 'Biographical notices', 172.
[43] Probably just resigned by Robert de Walton (**19, 1267**).

1272 BELHAGHE. Inst. of John de Ludham, priest, to the rectory of Belaugh (*Belahawe*) [N]; patrons, the abbot and convent of St Benet's, Hulme [N]. Thorpe next Norwich, 16 Dec. 1349.

1273 Inst. of William le Cook of Little Barningham [N], priest, to the vicarage of Horning [N]; patron in this turn, Edward III, because of the vacancy of the abbacy of St Benet's, Hulme [N]. Thorpe next Norwich, 16 Dec. 1349.

1274 Inst. of Nicholas del Islde, clerk with first tonsure, to the rectory of Tacolneston [N]; patron, Lady Margaret de Dovedale. Thorpe next Norwich, 20 Dec. 1349.

1275 Inst. of Walter Kempe of Narford [N], priest, to the vicarage[44] of East Walton [N]; patrons, the prior and convent of West Acre [N]. Thorpe next Norwich, 20 Dec. 1349.

1276 Inst. of John de Debenham, acolyte, to the rectory of St Etheldreda in Thetford [N]; presentation was by M. John de Oo, vicar-general of Bishop Thomas [de Lisle] of Ely, the patron. Thorpe next Norwich, 20 Dec. 1349.

1277 Inst. of M. Adam de Wykemere, acolyte, to the rectory of Hockwold [N]; patron, Michael de Ponyngges, knight. Note that Robert de Skales, knight, and Osbert de Mundeford renounced every right which they had had to the advowson of that rectory. Thorpe next Norwich, 21 Dec. 1349.

1278 Inst. of Nicholas Jerneys of *Wyndener'*, priest, to a moiety of St Matthias, Thorpe next Haddiscoe (*Thorp Sancti Mathie*) [N]; patron, John de Segrave, knight, lord of Folkestone (*Fulkestan*). Thorpe next Norwich, 22 Dec. 1349.

1279 Inst. of John de Chedistan, priest, to [a moiety[45] of] Little Glemham [S]; patron, William Phelipp of Dennington (*Dynyton*) [S]. Thorpe next Norwich, 13 [*sic*] Dec. 1349.

1280 Inst. of Richard del Grene,[46] priest, to the rectory of Babingley[47] (*Babbyngle*) [N]; patrons, Robert de Ufford, earl of Suffolk, and Thomas Chappe. Thorpe next Norwich, 24 Dec. 1349.

1281 [fo.117^v] Collation of the rectory of Badingham [S] to John de Wyneston, subdeacon; the bishop had patronage in this turn by right of devolution.[48] Thorpe next Norwich, 25 Dec. 1349.

---

[44] Vacant by resignation (**308**, **1224**).
[45] MS. *pro me*[dietate] added in margin; cf. **418**.
[46] *Alias* Atte Grene (**1775**).
[47] Vacant by resignation (Reg. Ayremynne fo.61^v, **1403**).
[48] At the last known institution, in 1329, the patron was Oliver de Ingham, knight (Reg. Ayremynne fo.26^v); his other advowsons were exercised by his widow, Elizabeth.

1282 QUARTUS IN GRATIA. Dispensation (as in **1256***) of Thomas de Walton, subdeacon, followed by his collation to the rectory of St James, South Elmham [S]. Thorpe next Norwich, 25 Dec. 1349.

1283 Inst. of John de Godewold of Woodford, priest, to the rectory of Markshall [N]; patron, Thomas Moyne. Thorpe next Norwich, 29 Dec. 1349.

1284 Collation of the deanery of Loes [S] to Stephen de Luton, priest. Thorpe next Norwich, 29 Dec. 1349.

1285 Inst. of Robert de Harpele, priest, to a moiety of Howe [N]; patron, John de Norwico, knight. Thorpe next Norwich, 29 Dec. 1349.

1286 Collation of the vicarage of Sapiston (*Sapeston*) [S] to Robert Parlet of Thompson [N], priest. Thorpe next Norwich, 30 Dec. 1349.

1287 Collation of the rectory of St Michael of Conisford[49] in Norwich, to Thomas atte Kyrke of Blofield [N], priest; patron in this turn by right of devolution,[50] the bishop. Thorpe next Norwich, 31 Dec. 1349.

1288 Collation of the vicarage of Castle Acre [N] to [omitted]; patron in this turn by right of devolution,[51] the bishop. Thorpe next Norwich, 31 Dec. 1349.

1289 Certificate of Bishop John [de Thoresby] of St David's that he has executed Bateman's commission (quoted in full; dated 1 Sept. 1349 at South Elmham) for an exchange of benefices between William de Horwych,[52] rector of *Launailok* in St David's diocese, and Henry de Campeden, rector of St Gregory's, Sudbury [S] with its annexed chapel. [fo.118] Bateman had nomination; the patrons, the prioress and nuns of Nuneaton, in Coventry and Lichfield diocese, agreed. London, 18 Oct. 1349.

1290 William [de Horwych] appeared personally before the bishop this day and gave oath of canonical obedience [for the rectory of St Gregory's, Sudbury [S], with its chapel]; order was sent [the archdeacon of] Sudbury to induct him. [Thorpe next Norwich], 31 Dec. 1349.

1291 Collation of the deanery of Hartismere (*Hertesmere*) [S] to Dns John de Horscroft, priest. Thorpe next Norwich, 1 Jan. 1350.

1292 Inst. of John le Neve of Stockton [N], deacon, to the vicarage of Hales [N]. The bishop had nomination; patrons, the prior and convent of St Olave, [Herringfleet] [S]. Thorpe next Norwich, 2 Jan. 1350.

---

[49] This rectory was incorporated to the Augustinian friary in 1368 (N. Tanner, *Church in Norwich*, 157, citing Watkin, *Inventory*, pt.1, 24, and Blomefield).
[50] The previous patron was Michael de Thorp (Reg. Ayremynne fo.12).
[51] Castle Acre priory had the appropriation (*Taxatio* 80).
[52] *Alias* Horwode (**1543**).

1293 Inst. of Geoffrey de Honeweton, clerk with first tonsure, in the person of his proctor, Dns Henry de Romeburgh, priest, to the rectory of Alpheton (*Alfetone*) [S]; patron in this turn, Edward III, the temporalities of the abbey of Aumale (*Albe Marle*) being in his hand. Thorpe next Norwich, 7 Jan. 1350.

1294 Inst. of William Ywar of Marham [N], priest, to a portion of West Bilney (*West Bylneye*) [N]; patrons, the prior and convent of Pentney [N]. Thorpe next Norwich, 8 Jan. 1350.

1295 QUINTUS IN GRATIA. Dispensation (as in **1256***) of James de Mortuo Mari, clerk with first tonsure, followed by his collation to the rectory of Syderstone (*Sydesterne*) [N]; patron in this turn by right of devolution,[53] the bishop. Thorpe next Norwich, 11 Jan. 1350.

1296* [fo.118ᵛ] BULLA SUPER DISPENSATIONE ETATIS PRO LX CLERICIS CONCESSE.[54] Letter of grace from Pope Clement VI to Bishop Bateman, authorizing him to dispense 60 clerks of Norwich diocese, who were at least 21 years old and otherwise suitable, from the requirement that they be 24 years old before receiving priests' orders and holding benefices with cure of souls. This grace was granted in response to a request from Bateman, claiming that pestilence had left many parishes without priests. Avignon, 13 Oct. 1349.

1297 Inst. of John son of Ralph le Smyth of Worstead (*Worstede*) [N], priest, to the vicarage of Ormsby [N]; patrons, the prior and convent of Holy Trinity, Norwich cathedral. Thorpe next Norwich, 12 Jan. 1350.

1298 Inst. of Thomas Rous, deacon, in the person of his proctor, William de Taterford, to the rectory of South Wootton [N]; patron, Queen Isabella. Thorpe next Norwich, 20 Jan. 1350.

1299 Collation of the mastership of the grammar school of Blofield [N] to William Buntyng. Thorpe next Norwich, 19 Jan. 1350.

1300 Inst. of Hugh de Lydgate, acolyte, to the rectory of Brisley [N]; patron, Hugh de Hastinges.[1] Thorpe next Norwich, 22 Jan. 1350.

1301 Inst. of William atte Medwe, priest, to a moiety of Ringstead Parva (*Ryngestede parva*) [N]; patron, Richard de Boylond. Thorpe next Norwich, 22 Jan. 1350.

1302 Inst. of John Jay, priest, to the vicarage of Witton [N] [in Waxham deanery]; patrons, the prior and convent of Bromholm [N]. Thorpe next Norwich, 22 Jan. 1350.

---

[53] The patrons were John de Grey, son of John de Grey of *Retherfeld*, knight, and Sir Milo de Stapelton (Bek 70ᵛ and **1812**).
[54] See *CPL* III, 331.
[1] Preceded by a space where, possibly, *do*[min]*i* had been erased. This was Hugh, heir of Sir Hugh (**392**).

1303   Inst. of Henry de Redesham, priest, to the vicarage[2] of Flitcham [N]. [fo.119] The bishop had nomination; patrons, the prior and convent of Flitcham [N]. Thorpe next Norwich, 24 Jan. 1350.

1304   Collation of the vicarage of Silverley[3] (*Sylverle*) [Cambs.] to Nicholas de Haneworth of Bungay [S], priest. Patron in this turn was the bishop, by right of devolution, because the prior and convent of Hatfield Broad Oak (*Hatfeld*) did not present to the benefice within the legal time limit. Thorpe next Norwich, 25 Jan. 1350.

1305   Letter patent of Edward III presenting John de Bury, priest, to the rectory of Hevingham [N]; the king had patronage in this turn because the temporalities of the see of Norwich had recently been in his hand.[4] Westminster, 6 Feb. 1350.

1306   Inst. of John de Bury, priest, to the rectory of Hevingham [N]; patron in this turn, Edward III, the temporalities of the see of Norwich having recently been in his hand. Thornage, 1 Mar. 1350.

1307   Preferment of Brother Baldwin de Sanston, priest and professed Augustinian canon of Kersey Priory [S], to the priorate of that house, vacant by the death of the preceding prior.[5] Thorpe next Norwich, 26 Jan. 1350.

1308   Collation of the rectory of Alteston[6] [S] to Dns John Graunger, chaplain; patron in this turn by right of devolution,[7] the bishop. Thorpe next Norwich, 26 Jan. 1350.

1309   Inst. of William Suclyng of Helmingham, priest, to the vicarage of Darsham (*Dersham*) [S]; patron in this turn by the king's grant,[8] Mary [Roos], countess of Norfolk and marshal of England. Thorpe next Norwich, 29 Jan. 1350.

1310   Inst. of John Peggon[9] of East Rudham [N], priest, to the vicarage[10] of Barmer (*Bermere*) [N]; patrons, the prior and convent of Coxford [N]. Thorpe next Norwich, 30 Jan. 1350.

---

    [2] Vacant by resignation (**962, 1344**).
    [3] Silverly was later united to Ashley [Cambs.] also in Fordham deanery (*Phillimore Atlas*, 107).
    [4] See Introduction, xvi.
    [5] No election is mentioned.
    [6] The village was near Grimston Hall, about a mile southwest of Trimley St Martin, with which its rectory was consolidated in 1362 (White, *Suffolk*, 127; Reg. Percy fo.5^v).
    [7] At the last registered institution the patron was Edmund Peverel, lord of Grimston (Reg. Ayremynne fo.35).
    [8] Usually St Mary priory, Thetford (White, *Suffolk*, 364).
    [9] *Alias* Pygeon (**1766**).
    [10] Corrected as from inst. to a rectory; see Reg. Ayremynne fo. 83^v for the appropriation in 1326.

1311 Inst. of William de Lyvermer' of Brandon (*Brandon ferie*) [S], priest, to the rectory of Croxton [N]; patrons, the prior and convent of Bromehill [N]. Thorpe next Norwich, 1 Feb. 1350.

1312 Inst. of John Rayson, acolyte, to the rectory of Hassingham [N]; patron, John de Ratlesden, knight. Thorpe next Norwich, 3 Feb. 1350.

1313 Inst. of Gilbert Arches, priest, to [fo.119ᵛ] the rectory of Bixley [N]; patron, Mary [Roos], countess of Norfolk. Thorpe next Norwich, 6 Feb. 1350.

1314 Inst. of John Spore of Barton, priest, to the rectory of Thompson [N]; patrons, the master and brothers of the chantry of Barton Mills[11] [S]. Thorpe next Norwich, 11 Feb. 1350.

1315 Inst. of William de Eggefeld, priest, to the rectory of Kirton (*Kyrketon*) [S]; patron, Mary [Roos], countess of Norfolk and marshal of England. Thorpe next Norwich, 11 Feb. 1350.

1316 Inst. of John son of Thomas de Caldecote, acolyte, to the rectory of Shingham [N]; patron in this turn, Edward III, because of his wardship of the lands and heir of Hugh le Dispenser.[12] Thorpe next Norwich, 14 Feb. 1350.

1317 Inst. of William de Pakynton, clerk with first tonsure, to the rectory of East Wretham [N]; patron [in this turn], Edward III.[13] Thorpe next Norwich, 19 Feb. 1350.

1318 Inst. of Andrew Bomond of Blythburgh [S], priest, to the rectory of Thurston [S]; patron, the abbot of Bury St Edmunds [S]. Thorpe next Norwich, 19 Feb. 1350.

1319 Inst. of John de Stok, acolyte, to the rectory of Caldecote[14] [N]; patron in this turn, Edward III, because of his wardship of the lands and heir of Hugh le Dispenser. Thorpe next Norwich, 20 Feb. 1350.

1320 Inst. of Gerard Ricarii, priest, to the rectory of Heveningham [S]; patron in this turn, Edward III, the temporalities of St Neot's Priory being in his hand. Thorpe next Norwich, 22 Feb. 1350.

---

[11] The chantry college of Thompson [N] (**1325**), founded in 1349 by Sir Thomas de Shardelow and his brother John for six chaplains, in the parish church of Thompson (*CPR 1348–1350*, 374). The rectory of Barton Mills was appropriated to the college (cf. **933**).

[12] See *Complete Peerage* IV, 271–4.

[13] Usually the prior of Ogbourne St George (**390**) as proctor of the abbot of Bec-Hellouin (Reg. Ayremynne fo.75).

[14] *Alias* Cocket, just southwest of Beechamwell and Shingham; the village declined and the church was in ruins by the early 16th century, its rectory united to Cockley Cley (*Ruined Churches*, 53; White, *Norfolk*, 6; Faden, sheet 4).

1321   Inst. of Thomas de Ellerton, priest, to the rectory of St Mary's, Stiffkey [N]; patron, Walter Mauney, knight. Thornage, 2 Mar. 1350.

1322   Inst. of Thomas son of Peter de Melborn, priest, to the rectory of Willingham St Mary [S]; patron, Edward III. Thornage, 3 Mar. 1350.

1323   Collation of the rectory of St Peter's in South Elmham [S] to Robert Morleword[15] of Moulton, priest. Thornage, 5 Mar. 1350.

1324   Collation of the deanery of Fincham [N] to Roger de Stalham[16] of Heigham (*Hegham*) [N]. Thornage, 4 Mar. 1350.

1325   Inst. of William de la Chaumbr' of Eriswell [S], priest, to the rectory of Thompson [N]; patrons, the master and chaplains of the chantry of Thompson[17] [N]. Thornage, 10 Mar. 1350.

1326   [fo.120] Inst. of Dns Edmund [de Byrston], recent perpetual vicar of Quarles (*Wharles*) [N], priest, to the vicarage of Colkirk[18] (*Colkyrk*) [N]. The bishop had nomination; patrons, the prior and convent of Weybourne [N]. Thornage, 1 Mar. 1350.

1327   Inst. of Roger de Wytlesham, priest, to the vicarage of Swilland [S]; patrons, the prioress and convent of Wix. Thornage, 4 Mar. 1350.

1328   Inst. of Richard son of John Richard of Kimberley [N], priest, to the vicarage of Wymondham [N]; patrons, the prior and convent of Wymondham [N]. Thornage, 7 Mar. 1350.

1329   Collation of the rectory of Brumstead [N] to Henry de Plumpstede,[19] priest; patron in this turn by right of devolution,[20] the bishop. Thornage, 8 Mar. 1350.

1330   Inst. of Robert de Croft, priest, to the rectory of Bittering Parva[21] (*parva Bytering*) [N]; patron, Robert de Causton, knight. Thornage, 13 Mar. 1350.

1331   Inst. of Richard de Olneye, priest, to the rectory of Gressenhall [N]; patron, John Cameys, knight. Thornage, 13 Mar. 1350.

---

[15] Cf. **840**.
[16] Order omitted.
[17] See **1314**.
[18] This vicarage had just been established (**1**).
[19] This name was written later, preceded (unusually) by *dilecto filio*. Cf. **1408**.
[20] See **669** for the usual patronage.
[21] The church of Bittering Magna (St Nicholas) had disappeared by 1368 (Watkin, *Inventory* 2, xxi; cf. *Ruined Churches*, 53); the parish had lain between Gressenhall and Beetley and was annexed to them (White, *Norfolk*, 329).

1332 Preferment of Brother David de Fornham,[22] priest and professed Augustinian canon of St Mary's Priory, Chipley (*Chyppeleye*) [S], to the priorate of that house,[23] vacant by the death of the previous prior, Brother Richard [de Norwico[24]]. The bishop committed both spiritual and temporal administration to Fornham, so far as lay with him, saving in all things the episcopal rights. Thornage, 15 Mar. 1350.

1333 Inst. of John de Wrotham, clerk with first tonsure, to the rectory of Stratton St Michael (*longa Stratton Sancti Michaelis*) [N], vac. by resig. of Dns Richard Markant, rector; patron [in this turn[25]], Edward III. Thornage, 15 Mar. 1350.

1334 Inst. of William Leche, priest, to the rectory of St Michael's, Fincham [N]; patrons, the prior and convent of Castle Acre [N]. Walsingham [N], 16 Mar. 1350.

1335 Collation of the deanery of Orford [S] to ([margin] Robert de Jernemuth of Kimberley [N], clerk with first tonsure); the usual notice of customary submission was sent. Thornage, 16 Mar. 1350.

1336 Inst. of Robert de Walsingham,[26] acolyte, to the church of[27] Thorpe next Haddiscoe [N]; patron in this turn, Edward III, the lands of John de Segrave, lord [fo.120ᵛ] of Folkestone, being in his hand. Thornage, 17 Mar. 1350.

1337 Inst. of John de Poringlond, clerk with first tonsure, to the rectory of Briston [N], vac. by resig. of Dns William de Motton, rector; patrons by right of acquisition, M. Richard de Lyng, M. Walter de Elveden, Dns Simon [de Rykynghale] of Babingley, Dns William de Cressingham, Dns John de Bury, Dns Stephen de Cressingham, Dns Robert de Walton, and Dns Thomas de Walton. Thornage, 20 Mar. 1350.

1338* Resignation by William de Motton, rector of Briston [N], into the bishop's hands, for reasons unspecified. n.d.

1339 Inst. of Thomas Dounham of Ely, priest, to the rectory of Southmere[28] N; patron in this turn, Edward III, the temporalities of Ivry Abbey (*Ybreyo*) being in his hand. Thornage, 22 Mar. 1350.

---

[22] Thornham in **1452**.

[23] No election is mentioned.

[24] Elected 1333 (Reg. Ayremynne fo.62).

[25] Usually Newton Longville priory (**369, 1688**).

[26] He held this benefice until his death in 1385 (*Norwich Wills* 2, 382).

[27] *Recte* a moiety of? (see **564, 1278**).

[28] The village of Southmere, *alias* Sutmere or Summerfield (*Domesday Gazetteer*, 288), was later deserted and the parish absorbed into Docking ('Lost Villages', 158; White, *Norfolk*, 636).

1340   Inst. of John Pers, priest, to the rectory of Whittington [N]; presentation was made by M. [John] de Oo, vicar-general of the patron, Bishop Thomas [de Lisle] of Ely. Thornage, 22 Mar. 1350.

1341   Inst. of John Hullyng of Burton, priest, to the rectory of Trimley St Mary [S]; patron, Mary [Roos], countess of Norfolk and marshal of England. Thornage, 24 Mar. 1350.

1342   Inst. of William Paty of Bodham [N], chaplain, to the vicarage of West Beckham [N]; patrons, the prior and convent of Holy Trinity, Norwich cathedral. Thornage, 21 Mar. 1350.

1343   [Margin] Memorandum that [John Balle,[29]] the vicar of Griston [N], was instituted at the bishop's nomination.[30] n.p., 18 Mar. 1350.

1344   Inst. of Thomas de Plumpstede, priest, to the vicarage of Halvergate [N]. The bishop had nomination; patrons, the abbot and convent of Tintern Abbey (*Tynterna*). Thornage, 25 Mar. 1350.

1345   Inst. of Edmund de Southcaldecote, priest, to the rectory of Akenham [N]; patron, Lady Katherine Latymer. Thornage, 26 Mar. 1350.

1346   [fo.121] Collation of the rectory of St Peter Hungate, Norwich (*Sancti Petri de Hounegate*), to Robert de Eton of Lincoln diocese, priest; patron in this turn by right of devolution,[31] the bishop. Order was sent [the archdeacon of] Norwich to induct Eton. n.p., 26 Mar. 1350

1347   Inst. of Roger Hamond of Charsfield [S], priest, to the rectory of St Matthew's, in Ipswich (*iuxta Gyppewicum*) [S]; patron, Edward III. Thornage, 31 Mar. 1350.

1348   Inst. of John de Hadenham, priest, to the rectory of Kennet [Cambs.]; patron, Mary [Roos], countess of Norfolk and marshal of England. n.p., 14 Apr. 1350

1349   Inst. of M. Robert de Heselbech, priest, in the person of his proctor, John de Haddon, clerk, to the rectory of Kedington [S], vac. by resig. of M. Richard de Retford,[32] in exchange [see next] for the rectory of Sturton le Steeple (*Stretton*), York diocese; patron, Thomas de Bernardeston, knight. Thornage, 14 Apr. 1350.

1350   Inst. of M. Richard de Retford, by commission of Archbishop William [de la Zouche], to the rectory of Sturton le Steeple, York diocese, vac. by resig. of

[29] See **1677**.
[30] See **22** for this recent appropriation.
[31] The usual patrons were the College of St Mary in the Fields, Norwich (N. Tanner, *Church in Norwich*, 175).
[32] Inst. in 1343 (Reg. Bek fo.70ᵛ).

M. Robert de Heselbech, in exchange for Retford's rectory of Kedington [S]; patrons, the abbot and convent of St Mary's, York. Thornage, 14 Apr. 1350.

1351 Inst. of John le Clerk, priest, to the rectory[33] of Fulmodeston (*Fulmerston*) [N]; patron, the prior and convent of Castle Acre [N]. Thornage, 17 Apr. 1350.

1352 Inst. of Walter Smyth of Wymondham [N], priest, to the rectory of South Pickenham [N]; patron in this turn,[34] Richard FitzWilliam of *Hales*.[35] Norwich, 19 Apr. 1350.

1353 Inst. of John de Weston, acolyte, in the person of his proctor, Thomas de Byntr', clerk, to a moiety of Sidestrand [N]; presentation was made by Dns Henry de Walton, attorney general of Henry, earl of Lancaster. Norwich, 19 Apr. 1350.

1354 Inst. of Thomas de Hoxhill, priest, to the rectory of Hengrave (*Hemegrave*) [S], vac. by resig. of Dns Nicholas de Aldham, in exchange for Hoxhill's rectory of Whatfield [S]; patron, Edmund de Hemegrave, knight. Thetford, 21 Apr. 1350.

1355 [fo.121ᵛ] Inst. of Nicholas de Aldham, priest, to the rectory of Whatfield [S], vac. by resig. of Thomas de Oxhill, in exchange for Aldham's rectory of Hengrave [S]; patron, Richard de Kokfeld. Thetford, 21 Apr. 1350.

1356 Inst. of Henry Lewin, priest, to the rectory of St Andrew's,[36] Blo Norton (*Blonorton*) [N]; patron, William de Middelton. Thetford, 21 Apr. 1350.

1357 Inst. of Thomas Fencr', priest, to the rectory of Plumstead (*Plompsted iuxta Holt*) [N], vac. by resig. of Dns Walter de Kent; patrons, the prior and convent of Merton. London, 28 Apr. 1350.

1358* Collation of the rectory of Blofield [N] to Robert de Stratton, BCL, clerk with first tonsure. Blofield was vacant by the free and simple resignation of the bishop, who had recently obtained it by papal authority, as united to his *mensa*. Order was sent to a certain unnamed chaplain to induct Stratton. London, 29 Apr. 1350.

1359 Inst. of John Robechon, priest, to the vicarage of Great Thurlow [S], vac. by resig. of Dns Edmund de Southcaldecote [**1345**]; patrons, the abbot and convent of Battle Abbey. London, 2 May 1350.

---

[33] St John the Baptist chapel at Croxton was annexed to this (*Taxatio* 90; Reg. Ayremynne ff.58ᵛ, 95*bis*ᵛ, Bek fo.20ᵛ; and see White, *Norfolk*, 653).

[34] This patronage was held by two men in turns (**1488**).

[35] Probably Hale [N], less than 3 miles northeast.

[36] There were two parishes here (*Taxatio*, 87), but St Margaret church was dilapidated by 1394 and the two were united in 1401 (A. Davison, *Six Deserted Villages in Norfolk*, East Anglian Archaeology report 44, Dereham 1988, 101; and see *Ruined Churches*, 53).

1360 Inst. of John Joye, priest, to the rectory of Great Bealings [S], vac. by resig. of Dns Nicholas de Lydgate, in exchange [**1362**] for the vicarage of Clare [S]; patrons, Walter de Wancy, Robert de Wancy, and Hugh de Penteneye. Chelmsford (*Chelmersford*), 3 May 1350.

1361 Inst.[37] of John de Totyngton priest, to the rectory of Elveden [S]; patron, the abbot of Bury St Edmunds [S]. London, 26 Apr. 1350.

1362 [fo.122] Inst. of Nicholas de Lydgate, priest, to the vicarage of Clare [S], vac. by resig. of John Joye, in exchange [**1360**] for the rectory of Great Bealings [S]; patron in this turn, Edward III, the temporalities of Stoke-by-Clare Priory [S] being in his hand. Chelmsford, 3 May 1350.

1363 Inst. of John de Boys of Worcester diocese, clerk with first tonsure, in the person of his proctor, Dns Richard [le Dyer[38]] of Kidderminster, priest, to the rectory of St Martin's, Fincham [N]; patrons, the prior and convent of Shouldham [N]. Terling, 13 May 1350.

1364 Inst. of Edmund le Gonvill, clerk with first tonsure, to the rectory of Thelnetham [S], vac. by resig. of Dns William Gonvill; patron, Robert de Benhal, knight. Terling, 14 May 1350.

1365 Inst. of John South, priest, to the rectory of Brancaster (*Brauncestr' iuxta mare*) [N]; patrons, the abbot and convent of Ramsey Abbey. Dover, 27 May 1350.

HEADING: Institutions and admissions by the prior of Norwich cathedral [Simon Bozoun], M. Richard de Lyng, archdeacon of Norwich, and M. Thomas de Meth[elwolde, archdeacon of Sudbury], vicars-general in the bishop's absence *in remotis*. Memorandum that their commission was in the same terms as their previous one and dated Dover, 28 May 1350.

1366 Inst. of Robert de Thernyng, priest, by vicar-general Methelwolde, to the rectory of Rushbrooke [S], vac. by resig. of Dns William de Lylleford; [fo.122ᵛ] patron, the abbot of Bury St Edmunds [S]. Chevington [S], 4 June 1350.

1367 Inst. of John de Esterford, priest, by vicar-general Methelwolde, to the vicarage of Ubbeston [S]; patron in this turn, Edward III, the temporalities of the alien priory of St Neot being in his hand. Cowlinge [S], 5 June 1350.

1368 Inst. of Roger le Yonge, priest, by the bishop, to the rectory of Stoke Ash [S], vac. by resig. of Dns Richard de Northcreyk;[39] patron in this turn, Edward III, the temporalities of Eye Priory [S] being in his hand. Norwich, 23 June 1350.

---

[37] A later addition in the lower margin.
[38] See **166**.
[39] For another benefice: **1484**.

1369 Inst. of Robert Donkan of Wormegay [N], priest, by vicar-general Methelwolde, to the rectory of Hawkedon [S]; patron, Walter de Bernyngham, [knight]. Norwich, 26 June 1350.

1370 Inst. of William de le Brok, priest, by vicar-general Methelwolde, to the rectory of Nettlestead [S]; patron, John Typtot, knight. Norwich, 26 June 1350.

1371 PER IPSUM PATREM. Collation by the bishop to Edmund le Strange, priest, of the rectory of Helmingham [S[40]], vac. by resig. of William de Askeby, in exchange for Strange's rectory of Staplehurst (*Stapelherst*) in Canterbury diocese. n.p., 24 June 1350.

1372 Inst. of William de Askeby, priest, to the rectory of Staplehurst in Canterbury diocese, vac. by resig. of Dns Edmund le Strange, in exchange for the rectory of Helmingham [S] as above, [fo.123] by commission of Archbishop Simon [Islip] of Canterbury; patron, John de Somery, knight. Norwich, 24 June 1350.

1373 Inst. of Walter Ubston of Hempnall (*Hemenhale*) [N], priest, to the rectory of St John, Dunwich [S]; patron in this turn, Edward III, the temporalities of Eye Priory [S] being in his hand. London, 21 May 1350.

1374 Inst. of John Syward of Middleton [S], priest, to the rectory of Hoo [S]; patron, Mary [Roos], countess of Norfolk and marshal of England. Terling, 6 July 1350.

1375 Collation of the deanery of Humbleyard [N] to M. Walter de Newehawe of Bacton [S], priest and inceptor in arts; the usual notice of customary submission was sent. Bacton [S], 12 July 1350.

1376 MULTON PARVA.[41] Inst. of William de Mendham, priest, to the rectory of Little Moulton [N]; patron in this turn, Edward III, because of the recent vacancy of the abbacy of St Benet's, Hulme [N]. Thorpe next Norwich, 15 July 1350.

1377 Inst.[42] of John son of Hugh de Kymburle, priest, to the rectory of Kimberley [N]; patrons by right of acquisition, M. Richard de Lyng, archdeacon of Norwich, M. Walter de Elveden, and Dns Simon de Rykenhale, rector of Rollesby [N]. Thorpe next Norwich, 17 July 1350.

1378 Preferment[43] of Brother Robert Duyt, priest and professed Augustinian canon of St Peter's Priory, Ipswich [S], to the priorate of Alnesbourn Priory [S], vacant by the death of Brother Henry [de Hawele[44]] of Finningham. The bishop

[40] For Helmingham [N] see **592**.
[41] *Parva* added by a contemporary hand.
[42] See **720**, **1404**.
[43] No election is mentioned.
[44] See **518**.

committed to Duyt both [fo.123ᵛ] temporal and spiritual administration, so far as lay with him; order to install Duyt was sent the archdeacon of Suffolk or his official. Thorpe next Norwich, 17 July 1350.

1379 CAPELLA MANERII DE CASTR' TRINITATIS. Inst. of James de Baynton, priest, to the free chapel or chantry of the manor of Caister next Yarmouth (*Castr' Sancte Trinitatis*) [N]; patron, William de Lee. Thorpe next Norwich, 18 July 1350.

1380 Inst. of William Uffe of Congham [N], priest, to the vicarage of St Mary's, South Walsham [N], vac. by resig. of Richard Grubbe; patrons, the master and brothers of St Giles Hospital, Norwich. Thorpe next Norwich, 21 July 1350.

1381 Inst. of Simon de Shotesham, priest, to the rectory of Little Hautbois (*Hauboys parva*) [N]; patron, Richard de Reppes. Thorpe next Norwich, 23 July 1350.

1382 Collation to William de Raumesholt, priest, of the rectory of St Mary's of Homersfield, South Elmham [S], vac. by resig. of William de Lopham, in exchange for the rectory of Carlton (*Carleton iuxta Keleshale*) [S]. Thorpe next Norwich, 24 July 1350.

1383 Inst. of William de Lopham, priest, to the rectory of Carlton [S], vac. by resig. of Dns William de Rammesholt, in exchange; patrons, the prioress and convent of Campsey Ash [S]. Thorpe next Norwich, 24 July 1350.

1384 Inst. of William de Hopton, priest, to the rectory of St Peter's, Thetford [N], vac. by resig. of Dns Hugh de Humylierd;[45] patrons, the prior and convent of Lewes. Thorpe next Norwich, 25 July 1350.

1385 Inst. of Peter de Neuton, priest, [fo.124] to a moiety of Brome (*Brom*) [S], vac. by resig. of Dns Richard Punch;[46] patron in this turn,[47] Edward III. Thorpe next Norwich, 26 July 1350.

1386 Inst. of William de Kynyngham, priest, to the vicarage of Wissington [S], vac. by resig. of John Large; patron,[48] the prior of Horkesley. Thorpe next Norwich, 26 July 1350.

1387 Inst. of William de Eboraco, acolyte, in the person of his proctor, Dns Henry Swalwe,[49] rector of Houghton on the Hill (*Houton*) [N], to a moiety of

---

[45] *Alias* Homelyerd, inst. 1343 (Reg. Bek fo.72ᵛ).

[46] He may have been instituted *sede vacante*, as the last known vicar was Henry de Shelton in 1330 (Reg. Ayremynne fo.35ᵛ).

[47] The heir of the previous patron, Brian de Hikelyng, tenant in chief, was his ward; see *CPR 1348–1350*, 368 (dated 17 Aug. 1349).

[48] Cf. **501**.

[49] Inst. 1336 (Reg. Ayr. fo.77).

Barford (*Berford*) [N], vac. by resig. of Dns William de Rudham; patron, Ralph de Nevill, lord of Raby.[50] Thorpe next Norwich, 25 July 1350.

1388 Inst. of John Mason of North Walsham [N], deacon, to the rectory of St Peter Southgate, Norwich; patron in this turn, Edward III.[51] Thorpe next Norwich, 26 July 1350.

1389 Collation of the deanery of Depwade [N] to John de Heygate of Trunch [N], fellow of Trinity Hall at Cambridge University; usual notice of customary submission was sent. Thornage, 27 July 1350.

1390 Collation of the deanery of Holt [N] to M. Richard de Corpsty, M.A., fellow of Trinity Hall at Cambridge University. Thornage, 27 July 1350.

1391* Notice that Brother Robert Dwyt,[52] prior of Alnesbourn [S], resigned his state and office of prior for reasons approved by the bishop into the bishop's hands, and swore on the Gospels to restore all things [belonging to the priory] which he had taken away or alienated, if there were any such. Thornage, 30 July 1350.

1392 [fo.124ᵛ] Inst. of Robert de Horwode, priest, to the [third part] of Shotford in Mendham parish [S], vac. by resig. of Gilbert de Arches [**1313**]; patron, Sir John le Straunge. Thornage, 31 July 1350.

1393 Inst. of Walter Amyas of Lidgate (*Lydgate*) [S], priest, to the free chapel or chantry of the manor of Badmondisfield (*Badmondesfeld*) in Wickhambrook [S]; patron, John Hakeluyt, knight. Thornage, 3 Aug. 1350.

1394 Inst. of John de Totyngton, priest, to the rectory of Little Barningham [N], vac. by resig. of Robert Wilymot, in exchange for the rectory of Brampton Ash (*Bramptone iuxta Dyngele*) in Lincoln diocese; patron, Ralph [de Stafford], baron of Stafford. Thornage, 8 Aug. 1350.

1395 Inst. of Robert Wylymot, priest, in the person of his proctor, Thomas Gayrstauk, clerk, to the rectory of Brampton Ash in Lincoln diocese, in exchange as above, by commission of Bishop John [Gynewell] of Lincoln; patron, Edward III. Thornage, 8 Aug. 1350.

1396 Preferment of Brother John de Lenn, priest and professed Augustinian canon of St Mary's Priory, Alnesbourn [S], to the priorate of that house, vac. by resig.[53] of Brother Robert Dwyt; no election was held because of a lack of canons there.[54] The bishop committed administration of the priory to Lenn; order was sent [the archdeacon of] Suffolk to install him. Thornage, 7 Aug. 1350.

---

[50] See *Complete Peerage* IX, 499–501.
[51] Because of the recent vacancy of the abbacy of St Benet's, Hulme: *CPR 1348–1350*, 558 (9 June 1350).
[52] See **1378**.
[53] See **1391**.
[54] MS. *Canonicorum in loco predicto carenciam*

1397   Inst. of Thomas de Wolterton,[55] priest, to the rectory of Briningham [N]; patrons by right of acquisition, Masters Richard de Lyng, Walter de Elveden, Simon [fo.125] de Rykynghale, and John de Wyneston. Thornage, 9 Aug. 1350.

1398   Inst. of Edmund Crestemesse, priest, to the vicarage of Hempnall [N], vac. by resig. of Dns John;[56] patrons, the prior and convent of Little Dunmow. Thornage, 10 Aug. 1350.

1399*   Memorandum that the prior and convent of Little Dunmow have made presentation to the vicarage of Hempnall [N] without nomination by the bishop of Norwich at least since 1303, although in the old register of the assessed payments of churches the vicarage is found listed among those to which the bishop has nomination. The instances of such presentation which were found in registers were: the institution of Robert de Nuttele, priest, by Bishop John [Salmon] on 3 July 1303 at Eccles [N]; the institution of Thomas Seward, priest, by Bishop W [William de Ayremynne] on 29 May 1328 at Thorpe next Norwich [N]; and the institution of Thomas atte Thorn of Cowlinge [S], priest, by bishop Anthony [de Bek] on 3 May 1342 at Thornage [N].[57] n.d.

1400   Inst. of William de Morton, priest, ([interlined] in the person of his proctor, Roger le March',) to the rectory of Briston [N]; patrons, the master and scholars of Trinity Hall at Cambridge University. Thornage, 11 Aug. 1350.

1401   Inst. of Roger Bengrant of Mildenhall [S], priest, in the person of his proctor, M. Nicholas de Dunstapl, clerk, to the rectory of Icklingham All Saints [S], vac. by resig. of Dns John de Manka; patron, John Fermer, knight. Thornage, 12 Aug. 1350.

1402   Inst. of William de la Chambre, [fo.125ᵛ] priest, to the rectory of Finningham [S]; patron, Nicholas Coners.[1] Thornage, 16 Aug. 1350.

1403   Inst. of Roger de Wortham,[2] priest, to the rectory of Tittleshall (*Tytleshale*) [N]; patrons, Richard Rokel, Dns Simon [de Rykynghale[3]] until recently rector of Babingley [N], Dns Richard [Syger[4]], rector of Oxwick [N], and Roger de Stalworth of Weasenham [N]. Thornage, 18 Aug. 1350.

1404   Inst.[5] of John son of Hugh de Kymburle, priest, to the rectory of Kimberley [N]; patrons, the master and scholars of Trinity Hall, Cambridge University. Thornage, 22 Aug. 1350.

---

[55] Cf. **715**.
[56] Cf. last known inst. shown in **1399**.
[57] See Reg. Salmon fo.12ᵛ, Reg. Ayremynne fo.22, and Reg. Bek fo.54ᵛ.
[1] His will was proved in 1375 (*Norwich Wills* 1, 99).
[2] See **22n**. for his inst. to this church in 1340.
[3] See **26**; *alias* de Babbyngle (**734**, *passim*).
[4] Inst. 1337 (Reg. Bek fo.5); see **1727** for surname.
[5] See **1377, 28**.

1405   Inst. of John atte Wynchel, priest, to the rectory of Little Wenham [S], vac. by resig. of Dns Walter Hert; patrons, Alice, the widow of Robert de Aspale, John de Aspale, knight, and Walter Hert. Thornage, 22 Aug. 1350.

1406   Inst. of Robert de Pypewell, priest, to the vicarage of Wickhambrook [S], recently established.[6] The bishop had nomination; patrons, the abbot and convent of Pipewell. Thornage, 23 Aug. 1350.

1407   Memorandum that on this date in the bishop's chamber, John de Subyr' acting as proctor for M. Simon de Subyr',[7] who was until this point the rector of Wickhambrook [S], resigned that benefice into the bishop's hands; present were Masters Walter de Elveden, Thomas de Honyng,[8] Simon [de Rykynghale] of Babingley, and unnamed others. Thornage, 22 Aug. 1350.

1408*   Inst. of Adam Charles, priest, to the rectory of Brumstead [N], vac. by resig. of Baldwin de Merwode; patron, Sir John Hakeluyt. There follows a memorandum that Dns Henry de Plumpstede, on whom the bishop had conferred Brumstead rectory, renounced his right in [fo.126] that benefice because the bishop had conferred it on him while Dns Baldwin de Merwode still held it.[9] Thornage, 23 Aug. 1350.

1409   Collation of the rectory of Mannington [N] to William son of Reginald Beverech of Itteringham [N], priest; patron in this turn by right of devolution,[10] the bishop. Thornage, 24 Aug. 1350.

1410   Inst. of Simon Broun, acolyte, to the rectory of Woolpit [S], vac. by conditional[11] resig. of M. John de Totyngton; patron, the abbot of Bury St Edmunds [S]. Thornage, 24 Aug. 1350.

1411   Inst. of Geoffrey de Berton, priest, to the rectory of Alpheton (*Alfeton*) [S]; patron [in this turn[12]], Edward III. Thornage, 25 Aug. 1350.

1412   Inst. of William atte Medwe, priest, to the rectory of a third part of East Beckham[13] (*Estbekham*) [N]; patrons, the prior and convent of Weybourne [N]. Thornage, 26 Aug. 1350.

1413   Inst. of Alexander Flemmyng, priest, to the rectory of Bildeston [S], vac. by resig. of M. John de Notyngham; patron in this turn,[14] Edward III. Thornage, 27 Aug. 1350.

---

[6] See **24–5**.
[7] See *BRUO* 3, 2218.
[8] Probably Thomas Willelmi of Honing, one of the bishop's clerks (*CPP* I, 138, 249).
[9] See **1329**.
[10] Usually the countess of Pembroke (**141**).
[11] MS. *per liberam resignationem . . . conditionaliter factam*
[12] See **1293**.
[13] See **45**; the church of St Helen was abandoned ca. 1700 and the few remaining parishioners used Aylmerton [N] (*Ruined Churches*, 53; White, *Norfolk*, 751).
[14] The heir was his ward (**459**).

1414   Inst. of John Shortwode, priest, to the vicarage of [a moiety of] Scarning [N]; patrons, the abbot and convent of Waltham. Thornage, 28 Aug. 1350.

1415   Inst. of Robert de Congham, subdeacon, to the rectory of Castle Rising [N], vac. by resig. of Hugh de Trikyngham; patron, Queen Isabella. Thornage, 30 Aug. 1350.

1416   VICARIA DE DITTON CAMIS. Inst. of William Auncel of Mildenhall [S], priest, to the vicarage [fo.126ᵛ] of Ditton Wood (*Dytton Camoys*) [Cambs.], vac. by resig. of Dns John Denlay; patron in this turn,[15] Mary [Roos], countess of Norfolk. Thornage, 30 Aug. 1350.

1417   Inst. of John Barkere, priest, to the rectory of Baylham (*Beylham*) [S], vac. by resig. of Dns William de Colyngham; patron, William Rothing, knight. Thornage, 31 Aug. 1350.

1418   Inst. of William de Haggesthorp, priest, to the vicarage of Kempstone [N], vac. by resig. of Dns Thomas Clog; patrons, the prior and convent of Castle Acre [N]. Thornage, 3 Sep. 1350.

1419   CRANEWITZ. Inst. of Robert Bysshop, priest, to the rectory of Cranwich [N], vac. by resig. of Dns William [Hulle] of Ketteringham [N], in exchange for a moiety of Hethersett [N]; patron, Adam de Clyfton, knight. Thornage, 5 Sep. 1350.

1420   Inst. of William [Hulle] of Ketteringham [N], priest, to a moiety of Hethersett [N], vac. by resig. of Dns Robert Bysshop, in exchange for the rectory of Cranwich [N]; patron, Edward III. Thornage, 5 Sep. 1350.

1421   Inst. of Robert son of Peter Gibbe of Kentford [S], deacon, to the vicarage of Rushmere [St Andrew[16]] (*Reysshemere*) [S]; patrons, the prior and convent of Holy Trinity, Ipswich [S]. Thornage, 8 Sep. 1350.

1422   [fo.127] Inst. of William de Bergh, priest, to the rectory of Cantley [N]; patron, John Bardolf, lord of Wormegay [N]. Norwich, 17 Sep. 1350.

1423   Collation to M. Laurence de Lyttelton, acolyte, of the rectory of Thorpe next Norwich [N], vac. by resig. of Dns John de Breyston,[17] in exchange for Lyttelton's deanery of Rockland [N]. The bishop then instituted Lyttelton to the rectory. Norwich, 19 Sep. 1350.

1424   Collation to John de Breydeston, priest, of the deanery of Rockland [N], vac. by resig. of M. Laurence [de Lyttelton], in exchange. Norwich, 19 Sep. 1350.

---

[15] Usually St Mary priory, Thetford (**254**).
[16] See **458***n*.
[17] *Alias* Breydeston, inst. 2 Jan. 1343 (Reg. Bek ff.64ᵛ–65).

1425 Collation of the prebend of the treasurer in the College of St Mary in the Fields in Norwich, to [left blank], chaplain. Order was sent the dean of the college to install him, as is customary. Norwich, 19 Sep. 1350.

1426 Inst. of M. Gregory de Hedersete, priest, to the rectory of Sculthorpe [N], vac. by resig. of Dns William de Bergh [**1422**]; patron, John de Norwico, knight. Hoxne, 21 Sep. 1350.

1427 Inst. of Lambert de Spaldyng, priest, to the vicarage of St German's, Wiggenhall [N]; patrons, the prior and convent of Holy Trinity, Norwich cathedral. Terling, 28 Sep. 1350.

1428 Inst. of James Beek, priest, to the rectory of [St Lawrence[18]], South Walsham [N]; patron, Mary [Roos], countess of Norfolk and marshal of England. London, 6 Oct. 1350.

1429 [fo.127ᵛ] Inst. of Thomas Gerond, priest, to the rectory of Great Bradley [S], vac. by resig. of Dns Richard Mercer of Briningham [N], in exchange for the rectory of Everdon in Lincoln diocese; patron, John Botourt, knight, lord of Weeley (*Weylegh*). Terling, 23 Oct. 1350.

1430 (i) Inst. of Richard Mercer of Briningham [N], priest, to the rectory of Everdon in Lincoln diocese, vac. by resig. of Dns Thomas Gerond, in exchange for Great Bradley [S], as above, by commission of Bishop John [Gynewell] of Lincoln; patron, Edward III. Terling, 23 Oct. 1350.
(ii) Gynewell's commission for the exchange, forwarding the enquiry made by the archdeacon of Northampton's official. [fo.128] Buckden, 7 Oct. 1350.

1431 CHATTEGRAVE. Inst. of Richard de Dysse, priest, to the vicarage of Chedgrave (*Chategrave*) [N], vac. by resig. of Dns Matthew [de Rendham[19]]; patrons, the prior and convent of Butley [S]. Hoxne, 6 Nov. 1350.

1432 Collation of the deanery of Rockland [N], vac. by resig. of Dns John de Breydeston, to Anthony de Goldesburgh, clerk with first tonsure. Hoxne, 7 Nov. 1350.

1433 Inst. of Robert de Derby, priest, to the rectory of Little Thurlow [S], vac. by resig. of Dns Henry Cook; patron in this turn, Edward III.[20] Hoxne, 7 Nov. 1350.

1434 Inst. of Robert Fox of Debenham [S], priest, to the chantry of St Mary in the parish church of Dennington [S], vac. by resig. of the chaplain, Dns William Galpyn; patron, Dns Thomas [Chyld of Debenham[21]], rector of Dennington. Hoxne, 8 Nov. 1350.

---

[18] Added later in margin.
[19] Inst. in 1342 (Reg. Bek fo.51).
[20] Usually Stoke-by-Clare priory (**1129**).
[21] See **587** and **1220**.

1435　Inst. of William Brithyeve of Braydeston [N], priest, to the vicarage of Great Plumstead (*Plumpsted magna*) [N], vac. by resig. of Dns Roger [Madour[22]] of Southrepps (*Reppes*); patrons, the prior and convent of Holy Trinity, Norwich cathedral. South Elmham, 12 Nov. 1350.

　　[Margin] It is not taxed.[23]

1436　Collation of the deanery of Ipswich [S] to M. Walter de Aldeby, fellow of Trinity Hall, Cambridge University, and priest. South Elmham, 12 Nov. 1350.

1437　Inst. of John de Sprotburgh, priest, [fo.128ᵛ] to the vicarage of Battisford (*Batesford*) [S]; patron, the prior of [the Knights Hospitallers of] St John of Jerusalem.[24] South Elmham, 13 Nov. 1350.

1438　Collation of the deanery of Wangford (*Waynforde*) [S] to John Hereward of [left blank], clerk with first tonsure;[25] usual notice of customary submission was sent. South Elmham, 15 Nov. 1350.

1439　Inst. of William Ranyld, priest, to the vicarage of Great Finborough (*Fynebergh magna*) [S], vac. by resig. of Dns John Harleye; patrons, the prior and convent of Butley [S]. South Elmham, 20 Nov. 1350.

1440　Inst. of Roger Mondegome, priest, to the rectory of Moulton (*Mouton*) [in Blofield deanery] [N]; patron, Alice de Bompstede.[26] South Elmham, 20 Nov. 1350.

1441　Collation of the rectory of Debach [S] to William, called le Clerc, of Debach, priest; patron by right of devolution,[27] the bishop. South Elmham, 20 Nov. 1350.

1442　Inst. of John de Dounhamstede, priest, to the rectory of Marlesford [S], vac. by resig. of Dns Geoffrey de Weston; patron, Matilda, widow of Robert de Saukevill. South Elmham, 24 Nov. 1350.

1443　Collation of the rectory of Spexhall [S] to William de Welton, clerk with first tonsure; patron in this turn by right of devolution,[28] the bishop. South Elmham, 29 Nov. 1350.

---

[22] See **490**.
[23] Great Plumstead was a peculiar of Norwich cathedral priory.
[24] There was a preceptory of the Knights Hospitallers at Battisford.
[25] Probably John de Ixworth, dean of *Wainford*, who accompanied Bateman to Avignon in 1354 (*CPP* 1, 277).
[26] See Millican, 'Biographical notices', 160.
[27] The king was patron (Reg. Ayremynne ff.35, 76).
[28] Usually the abbot and convent of St Mary's, York (e.g., **1235**).

1444 Collation of the vicarage of St Martin's at South Raynham[29] (*South-reynham*) [N] to Henry de Grafton, priest; patron by right of devolution,[30] the bishop. South Elmham, 1 Dec. 1350.

1445 [Common Pleas] writ[31] *admittatis non obstante reclamacione* ordering the bishop to admit a suitable presentee of Queen Philippa to the church of Horningtoft[32] [N] because she has recovered the presentation against Hugh son of Nicholas du Chastel, knight, by judgement of the court. Tested by J[ohn] de Stonore. Westminster, 24 Nov. 1350.
Trinity last, rot. xlv   Ditton

1446 [fo.129] Inst. of Robert Wygor, priest, to the rectory of Kirstead (*Kyrkestede*) [N], vac. by resig. of Dns Thomas de Scrouteby; patrons, the prior and convent of Butley [S]. South Elmham, 6 Dec. 1350.

1447 Inst. of Adam de Neubald, priest, to the rectory of Haverhill [S], vac. by resig. of Dns John de Tyngwyk,[33] in exchange for the rectory of Meppershall (*Mepereshale*) in Lincoln diocese; patrons, the prior and convent of Castle Acre [N]. South Elmham, 9 Dec. 1350.

1448 Inst. of John de Londe of Shotesham [N], priest, to the vicarage of Norton Subcourse [N]; patron,[34] the master of Raveningham College [N]. South Elmham, 10 Dec. 1350.

1449 Inst. of John Hamond, clerk with first tonsure, to the rectory of Roydon (*Rydon*) [N]; patron, Robert [de Ufford], earl of Suffolk. South Elmham, 10 Dec. 1350.

1450 Inst. of John Trendel of Guist [N], priest, to a moiety of Edgmere [N]; patrons, John de Wolterton, Roger Austyn, Adam Wortes, and Richard Ede.[35] South Elmham, 13 Dec. 1350.

1451 Inst.[36] of John Glanville, priest, to the rectory of Horningtoft [N]; patron, Queen Philippa, saving the rights of any other. South Elmham, 15 Dec. 1350.

1452 Preferment of Brother Reginald de Russheworth, priest and professed canon of St Mary Priory, Chipley [S], to the priorate of that house by the bishop of his special grace, no election having been held because of the lack of canons

---

[29] Not in *Taxatio* (81), which lists only *Reynham Sancte Margarete* and *Reynham Sancte Marie* (West and East Raynham).
[30] Usually the nuns of Blackborough (Reg. Ayremynne fo.77).
[31] Actual writ, measuring 24 by 6.2 cms., between ff.128–9.
[32] See **1451**.
[33] Last registered institution was of John Devennys (**386**); Tyngwyk's presentation to Meppershall is at *CPR 1350–1354*, 10.
[34] Cf. **23**.
[35] Cf. **1902**; and see these patrons in index.
[36] See **1445**.

there.[37] The previous prior, Brother David de Thornham,[38] had resigned. The bishop committed to Russheworth both spiritual and temporal administration, so far as it lay with him, and a letter of installation was sent [the archdeacon of] Suffolk. South Elmham, 17 Dec. 1350.

1453   Inst. of Robert de Norton, priest, to the rectory of Moulton [in Blofield deanery] [N], vac. by resig. of Dns Roger de Mondegome;[39] patron, Alice de Bompstede. South Elmham, 17 Dec. 1350.

1454   Collation to Roger Mondegome, priest, of the prebend of the dawn mass in the College of St Mary in the Fields, Norwich. Order for installation was sent to the dean of the college, as is customary. South Elmham, 18 Dec. 1350.

1455   Inst. of Robert Smyth of Hempnall [N], priest, to a moiety of Fishley [N]; patron, Roger Hardegrey. South Elmham, 20 Dec. 1350.

1456   [fo.129ᵛ] Inst. of William Bonyng, priest, to the rectory of Brundall [N]; patron, Thomas de Sancto Omero, knight. Hoxne, 23 Dec. 1350.

1457   Inst. of Roger Mondegome,[40] priest, to the rectory of Bracon Ash [N]; patron, Hugh Peverel, knight. Hoxne, 22 Dec. 1350.

1458   Collation to John son of Elias de Hoxn,[41] priest, of the vicarage of Hoxne [S], vac. by resig. of Dns Peter Osborne; the bishop also instituted him as vicar. Hoxne, 28 Dec. 1350.

1459   Inst. of Arnulf Sone, priest, to the rectory of Burgh next Aylsham [N]; patron, Robert [de Ufford], earl of Suffolk. Hoxne, 3 Jan. 1351.

1460   Collation of the archdeaconry of Sudbury to M. Henry la Zouche, subdeacon. Hoxne, 3 Jan. 1351.

1461   Inst. of Roger Pyllebergh, priest, to the rectory of Riddlesworth [N], vac. by resig. of Thomas Archer; patron, Roger Archer. Hoxne, 4 Jan. 1351.

1462   Inst. of Brother John de Hempstede, priest and canon of Hickling Priory [N], to the vicarage of Hickling (*Hykelingge*) [N]; patrons, the prior and convent of Hickling. Hoxne, 5 Jan. 1351.

1463   Inst. of John de Castr', priest, to the vicarage of Benhall [S]; patrons, the prior and convent of Butley [S]. Hoxne, 17 Jan. 1351.

---

[37] MS. *nulla electione de ipso facta propter carenciam canonicorum*
[38] See **1332**.
[39] See **1440**.
[40] See **1454**.
[41] Probably Elias de Hoxne, inst. as rector of Gisleham in 1340 (Reg. Bek fo.36).

1464 Inst. of Thomas Ry of Akenham [S], priest, to the vicarage of Tuddenham [St Martin[42]] [S]; patrons, the prior and convent of Holy Trinity Priory, Ipswich [S]. Norwich, 28 Jan. 1351.

1465* Collation to Dns Thomas de Claxton, priest, of the custody of St Mary Magdalene Hospital at Sprowston [N]. The power of compelling Claxton to render an account of his custody annually is reserved to the bishop and his successors. Saving in all things the episcopal customs and rights. Hoxne, 31 Jan. 1351.

1466* Copy[43] of writ of Edward III to Brother Michael Reynard, prior of Eye [S]. He had received custody of that priory from the king, as the king had the properties of all alien religious houses in his hand during the war in France, paying the king £140 annually according to letters patent.[44] Having learned that Bishop William of Norwich claimed first fruits or tax from the priory for their appropriated church of Laxfield [S] in each vacancy of the priory, and had sequestered its revenues for those fruits after the death of the last prior, the king had prohibited the bishop by writ from any action to his prejudice or the diminution or delay of his said farm. The business was referred to the king and council, and it appeared to the council that the bishop had a right to the first fruits of any vacant churches in his bishopric. Order, therefore, to the prior to pay the bishop and receive a quittance for the first fruits; an allowance in the same amount will be made in the sum due from Reynard to the Exchequer. Westminster, 16 May 1351.

1467 [fo.130] Inst. of John Jay, priest, to the rectory of Merton [N], vac. by resig. of Dns Robert Vaus, rector; patrons, the prior and convent of Lewes. Hoxne, 5 Feb. 1351.

1468 Inst. of William Baltrippe, priest, to the rectory of Diss [N], vac. by resig. of Dns Thomas de Coulyng, rector; patron, John FitzWauter,[45] knight. Hoxne, 7 Feb. 1351.

1469 Collation to Edmund Athelwold of Waterden [N], priest, of the vicarage of Langham Magna (*Langham Episcopi*) [N]. Hoxne, 8 Feb. 1351.

1470 Inst. of Roger Whitlok of Little Stonham (*Stonhamgernegan*) [S], priest, to the vicarage of Henley [S], vac. by resig. of Edmund Pomyrr[46] of Finningham [S]; patrons, the prior and chapter of Norwich cathedral. Hoxne, 8 Feb. 1351.
[Margin] He owes 5s. for letters of institution.

---

[42] *Taxatio* (117) shows Tuddenham St Martin appropriated to Trinity priory, Ipswich.
[43] Parchment measuring 26.2 by 11 cms. between ff.129–30. Written in a hand very similar to the adjacent folios: it is not a Chancery original.
[44] See *Calendar of Fine Rolls 1347–56*, 94 (dated 10 Sept. 1348); no other Chancery letters on this grant have been traced.
[45] FitzWalter of Woodham Walter; see *Complete Peerage* V, 472, 476–7.
[46] Cf. **725**.

1471 Inst. of Walter Colvyll,[47] clerk with first tonsure, to the rectory of Roydon [N], vac. by resig. of John Hamond; patron, Robert [de Ufford], earl of Suffolk. Hoxne, 8 Feb. 1351.

1472 Inst. of Robert son of John de Walsokne, priest, to the vicarage of Edwardstone [S], vac. by resig. of Roger Pillebergh [**1461**]; patrons, the prior and convent of Earls Colne. Norwich,[48] 26 Jan. 1351.

1473 Inst. of William de Whatton of Stoke to the rectory of Gisleham [S]; patron, Edward III, in right of his crown. Hoxne, 10 Feb. 1351.

1474 Inst. of Warren de Runhale, priest, to the vicarage of Ormsby [N]; patrons, the prior and convent of Norwich cathedral. Hoxne, 9 Feb. 1351.

1475 Inst. of Thomas de Branketr', priest, to the rectory of Newton [S], vac. by resig. of Dns Philip de Lenn, in exchange for the rectory of Finchley (*Fynchesleye*), London diocese; patron, William de Clopton. London, 17 Feb. 1351.

1476 Collation of the deanery of Samford (*Saunford*) [S] to Stephen son of Alexander Curson of Watton [N], clerk with first tonsure. London, 17 Feb. 1351.

1477 Collation of the deanery of Carlford [S] to Robert de Kymburle, clerk with first tonsure. London, 17 Feb. 1351.

1478 Collation of the deanery of Fincham [N] to Gilbert de Assheton, clerk with first tonsure. London, 20 Feb. 1351.

1479 [fo.130^v] Inst. of William Robyn, priest, to the vicarage of Swaffham [N]; patron, Dns Robert de Creyk, rector of Swaffham. London, 24 Feb. 1351.

1480 Inst. of John Akke, priest, to the rectory of Milden [S], vac. by resig. of Dns John de Wrottyngg; patron, Guy de Sancto Claro, knight. Hoxne, 11 Mar. 1351.

1481 Collation to Adam Grant, priest, of the vicarage of Carleton Forehoe [N]. Norwich, 15 Mar. 1351.

1482 Inst. of Simon Akewra,[49] priest, to the vicarage of Wroxham [N]; patrons, the prioress and convent of Carrow [N]. Norwich, 15 Mar. 1351.

1483 Inst. of Simon Norreys of Ferring, priest, to the free chapel of Caister Hall (*Castrehall*) [in Caister next Yarmouth] [N], with the obligation incumbent upon it; patron, William Boson of Caister. Blofield, 18 Mar. 1351.

---

[47] See **1147**, **1449**.
[48] Corrected from Hoxne.
[49] He was also chancellor of the College of St Mary in the Fields, Norwich (**847**, **1550**); Wroxham was about five miles distant.

1484   Inst. of Richard de Northcreyk, priest, to the rectory of Hitcham (*Hecham*) [S], vac. by resig. of Dns Martin de Ixnyng, in exchange for the rectory of Westmill, Lincoln diocese; patron, Bishop Thomas [de Lisle] of Ely. Blofield, 18 Mar. 1351.

1485   Inst. of William son of Nicholas Coupere of *Westricham*, priest, to the rectory of Clenchwarton [N], with the chapel annexed to it; patron in this turn,[50] William de Ingalesthorp, knight. Blofield, 21 Mar. 1351.

1486   Inst. of William de Hawe, priest, to the rectory of Banham [N]; patrons, the abbot and convent of St Mary's, York. Blofield, 21 Mar. 1351.

1487   Inst.[51] of James Bek, priest, to the rectory of Banningham [N]; patron, Mary [Roos], countess of Norfolk and marshal of England. Blofield, 23 Mar. 1351.

1488   Inst. of Henry de Dodelyngton,[52] priest, to the rectory of South Pickenham (*Southpykenham omnium sanctorum*) [N], vac. by resig. of Dns Walter Smyth; patron in this turn,[53] Richard de Holdych. Blofield, 23 Mar. 1351.

1489   Inst. of Hamo Gerard of Bawburgh [N], priest, to the vicarage of Runhall [N]; patrons, the prior and convent of West Acre [N]. Blofield, 24 Mar. 1351.

1490   [fo.131] Inst. of Richard Talbot, priest, to the manor chapel of Swaffham Market [N], with the obligation incumbent upon it; patron, Philippa, queen of England. Blofield, 26 Mar. 1351.

1491   Inst. of Hugh Cleres[54] of Ditchingham [N], priest, to the vicarage[55] of St Margaret's, Ilketshall (*Ilketeleshale*) [S], vac. by resig. of Dns Reginald Bysshop,[56] in exchange for the rectory of Winston [S]; patrons, the prioress and convent of Bungay [S]. Blofield, 28 Mar. 1351.

1492   Inst. of Reginald Bysshop, priest, to the rectory of Winston [S], vac. by resig. of Hugh Clerys, in exchange as above; patron, Edward de Monte Acuto, knight. Blofield, 28 Mar. 1351.

1493   Inst. of Robert Palmere of Ryburgh [N], priest, to the rectory of Wimbotsham (*Wymbotesham*) [N], vac. by resig. of Dns William Coupere;[57] patron, Lady Beatrice, widow of Sir Thomas de Ingalesthorp. Blofield, 1 Apr. 1351.

[50] Two laymen shared this advowson in turns (**1099**).
[51] Cf. **1006**.
[52] He held this benefice until his death in 1357 (*Norwich Wills* 1, 2).
[53] This patronage was held by two men in turns (**1352**).
[54] *Alias* de Dychingham (**703**).
[55] The usual phrase about the obligation of residence was omitted from this entry.
[56] He may have been instituted *sede vacante*, as the last known vicar was Philip Grenlyng of Yaxley, in 1334 (Reg. Ayremynne fo.63).
[57] See **1485**.

1494   Inst. of Hugh Dust, priest, to the rectory of Sweffling (*Swyftlyng*) [S]; patron, John Verdon, lord of Brixworth (*Brikelesworth*), knight. Blofield, 3 Apr. 1351.

1495   Inst. of Henry Olyver of Plumstead [N], clerk with first tonsure, to the rectory of St Clement of Conisford in Norwich; patron,[58] William de Myddelton. Blofield, 2 Apr. 1351.

1496   Inst. of Andrew Goldsmyth of Binham [N], priest, to the vicarage of Binham; patrons, the prior and convent of Binham. North Walsham, 6 Apr. 1351.

1497   Inst. of William de Wytton, priest, to the rectory of Lynford [N], vac. by resig. of Dns Edmund [de Waterden[59]]; patron, Lady Alice, widow of Robert de Aspale, knight. Blofield, 9 Apr. 1351.

1498   Inst. of Hubert Hubert, priest, to the rectory of Little Oakley[60] [S]; patron in this turn,[61] Mary [Roos], countess of Norfolk. Blofield, 11 Apr. 1351.

1499   Inst. of Robert Costard, priest, to the vicarage of St Martin's, Fincham [N]; [fo.131ᵛ] the bishop had nomination; patrons, the prior and convent of Shouldham. Blofield, 13 Apr. 1351.

1500   Inst. of John Stalker, priest, in the person of his proctor, Dns John Grundy, chaplain, to the rectory of Testerton [N], vac. by resig. of Dns Thomas de Eton; patron, Stephen de Hales, knight. Blofield, 20 Apr. 1351.

1501   Inst. of John Foderingeye of Bedford, priest, to the vicarage of Bures St Mary [S]; patron in this turn, Edward III, the temporalities of Stoke-by-Clare Priory [S] being in his hand. Newmarket, 29 Apr. 1351.

1502   Inst. of John Wryghte, priest, to the vicarage of Hempstead[1] [in Holt deanery] [N]; patrons, the prior and convent of Norwich cathedral. Hoxne, 23 May 1351.

1503   Inst. of Robert Shott of Blaxhall [S], priest, to the vicarage of Sudbourne-with-Orford [S]; patrons, the prior and chapter of Ely cathedral. Hoxne, 24 May 1351.

---

[58] Held by Wendling abbey in 1335 (Reg. Ayremynne fo.72ᵛ); see Tanner, *Church in Norwich*, 176, for the change.

[59] Inst. 1341 (Reg. Bek fo.43ᵛ).

[60] Little Oakley village and parish (St Andrew) disappeared through emparking; Great Oakley (St Nicholas) is now simply Oakley, its rectory united with Brome (White, *Suffolk*, 339, 459).

[61] Usually St Mary priory, Thetford (**133**).

[1] He held this benefice until his death in 1385 (*Norwich Wills* 2, 406).

1504   Inst. of Thomas de Bradeley, priest, to the rectory of Little Bradley [S], vac. by resig. of Robert Atte Crosse, in exchange for the vicarage of Billesdon, Lincoln diocese; patron in this turn, Edward III, the temporalities of Stoke-by-Clare Priory [S] being in his hand. Hoxne, 24 May 1351.

1505   Inst. of John le Spenser of Cretingham [S], priest, to the vicarage of Darsham [S], vac. by resig. of William Succlyng; patron in this turn,[2] Mary [Roos], countess of Norfolk and marshal of England. Hoxne, 30 May 1351.

1506   Inst. of John Trot of Houghton [N], priest, to the vicarage of Ashwicken (*Askywyken*) [N], vac. by resig. of William [Chapman] of Tostock [S]; patrons, the prior and convent of West Acre [N]. Hoxne, 31 May 1351.

1507   Inst. of Thomas de Wilton, priest, to a moiety of Barford [N], vac. by resig. of William de Eboraco; patron, Ralph de Neville, knight. Hoxne, 5 June 1351.

1508   Inst. of Ranulf de Friskeneye, priest, to the rectory of Barningham [S]; patron, John FitzWauter, lord of Woodham Walter. Hoxne, 8 June 1351.

1509   [fo.132] Inst. of John Conyn, priest, to the rectory of Garboldisham Parva[3] (*Garbotesham parva*) [N]; patron, John de Ufford, knight. Conyn immediately resigned his prior benefice [below], in accord with the constitution *Exsecrabilis*, in the presence of Walter de Elveden, Richard Honingham, and T. Dalton.[4] Hoxne, 8 June 1351.

1510   Inst. of Thomas Blower of Wiggenhall [N], priest, to the rectory of Pensthorpe [N], vac. by resig. of John Conyn [above]; patron, Hammond de Felton, knight. Hoxne, 10 June 1351.

1511   Inst. of Ralph Cok, priest, to the rectory of Onehouse [S]; patrons, John de Reppes, knight, and Geoffrey [Fausebroun[5]], rector of Buxhall (*Bucsahale*) [S]. Hoxne, 11 June 1351.

1512   Inst. of Nicholas de Hille of Woodton [N], priest, to the vicarage of Yoxford (*Jokesford*) [S], vac. by resig. of John Balle; patron in this turn,[6] Mary [Roos], countess of Norfolk and marshal of England. Hoxne, 12 June 1351.

1513   Collation of the deanery of Stow [S] to William de London, acolyte. Hoxne, 12 June 1351.

---

[2] Usually St Mary priory, Thetford (**1309**).
[3] There were two churches in the village, but only Parva (St John the Baptist) now stands; Magna (All Saints, see Reg. Ayr. fo.59ᵛ) was demolished in 1736 (*Ruined Churches*, 52).
[4] The last sentence was interlined later; on *Execrabilis* (*Ex.Ioh.XXII* 3, un.) see J. R. Wright, *The Church and the English Crown*, 12–14, 72–93.
[5] See **388***n*.
[6] Usually St Mary priory, Thetford (**1187**).

1514   Inst. of John Doget, priest, to the rectory of Edingthorpe [N], vac. by resig. of William de Boxgrave; patron, Joan de Barr', countess Warenne. Hoxne, 16 June 1351.

1515   PER VICARIOS GENERALES: TENOR COMMISSIONIS EIS FACTE. Commission of Bateman to M. Richard de Lyng, archdeacon of Norwich, and M. Walter de Elveden, precentor of Hereford, as vicars-general in spiritualities, together and severally, while the bishop was out of England or his diocese. He reserved to himself, however, the collation, nomination and provision of all ecclesiastical benefices, with and without cure of souls, as well as all dignities, parsonates and offices in the cathedral and elsewhere; in addition, he reserved the dispensation and absolution of all offences against the see or church of Norwich. London, 25 June 1351.

1516   Inst. of William de Stratton, acolyte, by M. Walter de Elveden, vicar-general, to the rectory of St Peter's, Upwell [N], vac. by resig. of William de Undele; patrons,[7] the abbot and convent of Ramsey Abbey. Norwich, 28 June 1351.

1517   Inst. of John de Dobaknay, priest, [fo.132ᵛ] by M. Walter de Elveden, vicar-general, to the vicarage of Henley [S], vac. by resig. of Roger Whitlok,[8] in exchange for the vicarage of Badley [S]; patrons, the prior and convent of Norwich cathedral. Norwich, 28 June 1351.

1518   Inst. of William de Wytton, priest, by the bishop (*sic*), to the rectory of Colney [N]; patron, Robert de Bumpstede. Norwich, 2 July 1351.

1519   Inst. of Raymond de Melcheborn, priest, by the said vicar-general[9] to the vicarage of Wissington [S]; patron, the prior of Horkesley [Esx.]. Norwich, 2 July 1351.

1520   Inst. of Thomas Walbot of Terrington [N], priest, by vicar-general Elveden, to the free chapel of St James at Terrington [N]; patrons, William Alexandr' and Thomas Howard. Norwich, 2 July 1351.

1521   Inst. of John de Bradeley, priest, by vicar-general Elveden, to the rectory of Little Thurlow [S], vac. by resig. of Dns Robert de Derby in exchange[10] for Bradeley's rectory of Aldbury (*Aldebury*), Lincoln diocese; patron in this turn, Edward III, the temporalities of Stoke-by-Clare Priory [S] being in his hand. Norwich, 3 July 1351.

---

[7] The king had presented M. John de Banyngham to Upwell on 15 July 1349 during the vacancy of Ramsey abbey (*CPR 1348–1350*, 345), but there is no mention in the register of his institution.

[8] See **1470**; Dobaknay may have been instituted *sede vacante*, as the last known rector (not vicar) of Badley was Roger de Norton in 1339 (Reg. Bek ff.31–31ᵛ).

[9] Corrected from *reverendum patrem*

[10] See Lincoln Reg. 9, fo.392, for the other side of this exchange.

1522 Inst. of M. Richard de Warmyngton, clerk with first tonsure, by vicar-general Elveden, to the rectory of Occold (*Ocolte*) [S] with the chapel of Benningham; patrons, the abbot and convent of St John's, Colchester. Norwich, 11 July 1351.

1523 Inst. of Richard de Matelask, subdeacon, by vicar-general Elveden, to the rectory of St Martin's, Shotesham [N]; patrons, the abbot and convent of St Benet's, Hulme [N]. Norwich, 12 July 1351.

1524 Inst. of William de Hunden, priest, by vicar-general Elveden, to the rectory[11] of Pattesley [N]; patron, William Bretoun. Norwich, 18 July 1351.

1525 Inst. of Richard Almot, priest, by vicar-general Elveden, to the vicarage[12] of Sibton [S] with Peasenhall chapel; patrons, the abbot and convent of Sibton [S]. Norwich, 18 July 1351.

1526 Inst. of Thomas de Burgh, priest, by vicar-general Elveden, to the rectory of Marlesford [S]; patron, Matilda, the widow of Robert de Saukevill. Norwich, 20 July 1351.

1527 [fo.133] Inst. of Bartholomew de Tacolneston, priest, by vicar-general Elveden, to the rectory of St Lawrence's, South Walsham [N]; patron,[13] Mary [Roos], countess of Norfolk and marshal of England. Norwich, 23 July 1351.

1528 Inst. of Henry de Burgh, priest, by vicar-general Elveden, to the rectory of Thelnetham [S]; patron, Robert de Benhale, knight. Norwich, 28 July 1351.

1529 Inst. of John Blisse, priest, by vicar-general Elveden, to the rectory of Lynford[14] [N]; patron, Lady Alice, widow of Robert de Aspal, knight. Norwich, 28 July 1351.

1530 MEDIETAS DE THORP IUXTA GEYTON.[15] [This marginal note is beside a blank space four lines long, left for an entry concerning a moiety of the parish of Gayton Thorpe [N]; the space was not filled.] n.d.

1531 Inst. of Roger de Eccleshale, priest, by M. Richard de Lyng, vicar-general, to the rectory of Theberton [S]; patron, John [de Segrave], Lord Segrave. Reedham, 12 Aug. 1351.

---

[11] Vacant by resignation (**792, 1564**).
[12] Vacant by resignation (**626, 1512**).
[13] On 7 July 1351, the countess had received licence to give this advowson to St Giles hospital in Norwich (*CPR 1350–1354*, 114).
[14] Vacant by resignation (**1497, 1518**).
[15] One moiety of Gayton Thorpe (*alias* Ayleswithorp, Aylesthorpe, Thorp) was appropriated to Dereham abbey, the other to Pentney priory (Reg. Bek ff.16, 49ᵛ, and *Taxatio*, 80).

1532 PER IPSUM PATREM. Inst. of Robert de Crandon, priest, by the bishop, to the chantry[16] of St Mary at Eyke [S]; patron, Dns Robert de Redenhal, rector of Eyke. Hoxne, 13 Sept. 1351.

1533 Collation to Henry Palmer,[17] clerk with first tonsure, of the rectory of Wiveton (*Wyveton*) [N]; patron in this turn by right of devolution,[18] the bishop. London, 22 June 1351.

1534 Collation to John Sparhauk of Norwich, acolyte, of St Botolph's rectory in Norwich; patron in this turn by right of devolution,[19] the bishop. London, 25 July 1351.

1535* Inst. of M. Laurence de Lyttelton, acolyte, to the rectory of St Mary's, Great Massingham [N]; patron in this turn, Edward III, the temporalities of the see of Norwich having been recently in his hand. London, 26 June 1351.

1536 Inst. of Alan Spark of Sporle [N], priest, to the rectory of Pettaugh[20] [S]; patron, Thomas de Gyppewico. Hoxne,[21] 26 Sept. 1351.

1537 Inst. of Roger Atte Heth, clerk with first tonsure, to the rectory of Tuddenham St Mary [S]; patron, Edmund de Hemegrave, knight. Rushworth, 20 Sept. 1351.

1538* [fo.133^v] Collation to William Gray,[22] priest, of the vicarage of Newton by Castle Acre [N]; patron in this turn by right of devolution,[23] the bishop. Gaywood, 27 Sept. 1351.

1539 Confirmation of the unanimous and harmonious election of Brother Vincent de Caldecote, priest and professed Augustinian canon of Pentney [N], as prior of that house, following the resignation of Brother Ralph de Framelyngham. Gaywood, 27 Sept. 1351.

1540 Confirmation of the harmonious election of Lady Cecilia de Well, professed Augustinian nun of Crabhouse [N], as prioress of that house, following the resignation of Lady Olive de Swafham. Gaywood, 28 Sept. 1351.

---

[16] 'Here was a *chantry*, called Bennet's Chantry, of the yearly value of £8' (White, *Suffolk*, 185).

[17] Unusually, described as *dilecto filio*

[18] At the last registered institution the patron was William de Brunne (Reg. Ayremynne fo.26^v).

[19] Various citizens held the advowson (N. Tanner, *Church in Norwich*, 173; and **1153**).

[20] See **1123**.

[21] A. H. Thompson suggested that either the date or the place is wrong here ('William Bateman', 136).

[22] Called *dilecto filio*

[23] The patrons were Castle Acre priory (**224**).

1541 Inst. of Ralph Randes of Kenninghall [N], priest, to the vicarage of Tibenham [N]; patron in this turn, Edward III, the temporalities of Horsham St Faith Priory [N] being in his hand. Gaywood, 28 Sept. 1351.

1542 Inst. of Robert Seyer, priest, to the rectory of Snailwell [Cambs.], vac. by resig. of Dns Thomas Dorrent, in exchange for Seyer's rectory of Stretham in Ely diocese; patron, Bishop Thomas [de Lisle] of Ely. Gaywood, 29 Sept. 1351.

1543 Inst. of Roger de Burton, clerk with first tonsure, to the rectory of St Gregory's, Sudbury [S], with the annexed chapel, vac. by resig. of William de Horwode.[24] The bishop had nomination; patrons, the prioress and nuns of Nuneaton.[25] Massingham, 1 Oct. 1351.

1544 Copy[26] of dispensation of Clement VI to M. John Barnet, canon of London, bachelor of laws.[27] Because he is a man of good reputation and character, he may receive one ecclesiastical benefice with cure of souls, even if he holds a dignity or parsonate or cathedral office, and he may freely retain this together with the rectory of Westwell (Canterbury dioc.) and canonries and prebends in Durham diocese and [St Paul's,] London; he may resign that parochial cure and exchange it for another, as often as he chooses, notwithstanding any universal or local canon laws or customs to the contrary. Barnet must ensure that due services are maintained in any benefice he holds. Avignon, 31 July 1350.
[Holograph note] Certified a true copy by W. de Elveden in the. king's chamber at Westminster, 27 Jan. 1352.

1545 [fo.134] Inst. of Adam Ketel, priest, to the vicarage of Corpusty [N]; patron,[28] Edward III. Hoxne, 5 Oct. 1351.

1546 Inst. of M. John Barnet, priest, to the rectory of East Dereham [N]; patron, Bishop Thomas [de Lisle] of Ely. Hoxne, 10 Oct. 1351.

1547 Inst. of John Smert, priest, to the rectory of Willingham [St Mary] [S], vac. by resig. of Thomas de Melborn, in exchange for a moiety of Howe [N]; patron, Edward III. Hoxne, 12 Oct. 1351.

1548 Inst. of Thomas de Melborn, priest, to a moiety of Howe [N], vac. by resig. of John Smert, in exchange [as above]; patrons, the prioress and convent of Carrow [N]. Hoxne, 12 Oct. 1351.

[24] See **1289**.
[25] See **62n**.
[26] Rather crudely written on a parchment measuring 29.6 by 8.8 cms., attached by glue under its left-hand margin across the lower margin of fo.134.
[27] See **1546**; *BRUO* 1, 112–13.
[28] Usually Horsham St Faith (**177, 874**).

1549 Inst. of Alexander de Boxn of Beccles [S], priest, to St John's rectory, Ilketshall [S], vac. by resig. of Robert Serle;[29] patrons, the prioress and convent of Bungay [S]. Hoxne, 12 Oct. 1351.

1550 Collation to Roger [left blank] of the prebend of the chancellor at the College of St Mary in the Fields, Norwich, vac. by resig. of Dns Simon Akewra; a letter of installation was sent the dean of the college. Hoxne, 12 Oct. 1351.

1551 Inst. of John Ode of Watton [N], priest, to the vicarage of Carbrooke Parva[30] (*Kerbrok parva*) [N], vac. by resig. of Hugh Herbert;[31] patron, the prior of the Knights Hospitallers in England. Hoxne, 12 Oct. 1351.

1552 Inst. of Robert Mast of West Lexham [N], priest, to the vicarage of Burston [N], vac. by resig. of John Martemer;[32] patrons, the prior and convent of Butley [S]. Hoxne, 14 Oct. 1351.

1553* Collation to William Olde of Debenham [S], priest, of the custody of St James Hospital, [fo.134ᵛ] Ipswich [S], including the administration of its spiritual and temporal goods; Olde gave the oath required by law and custom. Hoxne, 14 Oct. 1351.

1554 Collation to Thomas Godknape[33] of Redenhall [N], priest, of a fourth part of Antingham St Mary [N] (*beate Marie de Antyngham*); patron in this turn by right of devolution, the bishop. Hoxne, 16 Oct. 1351.

1555 Inst. of M. Thomas Loryng, priest, to the rectory of Terrington St Clement [N]; patron, Bishop Thomas [de Lisle] of Ely. London, 24 Oct. 1351.

1556 Inst. of Robert Kynche, priest, to the vicarage of Aldeburgh [S] with Hazlewood (*Haselwode*) chapel; patrons, the abbot and convent of St John's, Colchester. Hoxne, 14 Nov. 1351.

1557 The election of Brother Adam de Hokewold, priest and professed Augustinian canon of Ixworth [S], as prior of Holy Sepulchre Priory, Thetford (*Sancte Crucis Canonicorum Thefford*) [S], following the resignation of Brother Robert Edwyne [de Thefford[34]], was quashed by the bishop for defect of matter and form. The bishop then preferred the elect to that office by his special grace. A letter of induction [*sic*] was sent the archdeacon of Norwich. Hoxne, 14 Nov. 1351.

---

[29] Inst. 1341 (Reg. Bek fo.49).

[30] *Alias* West Carbrooke; the church was taken down in 1424 and the parish united to Carbrooke Magna (*Ruined Churches*, 53; White, *Norfolk*, 363). The Hospitallers had a preceptory and hospital at Carbrooke Parva (Knowles & Hadcock, 302).

[31] See **1559**.

[32] *Alias* Mortimer (**895**).

[33] Vicar of Roughton [N] (**1151**), and there is no sign that he gave it up; perhaps this portion of Antingham had no cure of souls.

[34] See **811**.

1558* Inst. of Robert de Isingwold, priest, to the rectory of Spexhall [S], vac. by resig. of William de Welleton; patrons, the abbot and convent of St Mary's, York. Isingwold swore on the Gospels that he would return to Spexhall around the feast of St Matthew next [21 Sept.], and thereafter serve the parish in person. Hoxne, 16 Nov. 1351.

1559* Preferment of Hugh Herbert, chaplain and brother of the College of St John the Evangelist, Rushworth [N], unanimously elected by the brothers of that college to be their Master, and then presented by the patrons of the college, Dns John de Gonevill, rector of East Harling [N], and his brother Edmund, to the mastership, following the resignation of Dns Nicholas de Wrotham. Hoxne, 17 Nov. 1351.

1560 Inst.[35] of John Leche, priest, to the rectory of Wood Dalling [N]; patrons, the master and fellows of Trinity Hall, Cambridge University. Thorpe next Norwich, 22 Nov. 1351.

1561 [fo.135] Inst.[36] of John de Chedestan, priest, to the vicarage of Chediston (*Chedestan*) [S], vac. by resig. of Dns Richard Pottere; patrons, the prior and convent of Pentney [N]. Thorpe next Norwich, 26 Nov. 1351.

1562 Collation to John de Shaftesbury, priest, of the rectory of Gaywood [N], and the bishop instituted him. Thorpe next Norwich, 27 Nov. 1351.

1563 Collation to Roger de Wortham, priest, of the custody of St John's Hospital in Lynn [N], [as in **1553***]. Hoxne, 28 Nov. 1351.

1564 Inst. of Henry Smyth of Billingford [N], to the vicarage of Little Ryburgh [N], vac. by resig. of Dns Robert Warner; patrons, the prior and convent of Binham [N]. Hoxne, 7 Dec. 1351.

1565 Inst. of Richard Claville, priest, in the person of his proctor, Dns Robert Burgeys, chaplain, to the rectory of Hilborough (*Hildeburghworth*) [N], vac. by resig. of Dns Peter de Lacy, in exchange for Claville's benefice, the first portion of Bisley (*Biselee*), Worcester diocese; patron, Robert de Ufford, earl of Suffolk. Hoxne, 11 Dec. 1351.

1566 Inst. of John Wodeward, acolyte, to the rectory of Bucklesham (*Boclesham*) [S], vac. by resig. of Dns John de Playforde; patron, Thomas de Holbrok, knight. Hoxne, 17 Dec. 1351.

1567 Inst. of William del Medwe, priest, to a moiety of Little Glemham [S], vac. by resig. of Dns John de Chediston;[37] patron, William Phelip of Dennington [S]. Hoxne, 19 Dec. 1351.

---

[35] Cf. **34** and **782**.

[36] MS. (unusually) *institutus fuit personaliter*

[37] See **1561**.

1568 Inst. of John de Bliclyngg, priest, in the person of his proctor, Dns William [Wolwyne], rector of Gunton [S], to the rectory of Flixton [St Andrew] (*Flixton in Luthinglond*) [S], vac. by resig. of Dns Walter Lemoc; patron, Sarah, widow of William de Lauveney.[38] Hoxne, 21 Dec. 1351.

1569 [fo.135ᵛ] Certificate[39] of Bishop John [de Trillek] of Hereford that he has executed Bateman's commission (quoted in full; dated Hoxne [S], 6 Dec. 1351) for an exchange of benefices between M. Michael de Northburgh,[40] rector of Pulham [N] with the annexed chapel,[41] and William de Kelleseye, portionary of Ledbury in Hereford diocese. He examined the enquiry of the commissary of the official of the archdeacon of Norfolk, and instituted Kelleseye to Pulham; the patron, Bishop Thomas [de Lisle] of Ely, had agreed. Prestbury [Cheshire], 13 Dec. 1351.

1570 William de Kelseye, rector of Pulham [N], gave oath of canonical obedience to the bishop and his ministers [for the rectory of Pulham]; the order [to induct] was sent [the archdeacon of] Norfolk. Newmarket, 10 Jan. 1352.

1571 Inst. of Richard Monnch, priest, to the vicarage of St Mary Magdalen, Wiggenhall [N], vacant by the death of Robert de Griston; patrons, the prior and convent of Castle Acre [N]. Hoxne, 8 Jan 1352.
  [Margin] He is obligated for his predecessor, to pay at Easter.

1572* [fo.136] Collation to John Colyn of Cranwich [N], priest, of the vicarage of Potter Heigham [N]; patron in this turn, the bishop, because the abbot and convent of St Benet's, Hulme [N] refused to present the bishop's nominee, as they are bound to do by the composition made between them and the bishop concerning this benefice.[42] Hoxne, 9 Jan. 1352.

1573 Inst. of Thomas Atte Gate of Thorndon [S], priest, to the rectory of Tunstall [S], vac. by resig. of William de Hales; patron, Edward de Monte Acuto, knight. London, 19 Jan. 1352.

1574 Inst. of Richard de Chesterfeld, priest, to the rectory of Horstead [N], vac. by resig. of Dns Roger de Chesterfeld; patron in this turn, Edward III, the temporalities of the abbacy of the alien abbey of Caen being in his hand. London, 28 Jan. 1352.

1575 Inst. of John de Stanton, priest, to the rectory of Westwick [N], vac. by resig. of Richard de Tuttebury; patron in this turn, Edward III, the lands and

---

[38] *Alias* Launay (**684**).
[39] See also *Registrum Johannis de Trillek*, edited by J. H. Parry, CYS 8 (1912), 407.
[40] *BRUO* 2, 1368–70.
[41] The episcopal registers and *Taxatio* (**84**) show no sign of the later division into two parishes (St Mary the Virgin and St Mary Magdalene); in the 19th century a school in Pulham St Mary the Virgin was kept in 'the Old Chapel' (*Norfolk*, 727).
[42] See **57**.

tenements of John de Segrave, knight, being recently in his hand. London, 4 Feb. 1352.

1576 Inst. of Peter de Lacy, priest, to the free chapel of St Margaret, Hilborough [N], with the responsibility incumbent upon it; patron, Adam de Clyfton, knight. London, 4 Feb. 1352.

1577 Inst. of William de Dyghton, priest, to the rectory of Trimingham [N], vacant by the death of James de Platea; presentation was made by Dns Henry de Walton, archdeacon of Richmond, attorney general in England and Wales for the patron, Henry [of Grosmont], duke of Lancaster, in his absence. London, 5 Feb. 1352.

1578 Collation to John de Carleton, clerk with first tonsure, of the deanery of Burnham [N], vac. by resig. of William de Hales.[43] Usual notice of customary submission was sent. London, 6 Feb. 1352.

1579 Confirmation of the unanimous election of Brother Robert de Dockyngg, priest and professed Augustinian canon of Creake Abbey [N], as abbot of that house, following the resignation of Brother John de Harpele.[44] Order to install him was sent the archdeacon of Norfolk or his official. London, 10 Feb. 1352.

1580 [fo.136^v] Inst. of John Foucher, priest, to the rectory of Sparham [N], vac. by resig. of Nicholas Janyn, in exchange for the rectory of All Hallows Barking (*Berkynggecherche iuxta Turrim*), London; patron, William de Clynton, earl of Huntingdon. London, 15 Feb. 1352.

1581 Inst. of Nicholas Janyn, priest, to the rectory of All Hallows Barking, London, vac. by resig. of John Foucher, in exchange, by commission of Bishop Ralph [de Stratford] of London; patrons, the abbess and convent of Barking. London, 15 Feb. 1352.

1582 Inst. of Thomas de Bolmere, priest, to the vicarage of Soham [Cambs.], vac. by resig. of William de Leverington, in exchange for the vicarage of Terling, London diocese. The bishop had nomination; patrons, the abbot and convent of Rewley. London, 21 Feb. 1352.

1583 Inst. [*sic*] of William de Leverington, priest, to the vicarage of Terling, London diocese, in exchange for the vicarage of Soham [Cambs.] as above, by commission of Bishop Ralph [de Stratford] of London; patron, Bishop Bateman. London, 21 Feb. 1352.

1584 Inst. of William de Keleby, priest, to the rectory of Kelling [N], vacant by the death of John le Baxstere; patron, John Avenel, knight. London, 22 Feb. 1352.

---

[43] See **1573** and App. II, p. 142.
[44] Elected 1334 (Reg. Ayremynne fo.67^v).

1585   Inst. of Robert de Wyngreworth,[45] priest, to the rectory of Forncett[46] [N]; patron in this turn, Edward III, the lands and tenements of John de Segrave, knight, being recently in his hand.[47] Hugh de Elvestowe last had possession of the rectory. London, 4 Mar. 1352.

1586*   Inst. of Giles de Wyngreworth, clerk with first tonsure, to the rectory of Lopham [N]; patron in this turn, Edward III, the lands and tenements of John de Segrave, knight, being recently in his hand, and by the recovery of judgement in the king's court, and the dismissal of the case from the Court of Arches. William de Atterton last had possession of the rectory.[48] London, 4 Mar. 1352.

1587*   Incomplete letter[49] appointing William de Blyclyngg, priest of Norwich diocese, to one of the three chantries in the chapel of the bishop's palace,[50] established by Bishop William de Ayremynne; patron, the bishop. Blyclyngg gave his oath to carry out the duties of the chantry faithfully. n.d.

1588   [Common Pleas] writ[51] *admittatis non obstante reclamacione* ordering the bishop to admit a suitable presentee of the king to Fritton (*Freton*) [N] because he has recovered the presentation against John de Segrave and his wife Margaret, by judgement of the court.[52] Tested by J[ohn] de Stonore, Westminster, 12 May 1352. Rot. [no. omitted] Berugh

1589   [Common Pleas] writ *admittatis* [as in **1588**] in favour of the king for Forncett [N] church, against John de Segrave,[53] by judgement of the court. Tested by J[ohn] de Stonore, Westminster, 3 Feb. 1352. Rot. iij Berugh

1590   [Common Pleas] writ *admittatis* [as in **1588**] in favour of the king for Lopham [N] church, against John de Segrave,[54] by judgement of the court. Tested by J[ohn] de Stonore, Westminster, 3 Feb. 1352. Rot. iij Berugh

1591   Copy[55] of dispensation of Clement VI to Robert de Wyngreworth,[56] rector of Shipden [N], to hold two benefices with cure of souls, even if one should be a cathedral benefice, and to exchange one or both benefices as he should see fit, notwithstanding all canon laws, statutes and customs to the

---

[45] See **1591**.
[46] See **385n.** and *Taxatio*, 84.
[47] See *Complete Peerage* XI, 609; also **1589–1591**.
[48] See **1590**.
[49] This is the first of five pieces sewn together between ff.136–7 (**1588–1591**).
[50] Not much is known about this college, founded by Bishop Ayremynne; see N. Tanner, *Church in Norwich*, 22f, 93.
[51] This, **1589** and **1590** are actual writs of the usual size; **1588** has a filing hole at the left-hand side, where **1589** and **1590** have tears.
[52] See **1630**.
[53] See **1585**.
[54] See **1586***.
[55] On parchment measuring 23 by 13.1 cms. The endorsement is in another hand; its last name, written larger with flourishes, is probably a signature. See also *CPL* 3, 398.
[56] See **1585**.

contrary, so long as the benefices be properly served and the cure of souls not neglected. Avignon, 10 Mar. 1351.

[Dorse] On 4 March 1352, in London, collated with the original and found correct by J[ohn] de Wyneston, in the presence of Giles de Wyngr'worth, rector of Lopham [N], and William de Mont Sorrell, literate. Wyneston.

1592 [fo.137] The peaceful election of Brother John de Lodene, OSA, of St Leonard's, Bricett[57] (*Bresete*) [S], as prior of that house by the canons, following the death of Brother John de Essex, the previous prior, was quashed by the bishop for defect of matter and form. The bishop then provided the elect, mindful of his merits and of the unanimity of the canons. Order to install was sent the archdeacon of Suffolk or his official. London, 4 Mar. 1352.

1593 Inst. of Richard de Thoresby, priest, to the rectory of Stalham [N]; patrons,[58] the master and fellows of Trinity Hall, Cambridge University. London, 4 Mar. 1352.

1594 Inst. of Henry de Fordham, priest, to [Pakefield St Margaret], a moiety of Pakefield [S], vac. by resig. of William Colvylle in exchange for Fordham's rectory of Gunby, Lincoln diocese; patron, Edmund Berry. London, 5 Mar. 1352.

1595 Inst. of William Colvylle, priest, to the rectory of Gunby in Lincoln diocese, vac. by resig. of Henry de Fordham in exchange for a moiety of Pakefield [S], by commission of Bishop John [Gynewell] of Lincoln; patrons, the prior and convent of Buckenham [N]. London, 5 Mar. 1352.

1596 Collation to Thomas de Assheborn, priest, of the rectory of Colveston [N], vac. by resig. of John de Creton; patron in this turn by right of devolution,[59] the bishop. Norwich, 17 Mar. 1352.

1597 Inst. of Richard de Upetoft of Suffield [N], acolyte, to the rectory of St Peter Southgate, Norwich, vac. by resig. of John Masoun; patrons, the abbot and convent of St Benet's, Hulme [N]. Blofield, 20 Mar. 1352.

1598 Inst. of John son of John Durant of Helpringham (*Hilpringham*), priest, to the rectory of Thelveton [N], vac. by resig. of Richard de Ely; patrons, the prior and convent of St Mary's, Southwark, Winchester diocese. Blofield, 20 Mar. 1352.

1599 Inst. of Henry de Taterforde, priest, to the vicarage of Tunstead [N]. The bishop had nomination, [fo.137ᵛ] and the prioress and convent of Campsey Ash [S], as patrons,[60] presented the nominee. Blofield, 20 Mar. 1352.

---

[57] *Alias* Great Bricett, a dependency of St Leonard de Noblat, Limoges diocese.
[58] See **1024, 36**.
[59] See **965**.
[60] See *CPR 1348–1350*, 560, and Appendix II.

1600   Inst. of John de Seton, acolyte, in the person of his proctor, Dns William de Weston, rector of a moiety of Taverham [N], to the rectory of Thwaite [in Brooke deanery,[1] N] vac. by resig. of Peter Aleyn; patron, William de la Pole, knight. Blofield, 23 Mar. 1352.

1601   Inst. of Peter Aleyn of Morningthorpe [N], priest, in the person of Dns William de Weston,[2] to a moiety of Taverham [N], vac. by resig. of Dns Edmund [Cotenham[3]]; patron, William de la Pole, knight. Blofield, 23 Mar. 1352.

1602   Inst. of Robert de Beston, priest, to the rectory of Kirby Cane (*Kyrkebycam*) [N], vacant by the death of Dns William Attemersh; patron in this turn, William de Wychingham, because Nicholas Gavel is his ward. Blofield, 23 Mar. 1352.

1603   Collation to Thomas Lewyn of Starston (*Sterston*) [N], priest, of the rectory of St Nicholas, Dunwich [S]; patron in this turn by right of devolution,[4] the bishop. n.p., 26 Mar. 1352.

1604   Inst. of Robert Spacy, priest, to the vicarage of Witton [in Waxham deanery] (*Wytton iuxta Bromholm*) [N], vac. by resig. of Hugh Wodeherde;[5] patrons, the prior and convent of Bromholm [N]. Blofield, 31 Mar. 1352.

1605   Inst. of Adam Wych, priest, to the rectory of Cotton [S], vacant by the death of John de Castr'; patron, the abbot of Bury St Edmunds [S]. Blofield, 28 Mar. 1352.

1606   Inst. of John Lucas, priest, to a moiety of Hillington [N], vac. by resig. of William Gerys; patron, John Aubyn of Hillington. Blofield, 29 Mar. 1352.

1607   Collation of the chantry[6] in the church of Beetley [N] [fo.138] to Walter Tronemere of Gressenhall [N], priest; patron in this turn by right of devolution, the bishop. Blofield, 29 Mar. 1352.
   [Margin] It is not taxed.

1608   Inst. of Elias de Kertlyng of St Edmund, priest, to the vicarage of Silverley [Cambs.], vac. by resig. of Nicholas de Haneworth; patrons, the prior and convent of Hatfield [Broad Oak[7]]. Blofield, 30 Mar. 1352.

---

[1] See **1906**.
[2] Rector of the other moiety (**551, 1600, 1712**).
[3] See **1228**.
[4] At the last registered institution the patrons were Eye Priory (Reg. Ayremynne ff.43–43ᵛ).
[5] His institution was unregistered (cf. **1302, 1467**).
[6] Founded in or shortly before 1311, in the time of Bishop John Salmon, to provide an annual mass and other services for the soul of M. Thomas de Biteryng; presentation was usually made by the abbot and convent of Wendling (Reg. Salmon fo.44ᵛ, Reg. Bek ff.45ᵛ–46, 52).
[7] *Alias* Hatfield Regis.

1609 Inst. of William Swete,[8] priest, to the rectory of Stoke Ash [S], vac. by resig. of Roger Yonge; patron in this turn, Edward III, the temporalities of Eye Priory [S] being in his hand. Blofield, 5 Apr. 1352.

1610 Inst. of John de Donyngton, clerk with first tonsure, to the rectory of Wacton Magna [N], vac. by resig. of Roger Perleman; patron in this turn, Edward III, because the lands and tenements of John de Segrave, knight, were recently in his hand. Blofield, 7 Apr. 1352.

1611 Inst. of Robert de Twyford, priest, to the rectory of All Saints in Gillingham [N], vac. by resig. of John de Tyvetteshal;[9] patron, John [de Segrave], Lord Segrave. Blofield, 17 Apr. 1352.

1612 Inst. of Edmund Torald, priest, to the vicarage of Chedgrave [N]; patrons, the prior and convent of Butley [S]. Blofield, 10 Apr. 1352.

1613 Inst. of Benedict de Estmor, priest, to the vicarage of Earlham [N], vac. by resig. of William de Worstede;[10] patrons, the prioress and convent of Carrow [N]. Blofield, 17 Apr. 1352.

1614 Inst. of John de Tyfveteshal,[11] priest, to the rectory of Hale[12] (*Holmhale*) [N], vac. by resig. of Robert de Burgwode; patron, Stephen de Tyfteshale. Blofield, 17 Apr. 1352.

1615 Inst. of William de Ellerton, priest, to St Mary's rectory, Stiffkey [N], vac. by resig. of Thomas de Ellerton; patron, Walter Mauny, knight. Blofield, 14 Apr. 1352.
[Margin] He is obligated for his predecessor.

1616 Inst. of John de Babrunne, priest, to the rectory of Gunton [N], vac. by resig. of Roger Bacon; patron, Walter de Walcote, knight. Blofield, 20 Apr. 1352.

1617 Inst. of John de Porynglond, clerk with first tonsure, to the rectory of Cowlinge [S], vac. by resig. of John de Melborne; patrons,[13] the master and scholars of Trinity Hall, Cambridge. Blofield, 21 Apr. 1352.

1618 Inst. of Walter Gyzon of Lynford [N], priest, to the vicarage of Havering-land [N]. The bishop had nomination; patrons, the prior and convent of Horsham St Faith [N]. Blofield, 31 Mar. 1352.[14]
[Margin] He owes 2s. 4d. for letters of institution.

---

[8] He held this benefice until his death in 1379 (*Norwich Wills* 2, 359).
[9] See **1614**; Tyvetteshal may have been instituted *sede vacante*, as the last known rector was Dns Simon de Kirkeby super Wrocke in 1342 (Reg. Bek fo.54).
[10] See **842** and App. II, p. 142.
[11] He held this benefice until his death in 1374 (*Norwich Wills* 2, 368).
[12] See **496n**.
[13] See **35**; the patronage was a gift of John son of John de Shardelowe and his brother Thomas (*CPR 1350–1354*, 195).
[14] This entry was added in lower margin and marked for insertion after **1608**.

1619 [fo.138ᵛ] The election of Brother Laurence de Leek, OSB, priest and professed monk of Holy Trinity Priory, Norwich cathedral, as prior of that house by the subprior and chapter, following the resignation of Brother Simon Bozoun, was quashed by the bishop because it went contrary to the canon of the general council, *Quia propter*.[15] The bishop then declared the chapter to have lost its right of election in this turn, which devolved upon him. Mindful of the merits of the elect, however, and of the agreement of the chapter, he provided Leek to the priorate by his ordinary right. Saving in all things the episcopal rights, and the right and dignity of the church of Norwich. Blofield, 24 Apr. 1352.

1620 [Cancelled] Repetition of inst. to Cowlinge [S] [**1617**], but dated Babraham (*Badburgham*), 26 Apr. 1352.

1621 Inst. of Richard de Whydenham, priest, to the rectory of Chelsworth [S], vac. by resig. of Adam Wych; patron, the abbot of Bury St Edmunds [S]. London, 1 May 1352.

1622 Inst. of Roger de Holm, priest, to the rectory of Stalham [N], vac. by resig. of Richard de Thoresby; Thoresby resigned both Stalham and his prebend of Llandegley[16] (*Landegle*), St David's diocese, in exchange for Holm's rectory of Oundle (*Undele*), Lincoln diocese. Patrons, the master and scholars of Trinity Hall, Cambridge University. London, 5 May 1352.

1623 Inst. of Richard de Thoresby, priest, to the rectory of Oundle (*Oundele*), Lincoln diocese, in exchange with Roger Holm as above, by commission of Bishop John [Gynewell] of Lincoln; patron, the abbot of Peterborough (*Burgo sancti Petri*). London, 5 May 1352.

1624 Collation to Roger de Holm[17] of the prebend of Llandegley (*Landegle*), St David's diocese, in exchange, by commission of Bishop Reginald [Brian] of St David's. London, 5 May 1352.

1625 Inst. of M. Walter de Elveden, DCL, precentor of Hereford cathedral chapter, to the rectory of Snetterton All Saints [N], vacant by the natural death (*mortem naturalem*) of John de Bokenham; patron, Lady Alice, widow of Hugh de Bokenham, knight. Terling, 9 May 1352.

1626 Inst. of William de Schiltwode, priest, to a moiety of Wetherden [S], vac. by resig. of John Baret in exchange for the rectory of *Thalamynghangel Crath*,[18] St David's diocese; patron, the abbot of Bury St Edmunds [S]. Terling, 14 May 1352.
[Margin] He is obligated for his predecessor.

---

[15] Canon 24 of the Fourth Lateran Council (1215), which entered the *Corpus iuris canonici* as *Extra* 1,6,42.
[16] In Abergwili collegiate church, Powys.
[17] See **1622**.
[18] A number of places in South Wales are called Llanfihangel.

1627 Inst. of John Baret, priest, to the rectory of *Thlamynhangel Crath*, St David's diocese, in the exchange noted above; patron, Edward [the Black Prince], eldest son of the king and Prince of Wales. Terling, 14 May 1352.

1628 Inst. of Robert de Kyngton, priest, to the rectory of St Margaret of Westwick, Norwich, vacant by the death of John de Walsham; patron, John de Norwico of Yoxford [S]. Terling, 17 May 1352.

1629 Inst. of Robert Atte Faldyate of Brisley [N], priest, to the rectory of Themelthorpe (*Thymelthorp*) [N], vac. by resig. of Geoffrey Skynner; patrons, the prior and convent of Walsingham [N]. Terling, 18 May 1352.

1630* Inst. of Robert Colston, clerk with first tonsure, to the rectory of Fritton [N], vacant by the removal of Thomas Ryvet, according to the decision of the royal court by which the king recovered the advowson of Fritton;[19] patron in this turn, Edward III, the lands and tenements of John de Segrave, knight, having recently been in the king's hand. Terling, 18 May 1352.

1631 Inst. of Roger Bacoun, priest, to the rectory of Baconsthorpe (*Bacounesthorp*) [N], vacant by the natural death of Dns Roger Bacon; patron, Thomas Bacoun. Terling, 19 May 1352.

1632 Inst. of Thomas de Gatele, priest, to the vicarage of Hacheston [S], vacant by the canonical removal of John Skacher;[20] patrons, the prior and convent of Hickling [N]. Terling, 25 May 1352.

1633 Inst. of Henry Albot,[21] priest, to the vicarage of the churches[22] of Holy Trinity and St Andrew, Marham [N], vac. by resig. of Roger Godwyne, in exchange for a moiety of St Mary of Rockland Minor[23] (*beate Marie de Rokelond Minor*) [N]; [fo.139ᵛ] patrons, the prior and convent of West Acre [N]. Terling, 29 May 1352.

1634 Inst. of Roger Godwyne, priest, to a moiety of St Mary of Rockland Minor [N], vac. by resig. of Henry Albot in exchange as above; patron, John de Segrave, knight. Terling, 29 May 1352.

1635 Inst. of Walter Anyas, priest, to the rectory of Brumstead [N], vac. by resig. of Adam Charles; patron, John Hakeluyt, knight. Terling, 2 June 1352.
[Margin] He is obligated for his predecessor and for Badmondisfield[24] (*Bodmondesfeld*) [S].

[19] See **1588**.
[20] See **1020**.
[21] *Alias* Henry de Hoghton (Reg. Bek fo.24ᵛ).
[22] See **926***n*.
[23] See **307***n*.
[24] See **1393**.

1636 Inst. of John Mayster of Burnham [N], priest, to the vicarage of Shernborne [N], vac. by resig. of Gilbert de Holkham;[25] patrons, the prior and convent of Pentney [N]. London, 13 June 1352.

1637 Inst. of William de Crosdale, priest, to the rectory of Cockthorpe [N], vac. by resig. of John [Bacoun[26]]; patron, Thomas Bacoun. London, 14 June 1352.

1638 Certificate of Bishop John [Gynewell] of Lincoln, that he has executed Bateman's commission (quoted in full; dated London, 31 Jan. 1352) for an exchange of benefices between M. Thomas Maresshall, rector of Scotter (*Scotere*), Lincoln diocese, and Thomas de Rasen, rector of Thornham Magna (*Thornham Pylecok*) [S]; he examined the enquiry of the archdeacon of Sudbury's official, and instituted Maresshall to Thornham Magna, to which he had been presented by Edward III.[27] [fo.140] Sleaford (*Lafford*), 12 June 1352.

1639 M. Thomas Maresshal appeared personally before the bishop at Terling and gave oath of canonical obedience [for the rectory of Thornham Magna [S], as above]. Order was sent [the archdeacon of] Sudbury to induct Maresshal. Terling, 17 June 1352.

1640* Inst. of Roger son of William de Wylby, priest, in the person of his proctor, Dns Simon [de Rykynghale], rector of Rollesby [N], to the rectory of West Bradenham [N], vacant because the former rector, M. John de Brynkele, has peacefully acquired possession of the archdeaconry of Nottingham; patrons by right of acquisition, Robert de Rokelond, Robert Bysshop, William Hulle, [all clerks] and Laurence Mendeware of Buckenham [N]. Terling, 23 June 1352.

1641 Inst. of William Kerre, priest, to the vicarage of Stanford [N], vacant by the death of John de Brokford. The bishop had nomination; patrons, the prior and convent of Shouldham [N]. Terling, 22 June 1352.

1642 Inst. of John de Stethenache, priest, to a moiety of Great Wreningham [N], vac. by resig. of John Akewra, [in exchange]; patrons, the prioress and convent of Carrow [N]. Terling, 12 July 1352.

1643 Inst. of John Akewra, priest, to the rectory of Framlingham Pigot (*Framyngham Pycot*) [N], vac. by resig. of John de Stethenache[28] [in exchange]; patrons, Nicholas de Castello and Matilda, his wife. Terling, 12 July 1352.

1644 Collation[29] to John Stanlak, subdeacon, of the rectory of Bacton (*Baketon Episcopi*) [S]. South Elmham, 13 Sept. 1349 [*sic*].

---

[25] *Alias* Holkham Holmes (**1046**).
[26] See **818**.
[27] Eye Priory was the usual patron (**663**); see *CPR 1350–1354*, 213, for the presentation.
[28] Last recorded inst. was of John son of Richard de Hemplond (**591**).
[29] Cf. **1077**.

1645 Collation to Henry Whyte, priest, of the rectory of Stratton St Peter [N]; patron in this turn by right of devolution,[30] the bishop. Hoxne, 10 Sept. 1351 [*sic*].

1646 Collation to Robert Drille, priest, of the rectory of Kenningham [N]; patron in this turn by right of devolution,[31] the bishop. Hoxne, 12 Sept. 1351.[32]

1647* [Margin] Contemporary note that the vicarage of Little Yarmouth[33] [S] had become vacant during the Plague, and that the resulting institution was not registered. n.d.

1648 [fo.140ᵛ] Admission of Brother William de Bello Monte, priest and professed Benedictine monk of Bec-Hellouin, Rouen diocese, as prior of Stoke-by-Clare [S], following the resig. of Brother John de Aqua Partita, at the presentation [**1649***] of the abbot of Bec Hellouin; the bishop preferred Bello Monte to that office and committed to him the care and administration of the priory, both spiritual and temporal. Saving all episcopal customs. Blofield, 20 Apr. 1352.

1649* Letter from Abbot Robert of Bec-Hellouin, Rouen diocese, to Bishop Bateman, presenting Brother William de Bello Monte, priest and professed Benedictine monk of Bec-Hellouin, as the new prior of Stoke-by-Clare [S]. The abbot asked Bateman to accept the resignation of the former prior, Brother John de Aqua Partita, *alias* Goullafr', and admit Bello Monte. Bec Hellouin, 17 Mar. 1352.

1650 The unanimous election of Brother John de Swafham, priest and professed Augustinian canon of St Mary Priory, Ixworth [S], by the subprior and canons, as prior of that house, following the resignation of Brother Roger [de Kyrkested[34]], was quashed by the bishop for defect of form. Mindful of the merits of the elect, however, the bishop preferred him to that office of his special grace. Blofield, 20 Apr. 1352.

1651 The peaceful election of Isabella de Hynton, professed Augustinian [*sic*] nun of Blackborough [N], by the subprioress and nuns, as prioress of that house, following the resignation of the last prioress [left blank[35]], was quashed by the bishop for defect of form. The bishop preferred the elect to that office by his special grace. Blofield, 20 Apr. 1352.

1652 Collation to Geoffrey Mirival, priest, of the rectory of Little Bricett[36] (*parva Bresete*) [S]; patron in this turn by right of devolution,[37] the bishop. Sudbury, 17 July 1352.

[30] Cf. **296** and **731**.
[31] Cf. **730**.
[32] MS. *Anno domini proximo supradicto*
[33] See **414***n*.
[34] Elected 1338 (Reg. Bek ff.11ᵛ–12ᵛ).
[35] Isabella de Stanton (**1086**).
[36] United to Offton parish in 1503 (White, *Suffolk*, 238).
[37] St Mary priory, Thetford, had advowson (Reg. Ayremynne fo.68ᵛ).

1653　Inst. of John de Lenne, priest, to the vicarage of [All Saints[38]], Wickle-wood (*Wyckelwode*) [N], vac. by resig. of William Grey;[39] patrons, the prior and convent of Holy Trinity, Norwich cathedral. South Elmham, 21 July 1352.

1654　[fo.141] Inst. of Semannus de Gyppewico, priest, to a moiety of Ring-stead Parva [N], vac. by resig. of William atte Mede; patron, Richard de Boylond, knight. South Elmham, 21 July 1352.

1655　Collation to William Debbe, priest, of a moiety[40] in the church of Holverston (*Holveston*) [N]; patron in this turn by right of devolution,[41] the bishop. South Elmham, 23 July[42] 1352.

1656　Inst. of John de Stowe, priest, in the person of his proctor, Dns William de Swyneflet, rector of Elsing [N], to the rectory of Brisley [N], vac. by resig. of Hugh de Lydgate; patron, Hugh de Hastynges, knight. South Elmham, 28 July 1352.

1657　Inst. of Nicholas Wolvenys, priest, to the vicarage of Tuttington [N], vacant by the death of Dns Clement [Tyllok]; patrons, the prior and convent of Bromholm [N]. South Elmham, 28 July 1352.

1658　Inst. of John Bakepol, priest, to the free chapel of St Andrew at Stradbroke [S], vac. by resig. of John de Lay; patron, Thomas de Wyngefeld. South Elmham, 28 July 1352.

1659　Inst. of Walter [Lyster[43]] of Dunwich, priest, to the rectory of Hevening-ham [S], vac. by resig. of Dns Gerard Ricar' in exchange for the vicarage of Tannington with Brundish chapel [S]; patron in this turn, Edward III, the temporalities of St Neot's Priory being in his hand. South Elmham, 29 July 1352.

1660　Inst. of Gerard Ricarii, priest, to the vicarage of Tannington with Brundish chapel [S], in exchange for the benefice of Walter [Lyster], as above; patron, Bishop Hamo [de Hethe] of Rochester.[44] South Elmham, 29 July 1352.

1661　Collation to Adam Shene of Peasenhall [S], priest, of the vicarage of Cransford [S]. He gave oath to reside according to the canon law.[45] South Elmham, 5 Aug. 1352.

---

[38] See **1088**.

[39] Inst. 1340 (Reg. Bek fo.34ᵛ); not William Gray, vicar of Newton by Castle Acre [N] (**1538**).

[40] The other moiety was annexed to Bergh Apton [N] (*Taxatio* 84).

[41] At the last recorded institution the patron was Thomas of Brotherton, earl of Norfolk and marshal of England (Reg. Ayremynne fo.32ᵛ).

[42] MS. *xxxiii Julii*

[43] See **748**.

[44] Hethe had died on 4 May 1352; his register is incomplete (*Registrum Hamonis Hethe*, ed. C. Johnson, CYS 48–9 [1948]).

[45] See **1736***.

1662 Inst. of Thomas Hannok, priest, to the rectory of Thorpe Parva [N], vacant by the death of Conrad (*Coraudi*) [de Metleys[46]]; patron, Edmund de Neketon. South Elmham, 6 Aug. 1352.

1663 [fo.141ᵛ] Inst. of John de Besthorp, priest, to the rectory of Moulton [in Blofield deanery] [N], vac. by resig. of Robert de Norton; patrons,[47] Richard Ive, Simon de Rykynghal, and John de Lympenhowe. South Elmham, 8 Aug. 1352.

1664 Inst. of Thomas Clement of Kirton [S], priest, to the rectory of St Peter of West Lynn (*Lenn sancti Petri*) [N], vac. by resig. of Fulk de Flete; patron, the prior and convent of Lewes. Hoxne, 12 Aug. 1352.
[Margin] He is obligated by oath for 24 marks in the next four years, 6 marks each year.

1665 Inst. of John de Asshedon, priest, to the rectory of Mundford [N], vacant by the natural death of Simon Wytherich;[48] patron, Gerard de Insula, knight. London, 18 Aug. 1352.

1666 Certificate of Bishop John [de Trillek] of Hereford that he has executed Bateman's commission (quoted in full; dated Terling, 17 June 1352) for an exchange of benefices between John Hope, prebendary of the subdeacon's prebend in Holdgate collegiate church (*Holgat*), and Thomas Crene,[49] dean of Fordham [S]; the deanery was in the bishop's advowson. Stretton Sugwas (*Sugwas*), 3 July 1352.

1667 John Hope, in the person of his proctor, M. Thomas Trillok,[50] rector of Adderbury (*Edburbury*), gave oath of canonical obedience [for Fordham [S] deanery]. London, 20 Aug. 1352.

1668 Inst. of William de Wanton, priest, to the rectory of Haverhill [S], vac. by resig. of Adam de Neubold, in exchange for the rectory of Clopton [fo.142] in Lincoln diocese; patrons, the prior and convent of Castle Acre [N]. London, 21 Aug. 1352.
[Margin] He is obligated for 60 marks, to pay in the Easter synod 30 marks and the Michaelmas synod £10 and at Christmas £10.

1669 Inst. of Adam Neubold, priest, to the rectory of Clopton in Lincoln diocese,[51] vac. by resig. of William de Wanton, in exchange for the rectory of Haverhill [S]; patron, Sir Edmund de Berforde. London, 21 Aug. 1352.

1670 Inst. of Henry Baffer of Gooderstone [N], priest, to the vicarage of Gooderstone, vac. by resig. of William Aunger in exchange for the vicarage of

[46] See **875**.
[47] Cf. **1453**, and *CPR 1350–1354*, 195, 292; Alice de Bumpstede had received royal licence to give this advowson to the College of St Mary in the Fields on 6 June 1352.
[48] Cf. **714**.
[49] Collated 1341 as Thomas Crene of Hereford (Reg. Bek ff.51ᵛ–52).
[50] *BRUO* 3, 1906–8.
[51] There is no mention of a commission from the bishop of Lincoln.

South Lynn [N]; patrons, the abbess and convent of Denney. South Elmham, 12 Sept. 1352.

[Margin] Ten marks at Easter and Michaelmas insofar as they are owed.

1671 Inst. of William Aunger, priest, to the vicarage of South Lynn [N], in exchange with Henry [Baffer, as above]; patrons, the prior and convent of West Acre [N]. South Elmham, 12 Sept. 1352.

[Margin] He is obligated for 12 marks at Easter and Michaelmas.

1672 Collation to Thomas de Mutforde, clerk with first tonsure, of the deanery of Bosmere [S], vacant by the canonical removal of William de Ocham.[52] South Elmham, 14 Sept. 1352.

1673 Inst. of William de Northwode, priest, to the rectory of Witnesham [S], vacant by the death of Simon de Assheby; patron, Lady Katherine Latymer. South Elmham, 20 Sept. 1352.

[Margin] 28 marks at Easter and Michaelmas.

1674 Inst. of John Bolt of Wangford [S], priest, to the rectory of Flempton [S], vacant by the death of William Payn; patron, John de Shardelowe, knight. South Elmham, 18 Sept. 1352.

[Margin] Eight marks at Easter and Michaelmas.

1675 Inst. of Henry de Lympenhowe, priest, to the rectory of St Michael of Coslany (*Coselanye*) in Norwich.[53] Massingham, 24 Sept. 1352.

[Margin] He is not obligated.

1676* Preferment of John de Aston, priest, as master of the collegiate chantry of the Annunciation at Campsey Ash [S], vac. by resig. of John de Caketon, with the obligation incumbent on that office; patrons, the prioress and convent of Campsey Ash. Massingham, 24 Sept. 1352.

1677 [fo.142^v] Inst. of William de Melton, priest of York diocese, to the vicarage of Griston [N], vac. by resig. of John Balle. The bishop had nomination; patrons, the prior and convent of Buckenham [N]. Gaywood, 28 Sept. 1352.

[Margin] Eight marks at Easter and Michaelmas.

1678 Inst.[54] of William Ernald of Apton[55] [N], priest, to the rectory of Carleton Rode [N], vacant by the death of Dns John Lyther; patron, Roger de Norwico, knight. Thornham[56] (*Thornham iuxta mare*), 4 Oct. 1352.

[Margin] 26 marks at Easter and Michaelmas.

[52] Collated in 1342 (Reg. Bek fo.63).

[53] No patron is named; N. Tanner shows the advowson of this parish belonged to a series of laymen from 1353 (*Church in Norwich*, 174). See also **1773**.

[54] MS. (unusually) *institutus fuit personaliter*

[55] St Martin church at Apton became a chapel in the 14th century, perhaps as early as 1316; the parish was united to Bergh (now Bergh Apton) (*Ruined Churches*, 53; 'Lost Villages', 142).

[56] Thornham Bishop (**226n.**).

1679 Inst. of Robert le Yonge, priest, to a moiety of Howe [N], vac. by resig. of Thomas Melburne; patrons, the prioress and convent of Carrow [N]. Thornham, 5 Oct. 1352.

[Margin] [He owes] 23 marks for first fruits and Willingham (*Wirlingham*), at Michaelmas, Easter and Michaelmas.[57]

1680 Inst. of Henry Fote of East Wretham [N], priest, to the vicarage of Hackford [in Hingham deanery] [N], vac. by resig. of Richard Sharp; patrons, the abbess and convent of Marham [N]. Blofield, 6 Oct. 1352.

[Margin] He is not obligated because it is not assessed.

1681 Collation to William de Brandon, clerk with first tonsure, of the deanery of Waxham (*Waxtonesham*) [N], vacant by the death of John Bermere. Hevingham, 6 Oct. 1352.

1682 Inst. of Walter de Fundenhale, priest, to the rectory of Lamas [N], vac. by resig. of Thomas Coyn; patron, Miles de Stapelton, knight. Blofield, 11 Oct. 1352.

[Margin] Eight marks at Easter and Michaelmas.

1683 Inst. of John Suwet, priest, to the rectory of All Saints, Gillingham (*Gylingham parva*) [N], vac. by resig. of Robert de Twyforde; patron, John de Segrave, knight. South Elmham, 14 Oct. 1352.

[Margin] Four marks at Easter and Michaelmas.

1684 Inst. of William de Drayton, priest, to the rectory of Great Bealings [S], vac. by resig. of John Joye in exchange for the vicarage of Felstead in London diocese; patrons, Walter Wauncy, Hugh Wauncy, Robert Wauncy and John de Lakynghithe. South Elmham, 18 Oct. 1352.

[Margin] Eleven marks at Michaelmas and Easter.

1685 Inst. of John Joye, priest, to the vicarage of Felstead in London diocese, in exchange [as above] with William de Drayton, by commission of Bishop Ralph [de Stratford] of London; patron in this turn, Edward III, the abbey of Caen being in his hand. South Elmham, 18 Oct. 1352.

1686 Collation to John de Berdewell, priest, of the chantry in the church of Ixworth Priory [S], founded by M. Nicholas de Norton, with the obligation incumbent upon that chantry; patron in this turn by right of devolution,[58] the bishop. South Elmham, 18 Oct. 1352.

1687 [fo.143] Inst. of Thomas de Marleforde, priest, to the vicarage of Friston (*Freston*) [S], vac. by resig. of John de Farnham; patrons, the prior and convent of Snape [S]. South Elmham, 21 Oct. 1352.

[Margin] Five marks at Michaelmas and Easter.

[57] MS. *in xxiii mar' pro ii fruct' et Wirlingham. Mich'. Pas et Mich'.* Cf. **1547** and **1716**.
[58] In 1342, the patrons were Nicholas Baillif de Norton and Katherine, widow of Eli Payk of St Edmunds (Reg. Bek fo.58ᵛ).

1688 Inst. of Richard Reyner, priest, to the rectory of Stratton St Michael [N], vac. by resig. of John de Wrotham; patron in this turn, Edward III, the temporalities of Newton Longville Priory being in his hand. South Elmham, 24 Oct. 1352.

[Margin] Sixteen marks: four at Easter, four at St Peter in Chains [1 Aug.], and eight at the next two synods.

1689 Inst. of Adam Belacombre, priest, to the rectory of Little Bealings (*Belyngg parva*) [S], vac. by resig. of Philip Yongman,[59] in exchange for the rectory of Twinstead in London diocese; patron in this turn,[60] Mary [de Roos], countess of Norfolk. South Elmham, 24 Oct. 1352.

[Margin] Five marks at Easter and Michaelmas.

1690 Inst. of Philip Yongman, priest, to the rectory of Twinstead in London diocese, vac. by resig. of Adam Belacombr', in exchange, by commission of Bishop [Ralph de Stratford] of London; patrons, the prior and convent of Merton. South Elmham, 24 Oct. 1352.

1691 Inst. of Peter Broun, priest, to the rectory of Chedburgh (*Chetebergh*) [S], vac. by resig. of Adam de Brandeston, in exchange for the vicarage of West Wratting in Ely diocese; patron, Edmund Verdoun, knight. Hoxne, 25 Oct. 1352.

[Margin] 100s. at Michaelmas and Easter.

1692 Inst. of Adam de Brandeston, priest, to the vicarage of West Wratting in Ely diocese, vac. by resig. of Peter Broun, in exchange, by commission of Bishop Thomas [de Lisle] of Ely; patrons, the prior and chapter of Ely cathedral. Hoxne, 25 Oct. 1352.

1693 Inst. of Richard Munch, priest, to the rectory of Fersfield [N], vac. by resig. of Andrew [Gylour[61]] of Wimbotsham [N], in exchange for the vicarage of St Mary Magdalen, Wiggenhall [N]; patron, John de Ufforde, knight. Hoxne, 25 Oct. 1352.

[Margin] Eight marks at Michaelmas and Easter.

1694 Inst. of Andrew [Gylour] of Wimbotsham [N], priest, to the vicarage of St Mary Magdalen, Wiggenhall [N], vac. by resig. of Richard Munch, in exchange [as above]; patrons, the prior and convent of Castle Acre [N]. Hoxne, 25 Oct. 1352.

[Margin] Seven marks at Michaelmas and Easter.

1695 Inst. of Hugh Wauncy, priest, to the rectory of Edgefield (*Eggefeld*) [N], vac. by resig. of Adam de Billokby,[62] in exchange for the rectory of Mulbarton (*Mulkerton*) [N]; patron, William de Symythweyt, knight. Hoxne, 26 Oct. 1352.

---

[59] His institution was not registered (cf. **872**).
[60] Usually St Mary priory, Thetford (Reg. Salmon fo.81^v).
[61] See **136**.
[62] Instituted in 1312 (Reg. Salmon fo.48^v).

[Margin] He is obligated to the bishop for 17 marks at Michaelmas and Easter.[63]

1696 [fo.143ᵛ] Inst. of Adam de Billokby,[64] priest, in the person of his proctor, William Bonyng, to the rectory of Mulbarton (*Mulkeberton*) [N], [see above]; patron, Lady Elizabeth de Sancto Omero. Hoxne, 26 Oct. 1352.
[Margin] Fourteen marks at Michaelmas and Easter.

1697 Inst. of Hugh Skorier,[65] priest, to the vicarage of Necton [N], vac. by resig. of John [Baxtere[66]] of Dunkirk (*Donchirch*) [N], in exchange for the rectory of Bowthorpe [N]; patron, Thomas [de Bello Campo], earl of Warwick. Hoxne, 30 Oct. 1352.
[Margin] Five marks at Michaelmas and Easter.

1698 Inst. of John [Baxtere] of Dunkirk [N], priest, to the rectory of Bowthorpe [N], vac. by resig. of Hugh Skorier, in exchange as above; patron, Avice de Wysham. Hoxne, 30 Oct. 1352.
[Margin] Six marks at Michaelmas and Easter.

1699 Inst. of Thomas atte Lathe, priest, to the rectory of St Michael's, Fincham [N], vac. by resig. of Dns William [Leche[67]] of Hapton [N]; patrons, the prior and convent of Castle Acre [N]. Hoxne, 1 Nov. 1352.
[Margin] Sixteen marks at Michaelmas and Easter.

1700 Inst. of Philip Martyn, priest, to the rectory of Mulbarton [N], vac. by resig. of Adam de Billokby;[1] patron, Lady Elizabeth de Sancto Omero. Hoxne, 5 Nov. 1352.
[Margin] Fourteen marks at Michaelmas and Easter.

1701 Collation to M. Roger de Holm, subdeacon,[2] of the rectory of Blofield [N], vac. by resig. of M. Robert de Stratton, in exchange for the rectory of Stalham [N]. Hoxne, 6 Nov. 1352.
[Margin] The bishop remitted 40 marks.

1702 Inst. of M. Robert de Stratton,[3] subdeacon, to the rectory of Stalham [N], vac. by resig. of Roger de Holm, in exchange; patrons, the master and college of Trinity Hall in Cambridge University. Hoxne, 6 Nov. 1352.
[Margin] He is not obligated.

---

[63] MS. *xvii. mar' Mich'is & Pas. ob' e' dno.*
[64] See **1700**.
[65] *Alias* Skyner; possibly the same as Hugh Skorier, parson of Raydon [S], whose will was proved in 1375 (*Norwich Wills* 3, 336).
[66] See **1090**.
[67] See **1334**.
[1] See **1696**.
[2] Possibly an error; cf. **1622**, **1702**.
[3] See **36** and **1706–7**.

1703　Collation to Dns John Valentyn of *Edrewell* [or *Odrewell*], priest, to the vicarage of St Mary's and St Botulph's, Shotesham [N], vac. by resig. of John de London.[4] Hoxne, 7 Nov. 1352.

[Margin] Not assessed in the register or the composition.[5]

1704　Inst. of M. Walter de Baketon, priest, to the rectory of Barnham Broom [N] with Riskes chapel, vac. by resig. of Thomas le Strange in exchange for the rectory of North Lynn (*sancti Edmundi de Lenn*) [N]; patron, [fo.144] Constantine de Mortuo Mari, knight. Hoxne, 11 Nov. 1352.

[Margin] Twenty marks at Michaelmas and Easter.

1705　Inst. of Thomas Strange, priest, to the rectory of North Lynn [N], vac. by resig. of M. Walter de Baketon in exchange for the rectory of Barnham Broom with Riskes chapel [N]; patron, the abbot of Bury St Edmunds [S]. Hoxne, 11 Nov. 1352.

[Margin] Fifteen marks at Michaelmas and Easter.

1706　Inst. of Robert Borewode, priest, to the newly-established vicarage[6] of Stalham [N]; patrons, the master and scholars of Trinity Hall, Cambridge. Hoxne, 17 Nov. 1352.

[Margin] 100s. at Easter and Michaelmas.

1707*　The letter of institution for Robert de Borewode of Aylsham [N], priest, as vicar of Stalham [N]. Borewode was one of two men presented to the bishop by the master and college of Trinity Hall, Cambridge University, in accord with the terms of the appropriation,[7] and he was the bishop's choice. Having received the oath of residence, the bishop instituted him. n.d.

1708　Inst. of Alan Spark, priest, to the vicarage of Walton (*Walton in Decanatum de Coln'*) [S] vac. by resig. of John [le Somenour[8]] of Garsington (*Gersyngdon*), in exchange for the rectory of Pettaugh (*Pethaghe*) [S]; patrons, the prior and chapter of Rochester cathedral. Hoxne, 17 Nov. 1352.

[Margin] Six and a half marks at Michaelmas and Easter, and J. de Gersingdon was instituted in this benefice about Ascension (26 May), 1351.

1709　Inst. of John [le Somenour] of Garsington, priest, to the rectory of Pettaugh [S], vac. by resig. of Alan [Spark] in exchange as above; patron, Thomas de Gyppewico. Hoxne, 17 Nov. 1352.

[Margin] Nine marks at Michaelmas and Easter.

1710　Inst. of William Butteveleyn, priest, in the person of his proctor, Dns Ralph de Chattegrave, chaplain, to the rectory of Tunstall [S], vac. by resig. of

[4] The patrons, Pentney priory [N], were not named.
[5] MS. *non taxatur in registro nec in compositione*, but cf. *Valor Ecclesiasticus*, 84, where all four Shotesham parishes are assessed.
[6] See **36, 1702, 1707**.
[7] See **36**.
[8] See **1740**.

Thomas [Atte gate[9]] of Thorndon (*Thornedon*) [S] in exchange for the rectory of Kelsale (*Keleshale*) [S]; patron, Sir Edward de Monte Acuto. Hoxne, 16 Nov. 1352.

[Margin] £10 at Michaelmas and Easter.

1711 Inst. of Thomas [Atte gate] of Thorndon [S], priest, in the person of his proctor, Ralph de Chattegrave, chaplain, to the rectory of Kelsale [S], vac. by resig. of Dns William Butteveleyn in exchange for the rectory of Tunstall [S]; patron, Edward de Monte Acuto, knight. Hoxne, 16 Nov. 1352.

[Margin] £20 at Michaelmas and Easter.

1712 Inst. of Thomas de Brom, priest, to a moiety of Taverham [N], vac. by resig. of William de Weston in exchange for the vicarage of Tunstall [N]; patron, Baldric de Taverham. Hoxne, 17 Dec. 1352.

[Margin] Eight marks at Michaelmas and Easter.

1713 Collation to William [fo.144[v]] de Weston, priest, of the vicarage of Tunstall [N], vac. by resig. of Thomas de Brom[10] in exchange for a moiety of Taverham [N]. Hoxne, 17 Dec. 1352.

[Margin] Eight marks at Michaelmas and Easter.[11]

1714* Certificate of Bishop John [de Thoresby] of Worcester, that he has executed Bateman's commission (quoted in full; dated London, 30 Nov. 1352) to test the literacy of John Edward of Fressingfield [S], the presentee of Castle Acre Priory [N] to the rectory of Trunch [N], found him suitably competent, and instituted him. London, 8 Dec. 1352.

[Margin] Sixteen marks at Easter and Michaelmas.

1715 William de Esthawe, priest, proctor of John Edward, appeared personally before the bishop and gave oath of canonical obedience [for Trunch [N] rectory]. Order was sent [the archdeacon of Norfolk] to induct Edward. Hoxne, 19 Dec. 1352.

1716 Inst. of John de Steyneston, priest, to a moiety of Howe [N], vac. by resig. of Robert Yonge; patrons, the prioress and convent of Carrow [N]. Hoxne, 30 Dec. 1352.

[Margin] Twenty marks, that is 7 marks for Willingham (*Wylingham*) and first fruits.[12]

---

[9] See **1573**.

[10] He may have been instituted *sede vacante*, as the last known vicar was William de Ryngelond in 1343 (Reg. Bek fo.66); the patrons were Sibton abbey (Philippa Brown, *Sibton Abbey Cartularies and Charters*, Suffolk Charters VII–X (Woodbridge 1985–1988), 1, 137).

[11] Archidiaconal visitation records of 1368 also give the taxation as 8 marks (Watkin, *Inventory* 1, 38).

[12] MS. *.xx.mar' viz pro vii mar' pro Wylingh' et .ii. fruct'*; cf. **1679**.

1717   Inst. of William Palmer, priest, to the vicarage of Pakenham [S], vac. by resig. of Robert de Pantele, in exchange for the rectory of Langham [S]; patron, the abbot[13] of Bury St Edmunds [S]. Hoxne, 4 Jan. 1353.

[Margin] Sixteen marks at Michaelmas and Easter.

1718   Inst. of Robert de Pantele, priest, to the rectory of Langham (*Langham iuxta Ixworth*) [S], vac. by resig. of [fo.145] William Palmere[14] in exchange for the vicarage [of Pakenham], as above; patron, the abbot of Bury St Edmunds [S]. Hoxne, 4 Jan. 1353.

[Margin] Ten marks at Michaelmas and Easter.

1719   Inst. of Nicholas Cunch, priest, to the rectory of Langford [N], vac. by resig. of John de Irlond;[15] patron, John de Hevenyngham, [knight]. Hoxne, 4 Jan. 1353.

[Margin] 60s. at Michaelmas and Easter.

1720   Collation to M.[16] John de Wyneston, priest, rector of Badingham [S], of the custody[17] of the Hospital of St Thomas the Martyr, Beck[18] (*le Bek*) [N], vac. by resig. of M. Roger de Hedersete. Wyneston gave oath in accord with the new constitution. Hoxne, 1 Jan. 1353.

1721   Inst. of Thomas de Dullyngham, priest, to the rectory of Wixoe (*Whidekesho*) [S], vacant by the natural death of Peter [de Asshewyk[19]] of Buntingford; patron, Edmund de Sutton.[20] n.p., 13 Jan. 1353.

[Margin] Nine marks at Michaelmas and Easter.

1722   Inst. of John de Buxton, priest, to the vicarage of Oulton [N[21]], vac. by resig. of John de Estfeld. The bishop had nomination; patrons, the prior and convent of Walsingham [N]. Hoxne, 16 Jan. 1353.

[Margin] Three marks at Michaelmas and Easter.

1723   Inst. of Ralph Urry, priest, to the rectory of Thurgarton (*Thurgerton*) [N], vac. by resig. of Edmund de Fresingfeld in exchange for the rectory of Clippesby [N]; patrons, the abbot and convent of St Benet's, Hulme [N]. Thorpe next Norwich, 10 Jan. 1353.

[Margin] Fourteen marks at Michaelmas and Easter.

---

[13] *et conventus* cancelled.

[14] His institution may have been *sede vacante*, as the last known rector was John Charles in 1337 (Reg. Bek fo.1^v).

[15] Cf. **924**.

[16] This is the only entry in which Wyneston was styled *Magister*.

[17] See **1728**.

[18] Listed in the Domesday Book (*Domesday Gazetteer*, 264), Beck lay between Billingford and Foxley; by the 18th century the place was marked only by Beck Hall on the site of the hospital (Faden, sheet 2; White, *Norfolk*, 346).

[19] See **474**.

[20] *Alias* Sutthton (**474**).

[21] See **904**.

1724 Inst. of Edmund de Fresyngfeld, priest, to the rectory of Clippesby [N], vac. by resig. of Ralph Urry in exchange as above; patron, Reginald de Eccles. Thorpe next Norwich, 10 Jan. 1353.

[Margin] Twelve marks at Michaelmas and Easter.

1725 Inst. of John Mareys of Saxmundham [S] to the rectory of Winston [S], vac. by resig. of Reginald Bysshop; patron, Sir Edward de Monte Acuto. Thorpe next Norwich, 11 Jan. 1353.

[Margin] 20s. at Michaelmas and Easter.

1726 Inst. of Nicholas de Beauchamppe,[22] priest, to the rectory of Whatfield [S], vac. by resig. of Nicholas de Aldham; patron, Richard son of Benedict de Cokefeld, knight. Thorpe next Norwich, 11 Jan. 1353.

[Margin] 24 marks at Michaelmas and Easter, 20 marks for his predecessor at Easter and Michaelmas.

1727 Inst. of John de Crosdale, priest, to the rectory of Oxwick [N], vac. by resig. of Richard Syger; patron, the same Richard Syger. Long Stratton, 9 Jan. 1353.[23]

[Margin] Ten marks at Michaelmas and Easter.

1728 [fo.145^v] Collation to Roger Oslak, vicar of Tottington [N], of the custody of the Hospital of St Thomas the Martyr, Beck[24] [N], vac. by resig. of John de Wyneston. Hoxne, 20 Jan. 1353.

1729 The election[25] of Brother William de Braunforde, priest and professed canon of Holy Trinity Priory, Ipswich [S], by the subprior and convent of that house, as prior, following the death of Brother John de Kentforde, was quashed by the bishop for defect of form. The bishop then preferred the elect to that office by his special grace, and sent order to Dns Simon de [Rykynghale] of Babingley, rector of Rollesby [N], to induct him. Hoxne, 31 Jan. 1353.

1730 CAPELLA DE MORINGTHORP.[26] Inst. of Adam de Redgrave, priest, to the free chapel of St Mary in Ashwellthorpe [N], vac. by resig. of Geoffrey Kempe;[27] patron, Lady Beatrice, widow of Sir Robert de Thorp. Hoxne, 1 Feb. 1353.

1731 Collation to Thomas de Hemenhale, acolyte, of the deanery of Breckles [N], vacant by the death of [left blank[28]]. Usual notice of customary submission was sent. Thetford, 6 Feb. 1353.

---

[22] He remained chaplain of St Nicholas chapel at Stoke Nayland [S], to which he had been instituted in 1340 (Reg. Bek fo.41^v); see **1735**.

[23] Followed by six unused ruled lines.

[24] See **1720***n*.

[25] MS. *canonice*, cancelled.

[26] Morningthorpe is some 3 miles east of Ashwellthorpe.

[27] Apparently he retained the rectory of Ashwellthorpe (**681**).

[28] The last dean collated was Robert de Aisterby, an acolyte, in 1340 (Reg. Bek fo.36^v).

1732* Commission to Prior Laurence [de Leek] of Norwich cathedral and M. Richard de Lyng, archdeacon of Norwich, together and separately, to be his vicars-general in spiritualities, until he should return to London. The bishop was about to cross to Calais to make a treaty of peace between the king and his French enemy [John II]. He reserved to himself the collation, nomination and provision which pertained to him as bishop, as well as the right of approving exchanges of benefices, and the right of absolving from offences against the see of Norwich. Dartford, 11 Feb. 1353.

1733 Inst. of Geoffrey Len, priest, in the person of his proctor, Adam de Chelesworth, clerk, by Prior Laurence [de Leek] as vicar-general, to the rectory of Whatfield [S], vacant by the death of Dns Nicholas de Beauchamp;[29] patron, Richard son of Benedict de Cokefeld, knight. Norwich, 20 Mar. 1353.
[Margin] 24 marks at Michaelmas and Easter.

1734 Inst.[30] of William de Mergate, priest, to the rectory of Braydeston [N] with the chapel of Brundall, vac. by resig. of Geoffrey Len; patrons, William de Bergh, rector of Cantley [N], and William de Felmyngham. Norwich, 21 Mar. 1353.
[Margin] Eight marks at Michaelmas and Easter.

1735 Inst.[31] of John Chamberleyn of Stoke Nayland [S], priest, to the free chapel[32] of Stoke Nayland (*Stokeneylond*), vacant by the death of Nicholas Beauchamp;[33] patron, Robert Gyffard of Shimpling (*Shymplingg*). Terling, 29 Mar. 1353.

1736* [fo.146] Collation to William Tuffin, priest, of the vicarage of Cransford [S], vacant by reason of the prolonged absence from the parish of Adam Shene.[34] Terling, 29 Mar. 1353.
[Margin] 40s. at Michaelmas and Easter. *Coll'.*

1737 Inst. of Henry de Burgh, priest, to the rectory of All Saints, Gillingham [N], vac. by resig. of John Suet; patron, John [de Segrave], Lord Segrave. Rochford, 20 Apr. 1353.
[Margin] Four marks at Michaelmas and Easter, and he owes 5s. for the letter, to be paid at the feast of St John [24 June?] by surety of S. de Ball' or by security.[35]

1738 Inst. of Oliver de Wytton, priest, to the vicarage of Worstead (*Worthstede*) [N], vac. by resig. of William de Aldeby in exchange for the rectory of Alderford

---

[29] See **1726**, **1735**.
[30] MS. *per dictum patrem*
[31] MS. *per dictum patrem*
[32] St Nicholas chapel, on a manor of the Giffards (Reg. Salmon ff.38, 50ᵛ).
[33] See **1726**, **1733**.
[34] See **1661**.
[35] MS. *vel caut'*

[N]; patrons, the prior and chapter of Holy Trinity, Norwich cathedral. Ipswich, 25 Apr. 1353.

[Margin] 100s. at Christmas and Easter.

1739   Inst. of William de Aldeby, priest, to the rectory of Alderford [N], vac. by resig. of Oliver de Wytton in exchange for the vicarage of Worstead [N]; patrons, the prior and chapter of Norwich cathedral. Ipswich, 25 Apr. 1353.

[Margin] Eight and a half marks at Christmas and Easter.

1740   Inst. of Roger de Godereston, priest, to the rectory of Pettaugh [S], vacant by the natural death of John le Somenour of Garsington;[36] patron, Thomas de Gyppewico. Ipswich, 25 Apr. 1353.

[Margin] Nine marks at Michaelmas and Easter.

1741   Inst. of William de Banham, clerk with first tonsure, to the rectory of Denton [N], vacant by the natural death of Richard de Bowgheyn; patron in this turn, Adam de Clyfton, knight. Hoxne, 26 Apr. 1353.

[Margin] 36 marks at Michaelmas and Easter.

1742   Inst. of Roger Pymbel, priest, to the rectory of Edingthorpe [N], vac. by resig. of John Doget in exchange for the rectory of Wrentham (*Wrantham*) [S]; presentation was made by the prior of Lewes and Thomas de Wyngefeld, attorneys general for Lady Joan de Barro, countess Warenne. Hoxne, 3 May 1353.

[Margin] 100s., also half a mark for the letter.

1743   Inst. of John Doget, priest, to the rectory of Wrentham [S], vac. by resig. of Roger Pymbel, in the exchange above; patron, Simon Pierepont, knight. Hoxne, 3 May 1353.

[Margin] 32 marks, also 5 shillings.

1744   Inst. of Roger Crees, priest, to the vicarage of Saxthorpe (*Saxtorth*) [N], newly appropriated;[37] patrons, the master and [fo.146ᵛ] scholars of Pembroke Hall, Cambridge University. Hoxne, 5 May 1353.

1745   Inst. of John Shirre, priest, to the rectory of West Lynn [N], vac. by resig. of Thomas Clement in exchange for the chaplaincy in the free chapel of St James on Molton manor in Frampton, Lincoln diocese; patrons, the prior and convent of Lewes. Hoxne, 7 May 1353.

[Margin] The said Thomas and John are obligated jointly for 19 marks, to be paid in 4 years, and John is obligated by himself for 12 marks for first fruits.

1746   Inst. of Thomas Clement, priest, to the free chapel of St James on the manor of John de Molton in Frampton, Lincoln diocese, vac. by resig. of John [Shirre] in the exchange noted above, by commission of Bishop John [Gynewell] of Lincoln; patron, Queen Philippa. Hoxne, 7 May 1353.

---

³⁶ See 1708–9.
³⁷ See 51.

1747   Confirmation of the election of Brother Thomas de Redham, priest and professed Augustinian canon of St Mary Abbey at Creake [N], canonically held by the subprior and canons of that house, to the abbacy of that house, following the free resignation of Brother Robert de Dockyngg. Order to install him was sent the archdeacon of Norfolk.[38] London, 17 May 1353.

1748   Confirmation of the unanimous and lawful election of John Grene of Thompson, perpetual chaplain of Thompson College [N] (recently founded by Thomas de Shardelowe, knight, and his brother John), as master, by the brothers of the college. Order to induct him was sent [the archdeacon of] Norwich.[39] London, 17 May 1353.

1749   Collation to John de Acre, priest, of the rectory of Gaywood [N], vac. by resig. of John de Shaftebury in exchange for the rectory of All Saints, South Elmham [S]. Acre was instituted in the person of his proctor, Dns Robert de Walton, rector of Thornage [N]. London, 20 May 1353.
[Margin] Five marks.

1750   Collation to John de Shaftebury, priest, of the rectory of All Saints, South Elmham [S], vac. by resig. of John de Acre in the exchange aforesaid. London, 20 May 1353.
[Margin] Twelve marks.

1751   Inst. of John son of Simon Jacob of Massingham [N], priest, to the rectory of Gunton [N], vacant by the death of Dns John Boton;[40] patrons, Bartholomew de Antyngham, knight, Thomas de Clopton, and Richard, rector of [Great] Sampford (*Sampforde*). London, 19 May 1353.
[Margin] Twelve marks.

1752   Inst. of William Stannard, clerk with first tonsure, to the rectory of Wacton Parva (*Waketon marie minor*) [N], vacant by the death of John atte Assh; patrons, Ralph de Shelton, Thomas de Shardelowe, and Richard de Boylond, all knights, William de Middelton, Hugh Cursen, and Thomas Caron, rector of Stratton St Mary [N]. London, 8 June 1353.
[Margin] 40s.

1753   Inst. of Giles Herny of Hindolveston [N], priest, to the vicarage of Guist [N], vacant by the death of John de Hatfeld; [fo.147] patrons, the abbot and convent of Waltham. London, 8 June 1353.
[Margin] 20s.

1754   Indult[41] from Pope Clement VI to John Bardolf, knight, and his wife Elizabeth, to have a portable altar and to have mass and other rites celebrated on

---

[38] *Norff' Archid's* added later.
[39] *Norwic* added later.
[40] The last recorded institution was to John de Babrunne (**1617**).
[41] See *CPL* III, 472.

it in their presence, in any fitting place, without prejudice to anyone else's right. Avignon, 7 Aug. 1352.

1755 Inst. of John de Kentforde, priest, to the rectory of Great Snoring[42] (*Naryngges magna*) [N], vacant by the death of Dns Thomas de Brecham; patron, Ralph de Shelton, knight. Terling, 18 June 1353.

[Margin] 40 marks.

1756 Inst. of M. John de Horseye, priest, to the rectory of Grundisburgh [S], vac. by resig. of Dns Walter Wauncy; patrons, the master and scholars of Michaelhouse (*domus sancti Michaelis*), Cambridge. Terling, 19 June 1353.

[Margin] 25 marks.

1757 Inst. of Alexander Vymen of Bramford [S], priest, to the rectory of Framlingham Earl (*Framelyngham parva*) [N], vacant by the death of Dns John de Bromholm; patron in this turn, Mary [de Roos], countess of Norfolk, because the king granted her the advowsons of all benefices pertaining to the prior and convent of the alien monastery at Thetford [N]. Terling, 20 June 1353.

[Margin] Four marks.

1758 Inst. of Nicholas Cranele of *Freston*, priest, to the rectory of Bradfield Saint Clare (*Bradefeld sencler*) [S], vacant by the death of Roger [de Debenham[43]]; patrons, Ralph de Hemenhale, knight, John son of Edmund, and Roger Aubry. Terling, 24 June 1353.

[Margin] Ten marks.

1759 Certificate of Archbishop John [de Thoresby] of York that he has executed Bateman's commission (quoted in full; dated Terling, 23 June 1353) for an exchange of benefices between M. Michael de Northburgh, archdeacon of Suffolk and prebendary of Dunnington (*Donyngton*) in York cathedral, and Dns William de Flisco, prebendary of Strensall (*Straneshale*) in the same cathedral.[44] [fo.147ᵛ] Westminster, 29 June 1353.

1760 Dns William de Flisco appeared personally before the bishop and gave oath of canonical obedience [for the archdeaconry of Suffolk]. Usual notice of customary submission was sent. Gaywood, 1 July 1353.

1761 Inst. of John de Langham, priest, to the vicarage of Gazeley [S], vacant by the resignation of the same John for certain reasons troubling his conscience; patron in this turn, Edward III, the temporalities of the alien priory of Stoke-by-Clare [S] being in his hand. Gaywood, 2 July 1353.

[Margin] Ten marks at Easter and Michaelmas.

---

[42] See **1779*** and **1844***.
[43] Inst. 1313 as Roger son of William son of Ralph de Debenham (Reg. Salmon fo.55).
[44] Patron is not mentioned.

1762   Inst. of Henry de Worthingg, priest, to the rectory of Copdock [S], vac. by resig. of John de Ketene in exchange for the vicarage of Bawdsey [S]; patron, William de Copedok. Gaywood, 3 July 1353.

[Margin] Twelve marks at Easter and Michaelmas.

1763   Inst. of John de Ketene, [priest], to the vicarage of Bawdsey [S], in exchange as above; patrons, the prior and convent of Butley [S].[45] Gaywood, 3 July 1353.

[Margin] Five marks at Easter and Michaelmas.

1764   Inst. of Simon de Sutton, priest, to the vicarage of Lakenheath (*Lakynghithe*) [S], vacant by the death of John [de Wreslyngworth[46]]; patrons, the prior and chapter of Ely. Thornage, 8 July 1353.

[Margin] Six marks at Easter and Michaelmas.

1765   Collation to Nicholas de Walsyngham, priest, of the vicarage of Quarles [N]; patron in this turn by right of devolution,[47] the bishop. Thornage, 9 July 1353.

[Margin] Five marks at Easter and Michaelmas.

1766   Inst. of John de Southgate of Barmer [N], priest, to the vicarage of Barmer, vac. by resig. of John Pygeon;[48] patrons, the prior and convent of Coxford [N]. Norwich, 16 July 1353.

1767   Confirmation of the election of Brother Peter Bysshop, priest and professed Augustinian canon of Pentney [N], as prior of that house, by the subprior and canons, following the free resignation of Brother Vincent de Caldecote. Order was sent [the archdeacon of] Norwich[49] to install him. Norwich, 16 July 1353.

1768   [fo.148] Inst. of Brother Roger de Toftes, priest and professed Augustinian canon of Hickling [N], to the vicarage of Hickling, vac. by resig. of Brother John de Hempstede; patrons, the prior and convent of Hickling [N]. Norwich, 16 July 1353.

[Margin] 10s.

1769   Inst. of William de Haverford, priest, to the rectory of Fodderston [N], vac. by resig. of Richard de Barenton; patrons, the prior and chapter of Ely cathedral. Hoxne, 7 Aug. 1353.

[Margin] . . . half for the letter, 40 . . . Michaelmas.

1770   Inst. of Richard de Penreth, priest, to the rectory of Lopham [N], vac. by resig. of Giles de Wyngreworth; patron in this turn, Edward III, the lands and

[45] The usual oath of residence is not mentioned.
[46] Inst. in 1337 (Reg. Bek fo.4).
[47] Creake abbey were patrons (**116**); the vicarage may have been vacant for several years (**1326**).
[48] See **1310**.
[49] *Norwych* added later.

tenements of the late John, Lord de Segrave, being in his hand. Hoxne, 7 Aug. 1353.

[Margin] 25 marks.

1771 Inst. of Thomas de Leverington, priest, to the rectory of All Saints, Hackford [in Sparham deanery] (*omnium sanctorum de Refham alias dicta Hakeforde*[50]) [N], vac. by resig. of M. John de Saxhendale;[51] patron, John Avenel, knight. Hoxne, 15 Aug. 1353.

[Margin] £10.

1772 Collation to Walter Ingalde of Wretham [N] of the prebend of the chancellor in the College of St Mary in the Fields, Norwich, vac. by resig. of [left blank[52]]. Hoxne, 17 Aug. 1353.

1773 Inst. of John [Porte[53]] of Morston [N], priest, to the rectory of St Michael of Coslany, Norwich, vac. by resig. of Henry de Lympenhowe in exchange for the vicarage of Holkham [N]; patron, Thomas Hobbe of Oakley (*Ocle*) [S]. Hoxne, 18 Aug. 1353.

1774 Inst. of Henry de Lympenhowe, priest, to the vicarage of Holkham [N], vac. by resig. of John [Porte] of Morston [N] in exchange for the rectory of St Michael [of Coslany], as above. The bishop had nomination; patrons, the abbot and convent of Dereham [N]. Hoxne, 18 Aug. 1353.

1775 Inst. of Bartholomew Norman of Grimstone [N], priest, to the rectory of Babingley [N], vacant by the death of Dns Richard atte Grene;[54] patron, John Boteler of Babingley. Hoxne, 28 Aug. 1353.

[Margin] Six marks, 10s.[55]

1776 Inst. of William Gernon,[56] priest, to the moiety formerly pertaining to the le Straunge family[57] in Fressingfield [S]; patrons, M. Walter de Elveden and Dns Simon de Rykynghale, by right of acquisition. Hoxne, 17 Sept. 1353.

1777 Confirmation of the unanimous election of Brother Alexander de Drenkeston, priest and professed canon of Butley Priory [S], as prior of that house, by the subprior and convent in the bishop's presence, following the free resignation of Brother Matthew de Pakenham. [fo.148ᵛ] Butley Priory, [blank] Sept. 1353.

---

[50] Whitwell, Reepham and Hackford shared a churchyard; when Hackford church burned down in 1543 the parish was united to Whitwell (*Ruined Churches*, 149, and see 150, note).

[51] Inst. 1340 (Reg. Bek fo.32ᵛ).

[52] See **1550**.

[53] See **611**.

[54] See **1280**.

[55] Below this marginal note is another, *hic act' de r' et d'no registr' apud Hoxn*

[56] Surname written by a different scribe.

[57] MS. *pro portione de Strange quondam*

1778   Collation to Walter Clere, priest, of the deanery of Flegg[58] [N], vac. by resig. of Robert Clere. Hoxne, 18 Sept. 1353.

1779*   Inst. of Nicholas le Millere of Honing [N], priest, to a moiety of Shelton [N], vac. by resig. of John de Kentforde on this condition: that if Kentforde is not able to hold the rectory of Great Snoring[59] [N] peacefully, he may return and hold this moiety in peace as before. This condition was accepted by the bishop and included in the letter given le Millere; patrons, the abbot and convent of Langley [N]. Newmarket, 21 Sept. 1353.

1780   Inst. of William de Sutton, priest, to the rectory of Gimingham [N], vac. by resig. of Dns William de Mirfeld in exchange[60] for the rectory of Rawreth (*Raureth*) in London diocese; patrons, the prior and convent of Lewes. London, 29 Sept. 1353.

1781   Inst. of William de Mirfeld, priest, to the rectory of Shipden (*Shipeden alias Crowemere*) [N], vacant by the death of Dns Robert de Wyngreworth; patron, Richard son of Philip Broun.[61] London, 30 Sept. 1353.

1782   Inst. of William de Tratynton, priest, to the rectory of Bergh[62] (*Bergh iuxta Hapeton*) [N], vacant by the death of Robert de Wynneferthingg, [Senior[63]]; patron, Marie de Sancto Paulo, countess of Pembroke. London, 29 Sept. 1353.

1783   Inst.[64] of John de Walcote of Merton [N], priest, to the vicarage of Silverley [Cambs.], vac. by resig. of Dns Elias [de Kertlyng[65]] of St Edmund; patrons, the prior and convent of Hatfield Broadoak (*Hatfeld Regis*), in London diocese. London, 27 Sept. 1353.

1784   Inst. of Robert Clere, clerk with first tonsure, to the rectory of Winterton [N] with the chapel of East Somerton, vac. by resig. of Walter Clere; patron, Robert Clere, father of Walter and Robert. London, 4 Oct. 1353.

1785   Inst. of William de Gyppewico, priest, to the rectory of Denton [N], vacant by the removal of William de Banham, incumbent, by judgement of the royal court;[66] patron in this turn, Edward III. Terling, 18 Oct. 1353.

1786   Inst. of John Aylmere, priest, to a moiety of Ingworth [N], vac. by resig. [fo.149] of Ralph Burgeys in exchange for the rectory of Lessingham [N]; patron, Edward III. Terling, 18 Oct. 1353.

---

[58] Including Great Yarmouth (183).
[59] See **1755**, **1844***, **1856–7**.
[60] Cf. **1781**.
[61] See **1788**.
[62] Annexed to Bergh were Apton [N] and a moiety of Holverston [N] (*Taxatio* 84).
[63] Inst. in 1343 (Reg. Bek fo.66).
[64] MS. (unusually) *institutus fuit personaliter*
[65] See **1608**.
[66] See **1787**.

1787 [Common Pleas] writ[67] *admittatis non obstante reclamacione* ordering the bishop to admit a suitable presentee of the king[68] to the church of Denton [N] because he had recovered presentation in the royal court against Adam de Clifton, knight. Tested by J[ohn] de Stonore, Westminster, 10 Oct. 1353.
    Pasch' ult' ro CLxij   Berugh

1788 [Chancery] writ[69] *ne admittatis* ordering the bishop not to admit a parson to the rectory of Shipden [N], said to be vacant and its advowson disputed in the king's court between the king and Richard son of Philip Broun.[70] Westminster, 18 June 1353.

1789 Inst. of Ralph Burgeys, priest, to the rectory of Lessingham [N], vac. by resig. of John Aylmere in exchange as above [**1786**]; presentation was by the prior of Ogbourne St George, attorney-general of the patron, the abbot of Bec-Hellouin. Terling, 18 Oct. 1353.

1790 Inst. of John de Thoresby,[71] subdeacon, in the person of his proctor, Robert de Wyndele, to the rectory of Lilford in Lincoln diocese, vac. by resig. of Richard de Hecham in exchange[72] for the rectory of Ashby [in Brooke deanery] [N]; patron, John de Wylughby, knight. Terling, 22 Oct. 1353.

1791 Inst. of Richard de Hecham of Limbury (*Lymbergh*), priest, to the rectory of Ashby [in Brooke deanery] [N], vac. by resig. of M. John de Thoresby in exchange as above; patrons, the abbot and convent of St Benet's, Hulme [N]. Terling, 22 Oct. 1353.

1792 Inst. of John de Wendlyngburgh, acolyte, to the rectory of Letton [N]; patrons, the prior and convent of Lewes. Terling, 22 Oct. 1353.

1793 Inst. of William Maghteld of Hedenham (*Hedyngham*) [N], priest, to the rectory of Sutton (*Sutton iuxta Shatesham*) [S], vac. by resig. of Robert Hotot; patron, John de Glanville of Shottisham (*Shatesham*) [S]. Terling, 24 Oct. 1353.

1794 Inst. of John Holm of Helmingham [S], priest, to the rectory of Shottisham [S], vac. by resig. of William Maghteld of Hedenham [N]; patron, Elaine, widow of Richard Glanville. Terling, 24 Oct. 1353.

1795 Collation to Robert Clere, clerk with first tonsure, of the deanery of Flegg[73] [N], vac. by resig. of Dns Walter Clere. London, 16 Dec. 1353.

---

[67] Actual writ, measuring 24.3 by 5 cms., sewn between ff.148–9 but now loose; it has a filing hole at the left-hand side.
[68] See **1785**.
[69] Actual writ, measuring 26.5 by 3.5 cms., sewn between ff.148–149; it has a filing hole at the left-hand side. See **1781** for the outcome.
[70] See **1780**.
[71] See *BRUO* 3, 1864–5.
[72] There is no mention of a commission from the bishop of Lincoln.
[73] Including Great Yarmouth (**183**).

1796   Commission to Brother Laurence [de Leek], prior of Norwich cathedral, and M. Richard de Lyng, archdeacon of Norwich, to serve as his vicars-general in spiritualities, together and severally, while he should be out of England. He reserved to himself the collation, nomination and provision of all ecclesiastical benefices, with and without cure of souls, as well as all dignities, parsonates and offices in the cathedral and elsewhere; in addition, he reserved the dispensation and absolution of all offences against the see or church of Norwich. The vicars-general were to accept any resignations of benefices [fo.149ᵛ] made before them by the incumbents, acting in person and not through proctors.[74] Dover, 13 Nov. 1353.

1797   Inst. of Richard de Barsham, priest, by Brother Laurence [de Leek], vicar-general, to the rectory of Melton Constable [N], vac. by resig. of John Mey in exchange for the vicarage of Bawburgh [N]; patron, Ralph de Astele, knight. Norwich, 27 Nov. 1353.

1798   Inst. of John Mey, priest, by Brother Laurence [de Leek], vicar-general, to the vicarage of Bawburgh [N], vac. by resig. of Richard de Barsham[75] in exchange as above; patrons, the prior and chapter of Norwich cathedral. Norwich, 27 Nov. 1353.

1799   Inst. by the vicar-general[76] of Thomas Larke, priest, to the vicarage of West Barsham [N], vac. by resig. of Stephen[77] in exchange for the rectory of Burgh Parva [N]; patrons, the prior and convent of Castle Acre [N]. Norwich, 28 Nov. 1353.

1800   BURGH PARVA IN HOLT. Inst. (*per dictum patrem*) of Stephen, former vicar of West Barsham [N], to the rectory of Burgh Parva [N], vac. by resig. of Thomas Larke in exchange as above; patron, Ralph de Astele, knight. Norwich, 28 Nov. 1353.

1801   Inst. by the vicar-general of Ralph [Brome¹] of Icklingham, priest, to the vicarage of Neateshead [N], vac. by resig. of Peter de Baldewell in exchange for the rectory of St John's, Beechamwell [N]; patrons, the abbot and convent of St Benet's, Hulme [N]. Norwich, 8 Dec. 1353.

1802   Inst. by the vicar-general of Peter de Baldeswell, priest, to the rectory of St John's, Beechamwell [N], vac. by resig. of Ralph [Brome] of Icklingham in exchange as above; patron, John de Denham. Norwich, 8 Dec. 1353.

---

[74] MS. *Proviso etiam quod renunciationes beneficiorum tam curatorum quam non curatorum coram vobis faciende per personas proprias incumbentes et non per earum procuratores si et quando fieri contigerint admittantur.*

[75] Cf. **762**.

[76] MS. *per dictum patrem vicarium generalem*

[77] He may have been instituted *sede vacante*, as the last known vicar was Richard de Wodeford in 1328 (Reg. Ayremynne fo.24).

¹ See **1057**.

1803 Inst. by Brother Laurence [de Leek], vicar-general, of Peter Dyke of Cheveley [Cambs.], priest, to the rectory of Swanton Novers (*Swanton Nowers*) [N], vac. by resig. of Robert [de Shudecampes[2]]; patron, John Nowers. Norwich, 6 Dec. 1353.

1804 Inst. (*per dictum patrem*) of Peter Lesse of Moreton-on-Hill[3] (*Helmyngham*) [N], priest, to the vicarage of Horsford [N], vac. by resig. of Richard le Cook;[4] patron [in this turn[5]], Edward III. Norwich, 7 Dec. 1353.

1805 Inst. by (*dictum patrem*) Prior Laurence [de Leek] of William de Kempstone, priest, to the vicarage of Kempstone [N], vac. by resig. of William [fo.150] de Hoggesthorp; patrons, the prior and convent of Castle Acre [N]. Norwich, 9 Dec. 1353.

1806 Inst. by the bishop of Thomas Peper of Catton [N], priest, to the vicarage of Wickham Market [S], vac. by resig. of John Wynter; patrons, the prioress and convent of Campsey Ash [S]. Terling, 21 Dec. 1353.

1807 Collation to Henry de Plumpstede, priest, of the custody of Hildebrand's Hospital in Norwich, vac. by resig. of Robert de Langele.[6] Terling, 21 Dec. 1353.

1808 Inst. of Walter Amyas, priest, to the rectory of Boxford [S], vacant by the death of Thomas Turnay; patron, the abbot of Bury St Edmunds [S]. Terling, 27 Dec. 1353.

1809 Inst. of Robert Flemmyng, priest, to the rectory of Scole [N], vac. by resig. of Richard [Atte Lane[7]] of Walton in exchange for the rectory of Rochford, London diocese; patron, Thomas de Shelton. Terling, 7 Jan. 1354.
[Margin] Note the oath given for the first fruits of his predecessor.

1810 Inst. of Richard [Atte Lane] of Walton, priest, in the person of his proctor, John de Hedersete, to the rectory of Rochford in London diocese, vac. by resig. of Robert [Flemmyng] in exchange as above, by commission of the bishop of London, [Ralph de Stratford]; patron, William de Bohoun, earl of Northampton. Terling, 7 Jan. 1354.

1811 Inst. of M. John de Wellewyk, priest, to the rectory of Forncett [N], vacant by the death of Robert de Wyngreworth; patron, Edward III. London, 12 Jan. 1354.

---

[2] Inst. in 1338 (Reg. Bek fo.16[v]).
[3] Moreton-on-Hill, *alias* Helmingham, is 3 miles from Horsford.
[4] The last recorded institution was of John Ingelond (**723, 746**).
[5] Usually St Faith priory, Horsham (**340, 723, 746**).
[6] His institution was unregistered, perhaps in 1349 (see **981**); the last known *custos* was John de Wykelwode in 1320 (Reg. Salmon fo.84).
[7] See **538**.

1812   Inst. of William de Aberforde, priest, to the rectory of Syderstone [N], vacant by the death of James de Mortuo Mari;[8] patrons, Miles de Stapelton and John le Gray, knights. Kelvedon (*Esterforde*), 22 Jan. 1354.

1813   Inst. of Henry de Rokelond, priest, to the vicarage of Gazeley [S], vac. by resig. of John de Langham in exchange for the rectory of Aston (*Aston iuxta Baldold*), Lincoln diocese; patron [in this turn[9]], Edward III. Ipswich, 24 Jan. 1354.

1814   Inst. of John de Langham, priest, to the rectory of Aston in Lincoln diocese, in exchange as above, by commission of Bishop John [Gynewell] of Lincoln; patrons, the abbot and convent of Reading. Ipswich, 24 Jan. 1354.

1815   PROTHOCOLLUM SUPER IURAMENTO RECTORIS DE ASTON. Memorandum that on this date in the house of the archdeacon of Suffolk, John [de Langham] swore upon the Gospels that he would pay 5 marks to the bishop at Norwich next Michaelmas or within 15 days thereafter, and another 5 marks the following Easter or within 15 days thereafter, and he so obligated himself in writing. Witnessed by Dns Stephen de Cressingham, rector of Belton [S], Dns John de Acr', rector of Gaywood [N], and Dns John Heved, chaplain. Wyneston.[10] [Ipswich, 24 Jan. 1354.]

1816   Inst. of Reginald Martyn of Sidestrand [N], priest, to the vicarage of Paston *iuxta Bromholm* [N], [fo.150[v]] vac. by resig. of Robert de Helgheton; patrons, the prior and convent of Bromholm [N]. Norwich, 30 Jan. 1354.

1817   Certificate of Bishop John [Pascal] of Llandaff that he has executed Bateman's commission (quoted in full; dated Terling, 18 Oct. 1353) for an exchange of benefices between M. William de Thinghvill,[11] rector of St Nicholas[12] of Feltwell [N], and Dns Henry Motelot, rector of Mitchel Troy (*Troia*) in Llandaff diocese. He examined the enquiry of the archdeacon of Norfolk's official. Thinghvill resigned and was instituted through his proctor, M. Roger de Horton; Motelot resigned and was instituted through his proctor, Richard de Kyngeston. [fo.151] The bishop's manor chapel at Bishton (*Lank*[adwallader][13]), 4 Nov. 1353.

---

[8] See **1295**.

[9] Usually Stoke-by-Clare priory: see **1761**.

[10] Apparently the signature of John de Wyneston, papal notary (and perhaps the bishop's registrar); as on the endorsement of **1591***, it is decorated with flourishes. The hand, however, seems to be the same throughout the folio.

[11] He may have been instituted *sede vacante*, as the last known rector was M. John de Keynesham in 1342, presented by Simon Montacute, bishop of Ely (Reg. Bek fo.58).

[12] There were two parishes in Feltwell: St Nicholas, in the bishop of Ely's advowson, and St Mary, in the advowson of Lewes Priory (Reg. Bek ff.20, 58, and see Appendix II). They were united in the 19th century (White, *Norfolk*, 393; *Ruined Churches*, 50).

[13] Llangadwaladyr (see W. Birch, *Memorials of the See and Cathedral of Llandaff*, Neath 1912, pp. 325, 344, 413).

1818   Collation to Nicholas Laurence of Little Blakenham [S], priest, of the chapel of St Edmund the Archbishop in Ipswich [S]. Ipswich, 24 Jan. [1354].

1819   Collation to M. Robert de Stratton[14] DCnCL, subdeacon, of the rectory of Marsham [N]. Hoxne, 9 Feb. 1354.

1820   Inst. of Roger Raundes, priest, to the rectory of Newton *iuxta Subiriam* [S], vac. by resig. of Thomas de Branketr' in exchange for the rectory of Great Leighs in London diocese; patron, William de Clopton. Hoxne, 15 Feb. 1354.

1821   Inst. of Thomas de Branketr', priest, to the rectory of Great Leighs, London diocese, in exchange as above, by commission of Bishop Ralph [de Stratford] of London; patron, Humphrey de Bohoun, earl of Hereford. Hoxne, 15 Feb. 1354.

1822   VICARIA DE KYMBURLE. [Five lines left blank.][15] n.d.

1823   Inst. of John de Redesham, priest, to the vicarage of Briston[16] [N]. The bishop had nomination; patrons, the master and scholars of [Trinity Hall, Cambridge University[17]]. Blofield, 20 Apr. 1351.

1824   Inst. of Thomas Trendel of Guist [N], priest, to the rectory of Wacton Parva (*beate Marie de Waketon*) [N], vac. by resig. of William Stannard; patron in this turn,[18] Edward III. Hoxne, 18 Feb. 1354.

1825   Inst. of Walter Clere, priest, to the rectory of Winterton [N] with East Somerton chapel, vac. by resig. of Robert Clere; patron, Robert Clere of Ormsby [N]. Hoxne, 20 Feb. 1354.

1826   [fo.151[v]] Inst. of William de Peek, priest, to the rectory of St Peter of Ringstead Magna [N], vac. by resig. of Richard Alwold in exchange for the perpetual chaplaincy at the altar of St John the Baptist in St Paul's cathedral, London; patrons, the abbot and convent of Ramsey. Hoxne, 21 Feb. 1354.

1827   Inst. of Warren de Runhale, priest, to the vicarage of Runhall [N], vac. by resig. of Hamo [Gerard[19]] of Bawburgh [N], in exchange for the vicarage of Ormsby [N]; patrons, the prior and convent of West Acre [N]. Hoxne, 4 Mar. 1354.

---

[14] See 28.

[15] Kimberley [N] was appropriated to Trinity Hall in 1350 (28); its rector apparently did not resign until July 1354 (1404, 1866).

[16] Like Kimberley, Briston [N] was appropriated to Trinity Hall (27, 28), and here also a space of 5 lines (incompletely used) was left for this institution.

[17] MS. *aule A.'*

[18] See 1120, 1752.

[19] See 1489.

1828 Inst. of Hamo [Gerard] of Bawburgh [N], priest, to the vicarage of Ormsby [N], vac. by resig. of Warren de Runhale in exchange as above; patrons, the prior and chapter of Norwich. Hoxne, 4 Mar. 1354.

1829 Inst. of John Reynald of Rendlesham [S], priest, to the rectory of Somerleyton (*Somerleton in Luth'*) [S], vacant by the natural death of Henry de Sothirton; patron, John Jernegan. London, 15 Mar. 1354.

1830 Inst. of John Abraham, priest, to the rectory of Brumstead [N], vac. by resig. of Walter Amyas;[20] patron, John Hakeluyt, knight. London, 16 Mar. 1354.

1831 Inst. of Henry de Welham, priest, to the rectory of Warham St Mary [N], vac. by resig. of M. William de Felton; patron, John de Norwico, knight. Terling, 24 Apr. 1354.

1832 Inst. of William de Wysete of Trunch [N], priest, to the rectory of Intwood [N], vacant by the death of John Boll;[21] patrons, Bartholomew de Appelyerd and John de Erpingham, citizens of Norwich. Terling, 27 Apr. 1354.

1833 Collation to Roger [Oslak[22]] of Helmingham (*Halmyngham*), priest, of the rectory of Threxton (*Threkestone*) [N], vac. by resig. of Robert Markant in exchange. Eccles, 16 May 1354.

1834* HOSPITALE DE BEK IN BILLINGFORDE. Collation to Robert Markant, priest, of the custody of Beck Hospital (*Hospitalis beati Thome de Bek*) [N] with the obligations incumbent upon it. [fol.152] Eccles, 16 May 1354.

1835 Inst. of Thomas de Brewouse, clerk with first tonsure, to the rectory of Framlingham (*Framelyngham Castri*) [S], vacant by the death of Richard de Brustede;[23] patron, Mary [de Roos], countess of Norfolk and marshal of England. Brewouse also has a licence to remain at university for two years, according to the constitution *Cum ex eo*.[24] Hoxne, 17 May 1354.

1836 Inst. of Peter de Baldeswell, priest, to the rectory of Gunton [S], vac. by resig. of William Wolwyne in exchange for the rectory of St John, Beechamwell [N]; patron, John, son of the late Roger de Ludham, knight. Hoxne, 19 May 1354.
[Margin] He owes 20d.

1837 Inst. of William Wolwyne, priest, to the rectory of St John's, Beechamwell [N], vac. by resig. of Peter de Baldeswell in exchange as above; patron, John de Denham. Hoxne, 19 May 1354.
[Margin] He owes 5s. 6d.

---

[20] See **1808**.
[21] *Alias* Boule (**721**).
[22] See **1728**, **1849**.
[23] *Alias* Richard de Burghstede, inst. 1328 (Reg. Ayremynne fo.24ᵛ).
[24] *Cum ex eo* (*Sext.* 1,6,34).

1838 Inst. of Thomas de Penreth, priest, to the rectory of Bowthorpe [N], vac. by resig. of John [Baxtere[25]] of Dunkirk (*Doncherch*) [N]; patron, Lady Avice de Wysham. Weybourne, 27 May 1354.

[Margin] And note that [he owes] for all first fruits of his predecessor.

1839 Inst. of Thomas Beneyt of Shefford, priest, to the vicarage of Carbrooke Parva [N], vac. by resig. of John Ode; patron, the prior of the Knights Hospitallers in England. Massingham, 30 May 1354.

[Margin] The Master of Carbrooke[26] mainperned for 5 marks.

1840 Inst. of John Larke, priest, to the vicarage of North Wootton[27] [N], vac. by resig. of John de Harpele in exchange for the rectory of Bawsey [N]; patrons, the prior and convent of Wymondham [N]. Massingham, 30 May 1354.

1841 Inst. of John de Harpele, priest, to the rectory of Bawsey [N], vac. by resig. of John Larke, in exchange as above; patron in this turn, Edward III, the temporalities of Eye Priory [S] being in his hand. Massingham, 30 May 1354.

1842 Inst. of Edward de Cugeho, priest, to the rectory of Outwell [N], vac. by resig. of Thomas Northerne in exchange for the vicarage of Hinton in Ely diocese; patron, Bishop Thomas [de Lisle] of Ely. Gaywood, 31 May 1354.

1843 Inst. of Thomas Northerne, priest, to the vicarage of Hinton in Ely diocese, vac. by resig. of Edward de Cugeho in exchange as above;[28] patron, M. Robert de Grymeston, rector of Hinton. Gaywood, 31 May 1354.

1844* [fo.152ᵛ] Inst. of Thomas Rous, priest, to the rectory of Great Snoring [N], vacant[29] because the king has recovered the advowson against Ralph de Shelton, knight. The king presented by the writ of judgement and by consultation about a prohibition [in respect of] a plea pending between Sir Ralph and his son Ralph, as the said writs show.[30] Gaywood, 1 June 1354.

1845 Inst. of John Aylmer, priest, to the rectory of Willingham [St Mary] [S], vac. by resig. of John Smert in exchange for the moiety of Ingworth [N]; patron, Edward III. Hoxne, 6 June 1354.

[Margin] He owes 6s. *pro bap'*.

1846 Inst. of John Smert, priest, to a moiety of Ingworth [N], vac. by resig. of John Aylmer in exchange as above; patron, Edward III. Hoxne, 6 June 1354.

[Margin] He owes 6s. *pro bap'*.

---

[25] See **1090**, **1697–8**.
[26] See **1551***n*.
[27] *Phillimore Atlas* lists as North Wotton (194).
[28] There is no mention of a commission from the bishop of Ely.
[29] Vacant by removal of John de Kentforde: see **1755**, **1779***.
[30] See **1856–7**.

1847   Inst. of William Palmere, priest, in the person of his proctor, Thomas de Blaby, to the rectory of Wood Rising [N]; patrons,[31] the prior and convent of Lewes. Hoxne, 6 June 1354.

1848   Inst. of John atte Faldegate of Barningham, priest, to a moiety of Fishley [N], vac. by resig. of William Chapman; patrons, Roger Hardegrey, John de Berneye, and Thomas de Bumpstede. Hoxne, 9 June 1354.

1849   Inst. of Richard Markant, priest, to the vicarage of Tottington [N], vac. by resig. of Roger [Oslak[32]] of Helmingham (*Helmyngham*); patrons, the prioress and convent of Campsey Ash [S]. Hoxne, 12 June 1354.

1850   Inst. of John Deye of Blakenham [S], priest, to the rectory of St Stephen's, Ipswich [S], vacant by the death of Robert de Beylham; patron, Andrew de Bures, knight. Hoxne, 17 June 1354.

1851   Thomas de Wattone, priest and brother of the College of St John the Evangelist in Rushworth [N], having been unanimously elected as master by the brothers of the college, following the death of Hugh Herbert, was presented by the patrons, Dns John de Gonevill, rector of East Harling [N], and Edmund de Gonevill, his brother. Wattone was then preferred to that office by the bishop. Hoxne, 21 June 1354.

1852   Inst. of John de Tyrington, priest, to the rectory of Scole [N], vac. by resig. of Robert Flemmyng; patron, Thomas de Sheltone. Hoxne, 21 June 1354.

1853   Inst. of Thomas de Harwe, priest, to the rectory of Bildeston [S], vac. by resig. of Alexander Flemmyng; patron in this turn,[33] Edward III, because the son and heir of John de Leveyne, knight, is his ward. Hoxne, 22 June 1354.

   [Margin] *R^e prothocoll' . . . g' p . . . fruct' inter l'ras inquis' . . . e . . . dce' eccl'ie.*

1854   Inst. of M. John de Thefforde, priest, to the rectory of Heigham (*Heygham iuxta Norwicum*) [N], vac. by resig. of Sylvester atte Gates in exchange for the rectory of Brinton [N] [**1858**]; [fo.153] patrons, the abbot and convent of St Benet's, Hulme [N]. Hoxne, 25 June 1354.

1855   [Common Pleas] writ[34] *admittatis non obstante reclamacione* ordering the bishop to admit a suitable presentee of the prior of Lewes to Wood Rising [N], because he has recovered the presentation against William de Wychyngham. Tested by R[oger] Hillary, Westminster, 18 June 1354. Rot. 41.

---

[31] See **1855**.
[32] See **1728**.
[33] Cf. **459**, **1413**.
[34] Actual writ, bound upside down, the larger part between ff.152–3 and the remainder between ff.156–7. See **1847**.

1856 [Chancery] writ[35] presenting Thomas Rous,[36] the king's clerk, to Great Snoring [N] church. The king had prohibited the bishop from making an institution while the advowson was disputed in his court between Ralph son of Ralph de Shelton and Ralph de Shelton, knight. The king, however, had recovered his presentation to the church against the said Ralph de Shelton by judgement of the justices of Common Pleas, as appears in their record called into Chancery; as Ralph thus has no title, the prohibition is void. Westminster, 24 May 1354.

1857 [Common Pleas] writ[37] *admittatis non obstante reclamacione* ordering the bishop to admit the king's suitable presentee to the rectory of Great Snoring [N], because he has recovered the presentation against Ralph de Shelton, knight. Tested by R[oger] Hillary, Westminster, 26 May 1354.
Mich' ult' Rot. 278

1858 Collation to Sylvester atte Gates, priest, in the person of his proctor, John Baxtere,[38] the rector of St Michael at Plea in Norwich, of the rectory of Brinton [N], vac. by resig. of M. John de Thefford in exchange as above [**1854**]. Hoxne, 25 June 1354.
[Margin] He owes for letters . . . .

1859 Inst. of John Skilman, priest, to the chapel of St Margaret, Melles [S], vac. by resig. of Henry Man;[39] patron, John de Norwico, knight. Hoxne, 27 June 1354.

1860 Inst. of John atte Forthe of Gissing [N], priest, to the vicarage of Rushall [N], vac. by resig. of John Pecok; patrons, the abbot and convent of Langley [N]. Hoxne, 29 June 1354.

1861 Inst. of John Herlond[40] of Kimberley [N], priest, to the rectory of Mutford [S]; patrons, the master and scholars of Gonville Hall, Cambridge. South Elmham, 8 July 1354.
[Margin] He does not owe . . . of first fruits.

1862 Collation to Dns John Leche, priest, of the rectory of St Mary's, Great Massingham [N], vac. by resig. of M. Laurence de Lyttelton in exchange for the rectory of Wood Dalling [N]. South Elmham, 7 July 1354.

---

[35] Actual writ, measuring 21.8 by 5.9 cms., bound with **1855** and **1857**. There is a filing hole at the left-hand side, where the seal tag has been torn off. There is no note of warranty. See **1844**.

[36] The king first presented him on 16 June 1353, in right of his wardship of the lands and heir of Hugh Burguillon (*CPR 1350–1354*, 468).

[37] Actual writ, also with filing hole (see **1856** and note); its insertion in the binding obscures part of the text.

[38] The last inst. to St Michael at Plea was of John de Heydon (**649**).

[39] His institution was not registered (see **871**).

[40] Cf. **995**.

1863   Inst. of M. Laurence de Lyttelton, subdeacon, to the rectory of Wood Dalling [N], vac. by resig. of Dns John Leche in exchange; patrons, the master and scholars of Trinity Hall, Cambridge. South Elmham, 7 July 1354.

1864   BRAUNFORDE VICARIA PRIMA INSTITUTIO.[41] Inst. of Robert Flemmyng, priest, to the vicarage of Bramford [S], newly established. The bishop had nomination; patrons, the abbot and convent of Battle Abbey, Chichester diocese. South Elmham, 2 July 1354.

1865   Inst. of John le Ferers, priest, to the rectory of South Wootton [N], vac. by resig. of Thomas Rous; patron, Isabella, the dowager queen. South Elmham, 13 July 1354.

1866   Inst. of John son of Hugh de Kymburle, priest, to the rectory of Skeyton [N], vacant by the removal of William de Whitewelle[42] by judicial sentence. Patrons are Dns Thomas de Buxton, clerk, Walter de Berneye, and William de Essex. South Elmham, 16 July 1354.

1867   Inst. of Edward de Attone, clerk, in the person of his proctor, Adam de Colby, chaplain, to the rectory of Thurning (*Thyrnyng*) [N], vac. by resig. of Henry de Becford;[43] patron, Lady Alma Burnel. South Elmham, 24 July 1354.

1868   Inst.[44] of John Bateman of Houghton [N], priest, to the vicarage of Honingham [N], vac. by resig. of Dns John Wippeseil. The bishop had nomination; patrons, the abbot and convent of Sawtry. South Elmham, 31 July 1354.

1869   Inst. of Robert atte Boure of Gimingham [N], priest, to the vicarage of Briston [N]; [fo.153ᵛ] patrons, the master and college of Trinity Hall, Cambridge. South Elmham, 5 Aug. 1354.

1870   Inst. of Hamo son of Walter Hamond, priest, to the vicarage of Sporle [N], vac. by resig. of Dns John de Bury; patron in this turn, Edward III, the temporalities of Sporle Priory [N] being in his hand. South Elmham, 16 Aug. 1354.

1871 CERTIFICATORIUM DOMINI WYGORNIENSIS EPISCOPI SUPER ECCLESIA DE RYKYNGHAL' INFERIOR. Certificate of Bishop Reginald [Bryan] of Worcester that he has executed Bateman's commission (quoted in full; dated Terling manor, 31 Aug. 1354) for an exchange of benefices between Dns Robert de Gersyngdon, rector of Rickinghall Inferior [S], and Thomas Godwyn, prebendary of St Mary collegiate church in Warwick. He examined the enquiry made by the archdeacon of Sudbury's

---

[41] See **54**.
[42] *Alias* Whytewell, inst. 1336 at the presentation of William de Whytewell and his wife Katherine, patrons in that turn (Reg. Ayremynne fo.77).
[43] See **1877**.
[44] There is a contemporary note, barely visible and illegible, in the margin.

official. The patron, the abbot of Bury St Edmunds [S], agreed. Bredon, 17 Sept. 1354.

1872 Thomas [Godwyn], acolyte, appeared personally before Bateman and gave oath of obedience [for the rectory of Rickinghall Inferior]; order was sent [the archdeacon of] Sudbury to induct [Godwyn]. London, 28 Sept. 1354.

[Heading for a section of acts by vicars-general Lyng and Elveden beginning on 5 Oct. 1354 (sic).]

1873* Commission to M. Richard de Lyng, archdeacon of Norwich, and M. Walter de Elveden, precentor of Hereford cathedral, as the bishop's vicars-general in spiritualities and temporalities, together and separately, [fo.154] conferring on them even the power of exercising, in person or by delegate, his own rights of collation, provision, nomination, presentation, or other disposition over benefices, dignities and offices, whether pertaining to him as bishop or by inheritance or in any other way. Dover, 6 Oct. 1354.

1874* Commission to M. Richard de Lyng, archdeacon of Norwich, and M. Walter de Elveden, DCnCL and precentor of Hereford, to enquire about men who, in the bishop's absence, might claim papal or even episcopal provision to benefices in Norwich diocese, whether 'in the form of poor clerks' or under another form, and, balancing the needs of all, to decide on appropriate fulfilment of the conditions of such provisions according to the enquiries made, to confer the benefices thus due to such men, to induct them, and to carry out all other required actions for the completion and execution of those graces, with the power of coercion. Dover, 6 Oct. 1354.

1875 Inst. of John de Cressingham, priest, by vicar-general M. Walter de Elveden, to the rectory of Frettenham [N], vac. by resig. of Dns Roger de Felthorp in exchange for the vicarage of North Elmham [N]; patron in this turn, John Bateman, because he has wardship of the lands of T. Bardolf,[45] the son and heir of John Bardolf of Spixworth [N]. Norwich, 8 Oct. 1354.

1876 Collation by vicar-general M. Walter [de Elveden], with the bishop's authority, to Roger [de Felthorp] of Frettenham, priest, of the vicarage of North Elmham [N], vac. by resig. of Dns John de Cressyngham in exchange as above. Norwich, 8 Oct. 1354.

1877 Inst. of Henry de Bekeforde, priest, by vicar-general M. Walter [de Elveden], to the rectory of Thurning (*Thrignyng*) [N], vac. by resig. of Edward de Atton;[46] patron, Lady Alma Burnel. Norwich, 8 Oct. 1354.
    [Margin] Henry is obligated for 1[4] marks on behalf of his predecessor and 14 marks on [his own] behalf.

---

[45] MS. *Bardold*
[46] See **1867**.

1878 Inst. of Peter Aleyn of Morningthorpe [N], priest, by the bishop (*sic*), to the rectory of Ashby (*Askeby in Luthinglond*) [S], vac. by resig. of Robert de Mundeforde; patron, John de Ingelose, knight. Norwich, 9 Oct. 1354.

1879 Confirmation by vicar-general M. Walter [de Elveden] of the election of Brother William de Spykesworth, priest and professed canon of St James Priory, Buckenham [N], as prior of that house by the subprior and convent, following the death of Brother Hugh de Brom; order to install him was sent [the archdeacon of] Norfolk. Buckenham Priory, 11 Oct. 1354.

1880 [fo.154ᵛ] Inst. of Richard de Cramforde, priest, by vicar-general M. Richard de Lyng, to a moiety of Taverham [N], vac. by resig. of Peter [Aleyn⁴⁷] of Morningthorpe [N]; patron, William de la Pol, knight. Norwich, 13 Oct. 1354.

1881 Inst. of John, son (*natus*) of Robert Lay of Brundish [S], priest, by vicar-general M. Walter [de Elveden], to the vicarage of Sibton [S] with Peasenhall chapel, vac. by resig. of Richard Almot; patrons, the abbot and convent of Sibton [S]. Ipswich, 14 Oct. 1354.
[Margin] He owes 4 marks on behalf of his predecessor.

1882 Inst. of John Cordewaner, priest, by vicar-general M. Richard [de Lyng], to the vicarage of South Creake [N], vac. by resig. of John son of Martin atte Grene of Beeston [N] in exchange for the moiety of Burnham Norton [N]; patrons, the prior and convent of Castle Acre [N]. Norwich, 20 Oct. 1354.

1883 Inst. of John son of Martin atte Grene of Beeston [N], priest, by vicar-general M. R[ichard de Lyng], to a moiety of Burnham Norton [N], vac. by resig. of Dns John Cordewaner in exchange as above; patrons, the abbot and convent of Wendling [N]. Norwich, 20 Oct. 1354.

1884 Inst. of Walter Stannard of Diss [N], priest, by vicar-general M. W. [Walter de Elveden], to the vicarage of Winfarthing [N], vacant by the death of John atte Bek;⁴⁸ patrons, the prior and convent of Butley [S]. Wetheringsett, 4 Nov. 1354.

1885 Inst. of Richard de Barsham, priest, by vicar-general M. R. [Richard de Lyng], to the rectory of Wickhampton (*Wychampton*) [N], vac. by resig. of John son of Richard de Wolter[t]on of Limpenhoe [N] in exchange for the rectory of Melton Constable [N]; patron, Edward Gerberge, knight. Reedham, 28 Oct. 1354.

1886 Inst. of John son of Richard de Wolterton of Limpenhoe [N], priest, by vicar-general M. Richard [de Lyng], to the rectory of Melton Constable [N], vac. by resig. of Dns Richard de Barsham in exchange as above; patron, Ralph de Astele, knight. Reedham, 28 Oct. 1354.

⁴⁷ See **1878**.
⁴⁸ See **1204**.

1887 Inst. of William de Bliclyng, priest, by vicar-general M. W. [Walter de Elveden], to the vicarage of East Winch [N], vacant by the removal of Henry Fleye; patrons, the prioress and convent of Carrow [N]. Norwich, 16 Nov. 1354.

1888 Inst. of Adam de Colby, priest, by vicar-general M. W. [Walter de Elveden], to the vicarage of Wood Dalling [N], newly established; patrons, the master and college of Trinity Hall, Cambridge. Norwich, 16 Nov. 1354.

1889 Inst. of Sylvester atte Yates,[49] priest, by vicar-general M. Walter [de Elveden], to the rectory of Heveningham [S], vac. by [fo.155] resig. of Dns Walter [Lyster[50]] of Dunwich in exchange for the rectory of Brinton [N]; patron in this turn, the king.[51] Norwich, 16 Nov. 1354.

1890 Collation by vicar-general M. Walter [de Elveden] to Walter [Lyster] of Dunwich, priest, of the rectory of Brinton [N], vac. by resig. of Dns Silvester [atte Yates] in exchange. Norwich, 16 Nov. 1354.

1891 Collation by vicar-general M. Walter [de Elveden] to Dns John de Roldestone, priest, of the rectory of Beetley [N], vac. by resig. of Dns Richard de Kneshale in exchange for the benefice at the altar of St Thomas the Martyr in the collegiate church of Southwell [Notts.]. Norwich, 16 Nov. 1354.

1892 Collation by vicar-general M. Walter [de Elveden] to Richard de Kneshale, priest, of the above benefice at Southwell, vac. by resig. of John de Roldeston in exchange;[52] Elveden acted on the authority of the patrons, the chapter of Southwell. Norwich, 16 Nov. 1354.

1893 Inst. of Richard Fylcot, priest, by vicar-general M. Walter [de Elveden], to the rectory of Sutton [N], vac. by resig. of Dns William de Draycote; patron, Juliana Hastyng, countess of Huntingdon. Norwich, 17 Nov. 1354.

1894 The election of Brother John de Surlyngham, priest and professed Augustinian canon of St John and St Olave Priory, Herringfleet [S], as prior of that house by the canons, following the death of Brother John de Porynglond, was quashed by vicar-general M. Walter [de Elveden] for defect of form. Elveden then preferred the elect to that office; order to install was sent [the archdeacon of] Suffolk. Norwich, 17 Nov. 1354.

1895 Inst. of William Pete of Swanton Morley [N], clerk with first tonsure, in the person of his proctor, Henry Botild, chaplain, by vicar-general M. Walter [de Elveden], to the rectory of Brandon Parva [N], vac. by resig. of John de Well;[53] patron, Robert de Morle, marshal of Ireland. Norwich, 18 Nov. 1354.

---

[49] *Alias* Atte Gates (**1858**).
[50] See **748**.
[51] Usually St Neot's priory (**1659**).
[52] There is no mention of a commission from the archbishop of York.
[53] *Alias* de Outewell (**281**).

1896 Inst. of John Tryg of *Hermesthorp*, priest, by vicar-general M. Walter [de Elveden], to the rectory of Brettenham [S], vac. by resig. of Dns John de Laniholm;[54] patron, Ralph [de Stafford], earl of Stafford. Norwich, 19 Nov. 1354.

1897 Inst. of Robert Dauns of Grundisburgh [S], priest, by vicar-general M. Walter [de Elveden], to the rectory of Wangford[55] [S], vac. by resig. of Dns John le Clerc, in exchange for the rectory of North Cove [S]; patron, Thomas de Ikworth. Little Saxham, 29 Nov. 1354.

1898 [fo.155^v] Inst. of John le Clerc, priest, by vicar-general M. Walter [de Elveden], to the rectory of North Cove [S], vac. by resig. of Dns Robert Dauns of Grundisburgh [S], in exchange; patron, Edward III. Little Saxham, 29 Nov. 1354.

1899 Inst. of William Somerd, priest, by vicar-general M. Walter [de Elveden], to the rectory of All Saints, Tatterset [N], vac. by resig. of Dns Adam Wortes in exchange; patrons, the prior and chapter of Norwich cathedral,[56] and the convent of Castle Acre [N]. Norwich, 9 Dec. 1354.

1900 Inst. of Adam Wortes, priest, by vicar-general M. Walter [de Elveden], to the vicarage of Hindringham [N], vac. by resig. of William Somerd in exchange as above; patrons, the prior and chapter of Norwich cathedral. Norwich, 9 Dec. 1354.

1901 Inst. of John Trendel, priest, by vicar-general M. Walter [de Elveden], to a moiety of Letheringsett [N], vac. by resig. of Dns Robert de Kylverstone, in exchange for a moiety of Edgmere [N]; patrons, the prior and convent of Binham [N]. Norwich, 9 Dec. 1354.

1902 Inst. of Robert de Kylverston, priest, by vicar-general M. Walter [de Elveden], to a moiety of Edgmere [N], in exchange as above; patrons, Dns John Leche and John de Eggemere. Norwich, 9 Dec. 1354.

1903 Inst. of John le Clerc, priest, by vicar-general M. W[alter de Elveden], to the vicarage of Wenhaston [S], vac. by resig. of Semanus Baron;[1] patrons, the prior and convent of Blythburgh [S]. Norwich, 10 Dec. 1354.

1904 Inst. of Warren Martel, priest, by vicar-general M. W[alter de Elveden], to the rectory of Thurington (*Thoryton*) [S], vac. by resig. of Dns William de Sneterton; patrons, the prior and convent of Blythburgh [S]. Norwich, 10 Dec. 1354.

1905 Inst. of John FrZeitunceys, priest, by vicar-general M. W[alter de Elveden], to the rectory of Boyton [S], vac. by resig. of Roger atte Brigge; patrons, Dns

---

[54] *Alias* Langeholm (**110**).
[55] Near Brandon (see **1039n.**).
[56] Cf. **835**.
[1] Inst. in 1338 (Reg. Bek fo.10).

Robert de Erpyngham, John de Berneye, John Horold, and Robert de Wotton. Norwich, 9 Dec. 1354.

1906   Inst. of William Balle, priest, by vicar-general M. W[alter de Elveden], to the rectory of Thwaite [in Brooke deanery] (*Twheyt iuxta Mundham*) [N], vacant by the canonical removal of John de Seton; patron, Hugh de Ulseby. Norwich, 13 Dec. 1354.

1907   Inst. of Edmund de Redgrave, priest, by vicar-general M. W[alter de Elveden], to the rectory of Bale (*Bathele*) [N]; patron, Edmund de Thorp, knight. Norwich, 19 Dec. 1354.

1908   M. R[ichard de Lyng] and M. W[alter de Elveden], vicars-general acting on the bishop's authority, collated to Dns Robert James of Whissonsett [N], priest, in the person of his proctor, William Cob of Lyng [N], the rectories of SS Simon and Jude, and St Swithin, in Norwich, with the rectory of Crostwick [N], all vacant by the death of Dns Walter de Banham. Norwich, 20 Dec. 1354.

1909   Inst. of Matthew son of Adam de Southbirlingham, priest, [fo.156] by vicar-general M. W[alter de Elveden], to the vicarage of Stoven [S]; patron in this turn, Edward III, the temporalities of Wangford Priory [S] being in his hand. Norwich, 21 Dec. 1354.

1910   Inst. of Andrew Wibbe, priest, in the person of his proctor, William de Usflet, clerk, by vicar-general M. W[alter de Elveden], to the rectory of South Acre [N]; patron, John Harsyk, knight. Norwich, 24 Dec. 1354.

1911   Inst. of Roger Drag of Bungay [S], priest, by vicar-general M. W[alter de Elveden], to the rectory of Carlton (*Carleton iuxta Saxmundham*) [S]; patrons, the prioress and convent of Campsey Ash [S]. Norwich, 5 Jan. 1355.

1912   Collation by vicar-general M. W[alter de Elveden] to Stephen Curson of Watton [N], clerk, of the deanery of Hartismere [S], vac. by resig. of Dns John de Horscroft in exchange for the deanery of Samford [S]. Norwich, 20 Dec. 1354.

1913   Collation by vicar-general M. W[alter de Elveden] to Dns J. de Horsecroft, priest, of the deanery of Samford[2] [S], in exchange as above. Norwich, 20 Dec. 1354.

1914   Inst. of John de Horsecroft, priest, by vicar-general M. W[alter de Elveden], to the vicarage of Brent Eleigh[3] [S]. The bishop had nomination, exercised in this turn by the vicar-general; patrons, the abbot and convent of St Osyth Abbey. Norwich, 5 Jan. 1355.

---

[2] In 1337 this deanery was considered to have cure of souls (p.xxvi; Reg. Bek fo.2[v]).
[3] This parish was ten miles from Samford deanery (**1913**).

1915 Inst. of Richard de Hornyngton, priest, by vicar-general M. W[alter de Elveden], to the rectory of Barrow [S]; patron, Guy de Brienne, baron.[4] Norwich, 11 Jan. 1355.

1916 Inst. of James de Ely, priest, by vicar-general M. W[alter de Elveden], to the vicarage of St German's, Wiggenhall [N]; patrons, the prior and convent of Norwich cathedral. Norwich, 16 Jan. 1355.

1917 Confirmation[5] of the election of Brother John Brandon of Weasenham [N], priest and professed canon of Great Massingham [N], as prior of that house. Norwich, 20 Jan. 1355.

1918 Inst. of William de Lavenham, priest, by vicar-general M. W[alter de Elveden], to the rectory of Lavenham [S]; patron, John Veer, earl of Oxford. Livermere, 19 Jan. 1355.

[The following notice of the bishop's death at Avignon on 6 Jan. 1355 follows four blank lines.]

Hic finitur Registrum bone memorie domini Willelmi de Norwico dudum Norwicensis Episcopi qui decessit Avinion' die Epiphanie domini anno domini Millesimo, CCC^{mo} quinquagesimo quarto circa horam tertiam eiusdem diei et sepultus est in ecclesia beate Marie iuxta Palacium Apostolicum. Et die .xxiiii. Januarii Anno domini supradicto primo innotuit vicariis generalibus Officiali et Correctori et ceteris ministris dicti patris de eius morte.

1919 [fo.156^v] [16th-century copy of an award by J. de Feryby, official of Bishop William (*sic*), dated 24 May 1277, concerning the rights of the bishop of Norwich and the vicar of Loddon [N] over St Andrew's chapel on Roger de Hales' manor of *Wrantishaghe* in Loddon parish.][6]

---

[4] See *Complete Peerage* I, 361.
[5] The entry does not say by whom.
[6] Text to be printed by C. Harper-Bill in *English Episcopal Acta*, British Academy VI, *Norwich*, part 3 (forthcoming).

APPENDIX I

These transcriptions of entries or parts of entries are numbered as in the calendar. The notes in this appendix deal only with textual issues. Each transcript begins with the number of the folio where it is found in the manuscript, followed by the centred or marginal heading (if any) in capital letters. Abbreviations have usually been expanded. The spelling of the scribes has been retained, except that when 'u' is a consonant it is rendered as 'v', and when 'v' is a vowel it is rendered as 'u'. Years have been reduced to Roman numerals. Punctuation and capital letters are added or modified for clarity; long passages are broken into paragraphs and sometimes punctuated with round brackets.

10

[fo.7^v] RESERVACIO FRUCTUUM ECCLESIE DE BLOFELD AD USUM COLLEGII SANCTE TRINITATIS IN UNIVERSITATE CANTEBRIG' USQUE AD TEMPUS.[1] Universis sancte matris ecclesie filiis ad quos presentes littere pervenerint Willelmus permissione divina Norwicensis episcopus salutem cum benedictione dextere salvatoris. Cum sacris canonibus sit sanctitum quod propter iustas et pias causas valeat episcopus cum consensu capituli sui usque ad certum tempus beneficiorum fructus vacancium reservare in usus pios durante dicto tempore convertendos; nos considerantes quod nulla causa magis poterit esse pia quam circa personas scolasticas indigentes pietatis opera excercere qui iuri insistunt canonico et civili ut divinarum ac etiam humanarum rerum noticiam iusti scienciam habeant et iniusti qua clericorum relevatur in opera sciencia dilatatur ecclesia defensatur et res pupplica gubernatur, quodque pestilencia pridium ingruens tot subtraxit in locis singulis et in nostra presertim diocese literatos quod pauci remanent hiis diebus per quos cura poterit ecclesiastica gubernari, idcirco ad honorem dei omnipotentis ac utilitatem commodum regimen et directionem rei publice et specialiter nostre ecclesie cathedralis Sancte Trinitatis nostreque diocesis Norwicen' unum collegium scolarium iuris canonici et civilis Sancte Trinitatis vocabulo insignitum in Universitate Cantebriggien' fundavimus, et illud incepimus aliqualiter iam dotare et quamquam dictum collegium ad plenum dotare perpetuis redditibus proponamus ac edificia pro habitacione competenti eiusdem collegii construere quam celerius poterimus deo duce.

Quia tamen ad presens sufficientibus dotatis redditibus non existit [fo.8] nec constructa habitacio pro eodem ut tam sanctum et pium propositum ad intentum facilius perducat habito tractatu cum capitulo nostro solempni ac iuris ordine qui in hac parte requiritur in omnibus observato, fructus redditus et

---

[1] The heading is centred, with no marginal heading.

proventus ecclesie de Blofeld nostre diocesis nostrique patronatus quam de gratia et privilegio sedis apostolice speciali habuimus et tenuimus tanquam mense nostre unitam pro vite nostre tempore possidendos per resignacionem nostram simplicem iam vacantis a die date presencium usque ad festum Sancti Michaelis proximo futurum et extunc per novem annos proximo tunc venturos, infra quos dictum collegium sufficienter dotare et edificia pro habitacione competenti construere curabimus altissimo annuente, tenore presencium de consensu dicti nostri capituli reservamus in usus dicti collegii; salva porcione rectoris qui pro tempore fuerit pro se et oneribus ecclesie ut inferius subiungitur convertendos, quod si forsitan infra dictorum novem annorum spacium dictum collegium in redditibus perpetuis sufficienter quod absit dotatum non fuerit pro vite necessariis custodi sociis et scolaribus[2] dicti collegii iuxta statutum et statuendum[3] per nos munitum atque modum ac edificacionis et aliis dicti collegii oneribus plenarie et perpetuo ministrandis, tunc eiusdem ecclesie de Blofeld fructus redditus et proventus exnu[n]c prout extunc per aliorum novem annorum spacium dictos novem annos immediate sequencium in usus dicti collegii necessarios salvis superius expressis integraliter convertendos de consensu eiusdem nostri capituli decrevimus reservandos, ac eos per tempus predictum de consensu dicti nostri capituli exnunc prout extunc tenore presencium reservamus.

Ne tamen dicta ecclesia[4] cura et regimine debitis negligatur, volumus et de consensu dicti nostri capituli ordinamus quod infra unius mensis spacium et extunc perpetuo ex nostra et successorum nostrorum collacione canonica ecclesia prefata rectorem habeat perpetuum qui curam habeat animarum et exnunc usque ad finem novennii reservacionis prefate in aula seu hospicio dicti collegii habitacionem suam habeat continuam si voluerit, sicut unus dicti collegii socius atque victum et ultra hoc pro vestibus et aliis neccesariis[5] ad suum proprium usum de proventibus ecclesie supradicte decem marcas sterlingorum, si moram et victum habuerit ut premittitur in collegio supradicto; alioquin decem libre sterlingorum pro omnibus[6] expensis suis propriis recipiet annuatim.

In secundo autem novennio si duraverit fructuum reservacio supradicta, decem libre cum habitacionis et victus commodo ut premittitur si in aula collegii voluerit commorari; alioquin viginti marcas si extra aulam stare voluerit recipiat annuatim de fructibus et proventibus ecclesie supradicte, toto residuo fructuum reddituum et proventuum dicte ecclesie ad usum dicti collegii reservato, salvo quod de dicto residuo fructuum reddituum et proventuum dicte ecclesie ministretur dicte ecclesie et parochianis eiusdem omnibus in divinis et alia ecclesie onera congrue supportentur; proviso tamen quod collegium supradictum durante dicte reservacionis tempore possit si voluerit absque rectoris contradictione qui pro tempore fuerit aliquem deputare in

---

[2] Written over an erasure by contemporary hand (but not S2). This same hand made several other corrections to the text.
[3] Interlined from *et*
[4] *Ecclesia* was written twice and the second one struck through.
[5] From *pro* written by the same correcting hand in the inner margin with an insertion mark.
[6] Interlined.

rectoria ecclesie supradicte ad recolligendum fructus redditus et proventus omnes dicte ecclesie [fo.8ᵛ] et ad disponendos libere de eisdem, qui onera ecclesie omnia ac pensionis predicto rectori debite de fructibus et proventibus dicte ecclesie supportabit et de toto residuo dicto collegio durante dicte reservacionis tempore fideliter et plenarie respondebit.

Post decursum vero temporum predictorum omnes fructus redditus et proventus dicte ecclesie integraliter extunc recipiet dictus rector qui pro tempore fuerit et de eisdem disponit libere pro suo libito iuxta canonica instituta. Volumus insuper et cum consensu dicti nostri capituli ordinamus quod per tota tempora quibus fructus redditus et proventus ecclesie prefate remanebunt ut premittitur in usus dicti collegii reservati, liceat rectori dicte ecclesie qui pro tempore fuerit a dicta se ecclesia absentare et in aula seu hospicio dicti collegii Universitatis Cantebr' studiorum causa continue residere et omnes fructus redditus et proventus dicte ecclesie ad firmam libere dimittere cum consensu collegii supradicti, super quibus etiam de consensu nostri capituli cum rectore quocumque qui pro tempore fuerit ecclesie supradicte tenore presencium dispensamus et auctoritate etiam nostra ordinaria specialem eisdem licentiam impartimur.

Cuicumque rectori dicte ecclesie qui pro tempore fuerit in virtute sancte obediencie et sub excommunicacionis pena quam sex dierum canonica monicione premissa in contradictores et rebelles quoscumque de consilio et assensu dicti nostri capituli ferimus in hiis scriptis firmiter iniungentes quatinus omnia et singula superius ordinata curet suis temporibus quantum in eo fuerit integraliter observare et in contrarium ne venire[t] puplice vel occulte ac omnia et singula impedimenta sique per eum ac suo nomine apposita fuerint contra premissa seu aliquem premissorum infradictorum sex dierum spacium revocare.

Datum in capitulo ecclesie nostre cathedralis predicte die vi Februarii anno domini MCCCXLIX et consecrationis nostre sexto.

11

[fo.8ᵛ] EXONERATIO CUIUSDAM CANTARIE PRO ECCLESIA DE REPP' FACTA MAGISTRO ET FRATRIBUS HOSPITALIS SANCTI EGIDII IN NORWICO.[7] Willelmus permissione divina Norwicensis episcopus dilectis in Christo filiis magistro et fratribus hospitalis Sancti Egidii in Norwico salutem gratiam et benedictionem. Petitio vestra nobis exhibita continebat quod licet Magister Willelmus de Suffeld archidiaconus Norwicensis vobis et hospitali vestro imperpetuum mesuagium suum in villa de Repp' in Fleg' iuxta mariscum cum terra in crofto adiacente et cum advocacione sive patronatu ecclesie de Repp' predicta et capelle de Bastwyk in pura et perpetua elemosina libere et absque omni onere per vos imponendo contulisset; vos tamen per vim laicalem oppresi onus trium capellanorum pro animabus Hugonis de Caly et Agnetis uxoris eius et successorum suorum, qui nichil iuris in dictis mesuagio crofto sive patronatu habuerint vel ad ea vel aliquod eorumdem, sumptibus vestris et dicti hospitalis celebrantium per aliqua tempora licet modica sine licencia et

---

[7] The entry has a marginal heading only.

consensu diocesani vestri in hac parte indebite submistis in vestri et dicti hospitalis preiudicium non modicum et gravamen, quare nobis humiliter supplicantes ut de oportuno remedio vobis in hac parte providere dignaremur.

Nos igitur attendentes quod bona dicti hospitalis in sustentationem pauperum Christi et precipue capellanorum debilium pro anima bone memorie domini Walteri quondam Norwicensis episcopi fundatoris dicte domus et pro animabus successorum suorum patronorum eiusdem distribui debeant et nullatenus in alios usus expendi maxime absque nostri vel successorum nostrorum licencia episcopali ac tam per exhibita vestra quam aliunde invenientes contenta in dicta petitione vestra vera esse, vobis tenore presencium intimamus quod decetero nullatenus ad onus tenemini memoratum.[8]

In cuius rei testimonium litteras nostras sigillo nostro patenti signatas vobis transmittimus has patentes. Datum apud Thorp' xxiii die mensis Julii anno domini MCCCL et consecracionis nostre septimo.

12

[fo.21] ACCEPTACIO PRO REDINTEGRACIONE ECCLESIE DE SCOTHOWE.[9] Universis sancte matris ecclesie filiis ad quos presentes littere pervenerint Robertus[10] miseratione divina abbas monasterii Sancti Benedicti de Hulmo Norwicensis diocesis et eiusdem loci conventus salutem et sinceram in domino caritatem. Universitati vestre tenore presencium innotescat quod cum Magister Thomas de Methelwold venerabilis patris domini Willelmi dei gratia Norwicensis episcopi officialis principalis et ipsius patris in ea parte commissarius specialis nos abbatem et conventum predictos ad possessionem ecclesie parochialis de Scothowe dicte diocesis, quam in proprios usus canonice obtinuimus et sine culpa nostra amisimus, iuris ordine in omnibus observato restituisset et redintegrasset sub hac forma:

In nomine domini Amen. Cum in negotio redintegracionis sive restitutionis ecclesie de Scothowe Norwicensis diocesis religiosis viris .. abbati et .. conventui monasterii Sancti Benedicti de Hulmo eiusdem diocesis primitus coram venerabili in Christo patre domini Willelmo dei gratia Norwicensi episcopo intentato fuisset ex parte dictorum religiosorum virorum quedam petitio dicto venerabili patri porrecta, cuius tenor talis est:

Reverende paternitati vestre domine Willelme dei gratia Norwicensi episcope supplicant et petunt vestri humiles et devoti filii abbas et conventus monasterii[11] Sancti Benedicti de Hulmo vestre diocesis quod cum ipsi ecclesiam parochialem de Scothowe dicte diocesis eis et eorum monasterio per bone memorie dominum Thomam nuper Norwicensem episcopum loci diocesanum predecessorem vestrum in proprios usus perpetuis temporibus possidendam interveniente consensu capituli sui ecclesie sue Norwicensis canonice appropriatam

---

[8] From *ad* written over an erasure.

[9] This entry has both a centred heading and a marginal heading. A contemporary hand noted beneath the latter, *pens' iii Mar'*. There is also a notation by a later-medieval, 'bastard' hand (S6) on fo.21ᵛ in the outer margin by line 25, *pens'*

[10] Corrected from *Willelmus*

[11] MS. *Manasterii*

obtinuissent et habuissent et eam sic appropriatam per tempora non modica tenuissent, ipsamque ecclesiam sine eorum culpa videlicet per curiam regalem in qua defensiones iuris iuxta morem ecclesiasticam eis non subsint proponendi et probandi facultatem¹² amisissent in eorum monasterii sui predicti enormem lesionem, hospitalitasque ac divina officia hac occasione diminuta extiterant necnon et alia onera eisdem inevitabiliter incumbencia quominus sustinere poterant et possunt in presenti, dictaque domus Sancti Benedicti plus solito extitit et existit per seculares onerata; quatinus eandem ecclesiam de Scothowe eisdem et eorum monasterio supradicto redintegrare restituere et in statum pristinum reducere et ex habundanti de novo appropriare annectere et unire dignemini favore religionis et in divini cultus augmentum ac intuitu caritatis, premissa proponunt et fieri petunt coniunctim et divisim vestrum officium humiliter implorando.

Dictus venerabilis pater prefatam petitionem admisit, factaque postmodum diligenti inquisitione auctoritate dicti patris ad informacionem consciencie sue per viros fidedignos in forma iuris iuratos et examinatos super omnibus et singulis in dicta petitione suggestis et contentis et aliis circumstantiis in ea parte debitis, factisque pontificali auctoritate dicti patris in dicta ecclesia de Scothowe et aliis ecclesiis circumvicinis diebus solempnibus et intra missarum solempnia premunitionibus proclamationibus et citationibus in vulgari, quod siqui se parochianos patrones vel interesse quodcumque aliud pretendentes voluerint aliquid dicere proponere vel allegare quare ad huius redintegrationem seu restitutionem procedi non debeat vel non possit, quod certis die et loco coram dicto patre vel eius commissario compareant dicturi facturi et proposituri quicquid velint in ea parte; religiosis viris dominis .. priore et capitulo seu conventu ecclesie Norwicensis necnon domino Hugone Peverel milite qui ad dictam ecclesiam dicitur ultimo presentasse ac domino Johanne rectori eiusdem ecclesie nichilominus ad dictos diem et locum ad hec facienda nominative et specialiter evocatis, quibus die et loco proposita quadam proposicione ex parte dictorum religiosorum virorum prioris et conventus ecclesie cathedralis Sancte Trinitatis Norwicensis, necnon Rogeri Verly et Johannis de Hevyngham parochianorum ecclesie de Scothowe supradicte ad informationem dicti patris, habitaque aliquale altercatione super eadem prefatisque dominis Hugone et Johanne in ea parte nullatenus se opponentibus. Deinde propositis et [fo.21ᵛ] exhibitis ex parte dictorum religiosorum abbatis et conventus quibusdam cartis et munimentis super appropriatione ecclesie de Scothowe per episcopum Norwicensem et confirmatione capituli Norwicensis eisdem religiosis factis, datus fuit terminus ad dicendum contra proposita et producta.

Deinde dicto negotio nobis Thome de Methelwold officiale principali dicti patris audiendo et fine canonico terminando commisso, nos commissarius antedictus datis terminis competentibus et auditis propositis et allegationibus partium hinc inde, datoque termino ad nostram pronunciationem seu sentenciam audiendam ad diem hodiernum in ecclesia cathedrali Norwicensi presente procuratore dictorum abbatis et conventus accusataque contumacia citatorum omnium aliorum, visis auditis et diligenter rimatis ac plenius intellectis meritis dicti negotii, Christi nomine invocato pro tribunali sedentes, pronunciamus decrevimus et declaramus dictos abbatem et conventum Sancti Benedicti de

---

¹² MS. *facultas*

Hulmo fore redintegrandos et restituendos ad possessionem ecclesie de Scothowe Norwicensis diocesis tanquam eisdem appropriate iuxta formam et modum quibus dudum eam tenuerunt et possederunt ut appropriatam et unitam virtute unionis et appropriationis eis facte per bone memorie dominum Thomam quondam episcopum Norwicensem, dictosque abbatem et conventum, salvis iure et possessione rectoris iam incumbentis pro tempore vite sue nisi eam aliter voluntarie duxerit resignandus, per hanc nostram sentenciam restituimus[13] et redintegramus ad possessionem ecclesie supradicte.

Salva etiam reverendo patri domino episcopo Norwicensi qui nunc est et successoribus suis libera potestate ordinandi et assignandi in dicta ecclesia vicariam perpetuam ac portionem debitam et sufficientem pro vicario perpetuo usque ad quadragintas marcas in vero valore annuali de redditibus fructibus et proventibus ecclesie supradicte cum habitatione etiam competenti, quam vicariam ad decem libras taxandam decernimus.

Salva etiam dicto patri et suis successoribus libera nominacione ydonee persone ad dictam vicariam cum vacaverit perpetuis temporibus in futurum, quam personam per prefatum patrem ac successores suos qui pro temporibus fuerint dictis abbati et conventui nominandam abbas et conventus predicti tenebuntur infra trium dierum spacium a die nominationis eis note domino episcopo Norwicensi[14] qui pro tempore fuerit presentare, alioquin collatio dicte vicarie ad prefatum dictum episcopum qui pro tempore fuerit illa vice libere devolvatur.

Salvis[15] etiam domino episcopo et eius successoribus annua pensione perpetua videlicet quadraginta solidorum per dictos abbatem et conventum episcopo qui pro tempore fuerit perpetuis temporibus exsolvenda in recompensationem primorum fructuum episcopo debitorum ratione vacationis et aliorum dampnorum que occasione appropriationis unionis et redintegrationis predictarum episcopis Norwic' qui pro tempore fuerint[16] contingere poterunt in futurum, et summo altari ecclesie cathedralis predicte quinque solidorum annua pensione,[17] quas pensiones annuas in duabus synodis singulis annis perpetuis temporibus pro equalibus portionibus per sequestrationem fructuum dicte ecclesie et censuras ecclesiasticas in abbatem et conventum fulminandas decernimus persolvendas.

Salvo etiam quod dicti religiosi viri omnia onera ordinaria et extraordinaria pro portione dicte ecclesie eos concernente et vicarii qui pro tempore fuerint pro portione dicte vicarie singulis temporibus futuris agnoscent et subibunt.

Et in testimonium omnium premissorum sigillum officialitatis ecclesie Christi Norwicensis quo in officio dicte officialitatis utimur presentibus apposuimus. Datum apud Norwicum xix die Maii anno domini MCCCXLVIII. Lecta et lata fuit hec sentencia in ecclesia cathedrali Norwicensi per nos officialem et commissarium antedictum anno et die supradictis.

Nos abbas et conventus memorati omnia et singula in dicta restitutione et redintegratione contenta et per prefatum [fo.22] commissarium acta habita et

---

[13] MS. *restituinmus*
[14] Interlined.
[15] MS. *Salva*
[16] MS. *fuerunt*
[17] MS. *annuam pensionem*

ordinata iuxta omnem vim formam et effectum eorumdem quatenus in nobis est[18] admittimus et acceptamus, et ad maiorem securitatem eorumdem nos successores nostros et monasterium nostrum predictum ad soluciones[19] dictorum quadraginta solidorum dicto venerabili patri et suis successoribus necnon dictorum quinque solidorum summo altari ecclesie cathedralis Norwicensis per nos et successores nostros terminis supradictis ex causis premissis bene et fideliter annuatim perpetuo faciendas obligamus per presentes sub penis et censuris superius annotatis, renunciantes in hiis omnibus appellationibus exceptionibus iuris remediis et subterfugiis quibuscumque per quas seu que dicte solutiones impediri poterunt quomodolibet vel deferri. In quorum omnium testimonium sigillum nostrum communem fecimus hiis apponi. Datum apud monasterium predictum in domo nostro capitulari ii kalendas Januarii anno domini MCCCXLVIII.[20]

17

[fo.25] [*Transcription of the letter of Clement VI authorizing Bishop Bateman to appropriate parishes to poor religious houses and hospitals, contained in this entry.*] Clemens episcopus servus servorum dei venerabili fratri Willelmo episcopo Norwicensi salutem et apostolicam benedictionem. Etsi ex iniuncto nobis apostolatus officio ecclesiarum ac hospitalium pauperum ac aliorum piorum locorum ecclesiasticorum omnium sollicitudo nobis immineat generalis, certa ea tamen diligencius vigilare nos convenit que ad suorum supportationem onerum sufficientes[21] non habent secundum eorum decentiam facultates.

Cum itaque sicut petitio pro parte tua nuper nobis exhibita continebat, nonnullorum ecclesiarum collegiatarum ac hospitalium et aliorum piorum locorum ecclesiasticorum tue diocesis redditus et proventus ad incumbentis eis hospitalitatis et pietatis opera ac alia onera eis incumbentia supportanda sufficere minnime[22] dinoscuntur; [fo.25ᵛ] nos eorum cupientes inopie quantum cum deo possumus subvenire ac gerentes de tue circumspectionis industria in hiis et aliis fiduciam in domino specialem, tuis supplicationibus inclinati, uniendi et annectendi in perpetuum auctoritate apostolica parochiales ecclesias dicte tue diocesis ecclesiis collegiatis ac hospitalibus et aliis piis locis predictis de quibus tibi videbitur expedire super quo tuam conscienciam oneramus ex causis veris et legitimis cum omnibus iuribus et pertinenciis, (ita quod post unionem et annexionem huiusmodi cedentibus vel decedentibus rectoribus ipsarum ecclesiarum parochialium qui nunc sunt vel cum ipse quocumque alia modo vacabunt, rectores collegiatarum ecclesiarum ac hospitalium et aliorum piorum locorum predictorum[23] auctoritate propria per se vel alium seu alios ipsarum parochialium ecclesiarum possessionem libere apprehendere et etiam retinere fructusque ipsarum parochialium ecclesiarum in usus proprios

---

[18] Interlined.
[19] MS. *solucionem*
[20] MS. *Octouo* for *Octavo*
[21] Corrected from *sufficientem*
[22] *Sic*
[23] Corrected from *predictarum*

ecclesiarum collegiatarum ac hospitalium et aliorum piorum locorum predictorum convertere possint tua vel cuiuscumque alterius licentia minime requi-
sita; reservatis tamen per te primitus et etiam assignatis ipsarum singularum
parochialium ecclesiarum proventibus pro singulis perpetuis vicariis instituendis
canonice in eisdem et in ipsis virtutum[24] domino servituris congruis portionibus
ex omnibus possunt commode sustentari iura episcopalia solvere et alia
incumbentia eis onera supportare; non obstantibus si aliqui super provisionibus
sibi faciendis de huiusmodi parochialibus ecclesiis vel aliis beneficiis ecclesias-
ticis in eadem diocese speciales vel in illis partibus generales sedis apostolice vel
legatorum eius literas inpetraverint, etiam si per eas ad inhibicionem reserva-
cionem et decretum vel alias quomodolibet sit processum, quas literas et
processus habitos per easdem post uniones huiusmodi si eas per te fieri
contigerit ad easdem parochiales ecclesias volumus non extendi sed nullum[25]
per hoc eis quoad assecutionem ecclesiarum et beneficiorum aliorum preiudicium generari seu quibuslibet privilegiis indulgenciis et literis apostolicis
generalibus vel specialibus quorumcumque tenor existant per que presentibus
non expressa vel totaliter non inserta effectus earum impediri valeat quomodolibet vel differi et de quibus quorumque totis tenoribus habenda sic in nostris
literis mentio specialis) fraternitati tue auctoritate predicta tenore presencium
plenam et liberam concedimus facultatem.

Nos enim si uniones huiusmodi per te ut prefertur fieri contigerit, irritum
decernimus et inane. Si secus super hiis a quoquam quavis auctoritate scienter
vel ignoranter contigerit attemptari.[26] Datum Avinon' xvii kalendas Decembris
pontificatus nostri anno septimo.

20

[fo.28] ASSIGNACIO VICARIE ECCLESIE DE REDENHALE.[27] Universis
sancte matris ecclesie filiis ad quos presentes littere pervenerint, Willelmus
permissione divina Norwicensis episcopus salutem et perpetuam memoriam rei
geste. Nos nuper dilectis in Christo filiabus priorisse et conventui de Bongeye
ordinis Sancti Benedicti nostre diocesis ecclesiam parochialem de Redenhale
dicte nostre diocesis certis et legitimis de causis auctoritate apostolica nobis in
hac parte commissa appropriavimus univimus et in usus proprios concessimus
perpetuis temporibus possidendam, salvis[28] tamen vicaria perpetua in ecclesia
predicta et vicario ibidem pro tempore servituro debita et sufficienti habitacione
ac congrua porcione de fructibus et proventibus dicte ecclesie usque ad viginti
librarum sterlingorum summam in vero valore annuo per nos imposterum
assignandis. Verum quia dicte habitacio et porcio nondum per nos fuerant
assignate, ne com[m]unis pareat discordiam in futurum ad assignacionem
dictarum habitacionis et porcionis in forma procedimus infrascripta.

In primis volentes tam dilectis filiabus priorisse et conventui predictis

---

[24] MS. *virtutium*
[25] MS. *nullium*
[26] This sentence seems to be incomplete: cf. **1296***.
[27] Centred heading.
[28] MS. *Salva*

rectoribus et vicario qui pro tempore fuerit ecclesie supradicte de mansis seu habitacionibus sufficientibus iuxta utriusque partis indigenciam infra rectorie limites providere, statuimus et ordinamus quod ad divisionem mansorum seu habitacionum rectorum et vicarii predictorum fiat unus murus a parte boriali portarum magnarum pretendens et fossata exteriori dicte rectorie iuxta dictas portas recta linea versus orientem usque ad fossatum interiorem circumdantem motam dicte rectorie excepto septem pedum spacio, et sic linialiter a parte altera orientali dicte mote fiat unus alius murus pretendens linialiter a dicta fossata interiori excepto septem pedum spacio usque ad sumitatem et finem partis orientaliis dicte rectorie. Et volumus et ordinamus quod dicte porte magne et totus ingressus per eas una cum pecia terre cum uno stagno ex opposito dicte rectorie quatuor acras vel circiter continente cum arboribus et quodam Tygurrio in ea contentis et tota mota cum omnibus edificiis in ea contentis et cum tota fossata aque dictam motam circumdantis, necnon tota porcio rectorie extra motam ex parte australi dicte rectorie cum omnibus edificiis arboribus et curtilagiis in ea [fo.28ᵛ] infra dictos duos muros contentis una cum fossata exteriori dictam porcionem exteriorem circumdante necnon spacium septem pedum ex parte boriali dicte rectorie circa fossatam aque motam ut premittitur circumdantis in quo septem pedum spacio poterunt vicarii qui pro tempore fuerint dictam fossatam circumquaque purgare retia libere ponere et ea etiam desiccare, ad vicarios qui pro tempore fuerint dicte ecclesie solos et in solidum libere pertineant perpetuus temporibus in futurum. Alia vero porcio rectorie predicte extra fossatam interiorem aque circumdantis motam predictam ex parte boriali dicte rectorie cum omnibus grangiis granario domibus arboribus et curtilagiis inter dictos duos muros contentis, septem pedum spacio circa fossatam interiorem predictam ut premittitur dumtaxat excepto una cum fossata exteriori dictam porcionem exterius circumdante, ad dilectas in Christo filias priorissam et conventum predictas rectores ecclesie prefate solas et in solidum pertineat perpetuis temporibus in futurum.

Item statuimus ac etiam ordinamus quod vicarius qui nunc est et qui pro tempore fuerit habeat pro porcione sua omnes fructus redditus et proventus ad dicte ecclesie alteragium pertinentes, videlicet redditus assise et tres gallinas de reddituum unam acram unam rodam et octo pedes prati et pasture;[29] item decimas feni lano lactis lini et canabi pullanorum vitulorum agnorum porcellorum ovorum pullorum gallinarum et columbarum aucarum cignorum anatum mellis cere et ceragii pomorum pirorum et fructuum quorumcumque arborum ortorum tam satorum quam plantatorum quocumque nomine censeantur, etiam si blada in dictis ortis fuerint seminata molendinorum piscariorum silvarum et boscorum turbarie oblacionum mortuariorum seque-larum et omnium altarum obvencionum cuiuscumque generis fuerint que debent ad alteragium pertinere de consuetudine vel de iure, una cum triginta acris terre de dote ecclesie iacentibus in campo australi dicte parochie ex parte aque vocata Le Bek sive sit ibi plus sive minus. Item statuimus et ordinamus quod vicarius qui pro tempore fuerit percipiet omnes et singulas decimas que de dicto campo australi perveniunt qui pretenditur a ponte de Alderforde usque ad Manerium vocatum Le Bekhalle in villa de Striston qui quidem

---

[29] Since the rents and lands described do not define the *alteragium*, they must be intended to supplement it.

campus habet tres partes vulgariter nuncupatas Harlestonfeld Overgatefeld et Wettewalefeld.

Et quia[30] in dicte appropriacionis litteris ordinavimus porcionem vicarie predicte ad viginti librarum sterlingorum[31] in vero valore summam dumtaxat extendi, volumus quod liceat dictis religiosis mulieribus vicario qui pro tempore fuerit viginti libras singulis annis in festis Sancti Luce Evangeliste et Purificacionis Beate Marie pro equalibus porcionibus persolvere et porcionem vicarii predictam, excepta habitacione pro vicario superius designata et dicta pecia terre cum stagno ex opposito rectorie ut premittitur situata (cum quibus possit vicarius qui pro tempore fuerit habere in dicta villa communionem animalium et pasture[32]) per tempora quibus dictam pensionem dictis terminis plenarie persolverint ad usus proprios retinere.

In casu autem quo[33] dicte religiose mulieres in aliqua solucione in dictis terminis vel saltim per quindecim dierum spacium post terminos supradictos in toto defecerint vel in parte, tunc dictam porcionem totam superius pro vicario assignatam decernimus ad vicarium qui pro tempore fuerit extunc perpetuo et incommutabiliter pertinere, et extunc liceat vicario qui pro tempore fuerit totam porcionem predictam auctoritate propria ingredi et eam plenarie et incommutabiliter in perpetuum possidere. Siquis autem dictum vicarium qui pro tempore fuerit impedierit quominus dictam porcionem in illum eventum ingredi valeat et eam ut premittitur pacifice possidere, aut hanc ordinacionem nostram seu eiusdem plenariam execucionem impedierit in toto vel in parte, sentenciam maioris excommunicacionis incurrere volumus ipso facto.

Volumus etiam et ordinamus quod dicte religiose mulieres [fo.29] pro tempore quo alteragium et ea que ad alteragium pertinent prout superius describuntur perceperint ut prefertur et teneantur, continuo unum parochialem presbiterum in dicta ecclesia et parochia continue ministrantem invenire propriis earum sumptibus.[34] Et hoc idem fieri volumus per vicarium qui pro tempore fuerit si et cum ad eum pertinuerint iuxta formam superius descriptam proventus alteragii supradicti. Ceterorum autem omnium et singulorum onerum ordinariorum et extraordinariorum ecclesie supradicte due partes ad dictas religiosas mulieres et tercia pars ad vicarium qui pro tempore fuerit pertineant perpetuis temporibus in futurum. In cuius rei testimonium sigillum nostrum fecimus hiis apponi. Datum apud Southelmham xvj die Octobris anno domini MCCCXLIX et consecracionis nostre sexto.

---

[30] At this point in the entry there is an insertion mark, which corresponds to a marginal note, *Et quia*. This is apparently a sign for the scribe himself, and marks the beginning of the modification of the vicarage assignment, noted in the calendar.

[31] Interlined.

[32] This clause is found in the outer margin, with an insertion mark to this point in the text; the hand is contemporary and it may be the same scribe.

[33] MS. *que*

[34] MS. *sumptibus invenire*

30

[fo.12] LITTERA ATTORNATUS AD TRACTANDUM ET COMPONEN-
DUM PRO MAIORI ET COMMUNITATE LENN.[35] Sachent toutz yceaux
qui cestes presentes lettres verront ou orront que nous Thomas Rythwys mair de
la ville de Lenn' et tote la comunalte de meisme la ville de comun assent et dune
entiere volunte avons fait establi et ordine noz chiers et biens ameez comburgeys
Geoffroy Drewe alderman de la dite ville, William de Brynton', Thomas Drewe,
Johan de Couteshale, Robert Braunche, William de Byteringge, Auncel
Braunche, Thomas Cook', Johan de Sustede, Simon de Gunton', Johan de
Thirsforde, William de Swanton', Geoffray de Hautboys et Johan Lomb de
parler et bone accord trere et final fyn faire ove nostre treshonure seignur
William par la grace de dieux evesque de Norwicz de la suyte que le dit seignur
fait vers le dit Geoffray Drewe alderman et la comunalte[36] de la ville de Lenn
avantdite et des toutes autres des choses des qux' le dit nostre seignur evesque
vers [fo.12ᵛ] la[37] dite comunalte se sente grevez, eyauntz ferm et estable
quecomque les avant nomez ferront en les choses avantdites. En tesmoignance
des quelles choses as ycestes noz lettres avons mys nostre comun seal, escrit a
Lenn avantdit' le vintisme tierce iour de Martz lan du regne le Roy Edward
tierce puys laconquest' dengleterre vintisme sysme.

31

[fo.12ᵛ] LITTERA OBLIGATIONIS COMMUNITATIS LENN IN QUIN-
GENTIS MARCIS. Pateat universis per presentes quod nos Maior et communitas ville Lenn episcopi tenemur et per presentes obligati sumus venerabili patri
et domino domino Willelmo dei gratia Norwicensi episcopo et successoribus
suis episcopis in quingentis marcis argenti bone et legalis monete solvendis
eidem domino episcopo et successoribus suis episcopis apud Norwicum in festo
Sancti Michaelis Archangeli proximo futuro post diem confectionis presencium
sine dilacione ulteriori, ad quam quidem solucionem dictis die et loco fideliter
faciendam obligamus nos successores succedentes nostros et communitatem
nostram ville de Lenn predicte per presentes. In cuius rei testimonium sigillum
nostrum commune presentibus est appensum. Datum apud Lenn Episcopi die
Lune in septimana Pasche videlicet proximo post festum Sancti Ambrosii
episcopi et doctoris anno regni Regis Edwardi tercii post conquestum Anglie
vicesimo sexto et regni sui Francie terciodecimo.

32

[fo.12ᵛ] INDENTURA COMPOSICIONIS FACTE SUPER LETA HUS-
TINGO ET ARTICULIS ALIIS. Hec indentura testatur quod orta pridem

---

[35] There is also a marginal heading *Lenn*.
[36] MS. *cominalte*
[37] MS. *vers la*

contencione dissensione et discordia inter reverendum in Christo patrem dominum Willelmum de Norwico dei gracia Norwicensem episcopum dominum ville seu burgi Lenn pro se et ecclesia sua Norwicensi ex parte una, ac maiorem burgenses et communitatem dicte ville Lenn Episcopi ex altera, super visu franciplegii hustingo et cognicione placitorum ac aliis articulis contentis in quadam composicione dudum inita atque facta inter bone memorie dominum Johannem de Ely tunc episcopum Norwicensem ex parte una et maiorem et communitatem dicte ville ex altera, et super eo quod ad suggestionem promocionem et excitacionem dictorum burgensium et communitatis prefatus dominus Willelmus episcopus erat per dominum regem et curiam regiam de et super premissis visu hustingo et cognicione placitorum impetitus turbatus inquietatus et graviter molestatus, dictaque visus hustengum et cognicio placitorum ad manum regiam capta et per eam tenta et occupata fuerunt; tandem dictus dominus episcopus obtinuit pro se et succesoribus suis et ecclesia sua Norwicensi dicta[38] visum franciplegii hustengum et cogniciones placitorum per dictum dominum nostrum regem et cartam suam regiam eidem episcopo et successoribus suis restitui dari concedi ac etiam plenarie confirmari perpetuis temporibus duraturis, prout in carta predicta plenius continetur.

Occasione igitur postmodum premissorum inter partes predictas rancoribus[39] dissensionibus et questionibus variis suscitatis; finaliter annuente pacis auctore est super premissis et eorum singulis inter eos taliter compositum consensum et unanimiter concordatum [est] quod dicti maior communitas et burgenses pro se et communitate ac successoribus eorum promiserunt quod nunquam decetero inquietabunt vexabunt nec molestabunt per se nec per alios publice nec occulte prefatum dominum episcopum nec aliquem de successoribus suis episcopis Norwicensibus super premissis visu franciplegii hustengo aut cognicione placitorum nec super aliquo iure libertate dominio articulo commodo seu proficuo contentis seu quocumque modo descriptis in dictis composicione et carta regia nec super aliquo premissorum neque quovismodo occasione premissorum, nec ad impediendum turbandum seu molestandum aliquem episcoporum super premissis vel aliquo premissorum dabunt auxilium consilium vel favorem publice nec occulte.

Et licet maior et communitas predicti per scriptum suum obligatorium sigillo communitatis sigillatum teneantur predicto domino episcopo et successoribus suis episcopis Norwicensibus in quingentis marcis sterlingorum prout in scripto obligatorio predicto contineatur; voluit tamen et concessit predictus dominus episcopus pro se et succesoribus suis quod quamdiu nec ipse nec aliquis successorum suorum fuerit inquietatus turbatus vel molestatus super [fo.13] premissis aut aliquis premissorum seu eorum occasione per ipsos burgenses aut communitatem aut per aliquam singularem personam communitatis predicte aut per alium seu alios eorum aut alicuius eorum nomine procuracione aut excitacione, tam diu dicta obligacio remaneat in suspenso et nulla penitus inde fiet execucio quovismodo.

Si autem contigerit quod absit quod prefatus dominus episcopus aut aliquis successorum suorum fuerit super premissis aut eorum aliquo aut eorum occasione per burgenses [aut] communitatem dicte ville qui pro tempore fuerint

---

[38] MS. *dictam*
[39] MS. *ranicoribus*

aut per alios eorum nomine ad instanciam procuracionem aut excitacionem eorum publicam vel occultam dumtamen super hoc probabiliter poterint[40] convinci, aut etiam per aliquam singularem personam communitatis ville predicti vel alium eius nomine mandato aut procuracione publica vel occulta dumtamen super hoc probabiliter poterit convinci, nisi dicta persona singularis dicte communitatis fuerit per burgenses et communitatem dicte ville abiudicatus et expulsus pro suo perpetuo ab omni iure commodo proficuo et libertate dicte communitatis et ville infra tres menses a die qua maior et communitas dicte ville per episcopum Norwicensem qui pro tempore fuerit aut per senescallum suum ville sue Lenn predicte seu alium eius nomine specialem ad hoc potestatem habentem fuerint requisiti, dicta summa quingentarum marcarum plenarie et incommutabiliter incurratur, et extunc liceat episcopo qui tunc fuerit et successoribus suis episcopis Norwicensibus dictam pecunie summam in virtute et iuxta formam dicti scripti obligatorii libere exigere et exigi facere et levare. In cuius rei testimonium huic parti indenture penes dictum dominum episcopum remanenti dicti maior et communitas sigillum commune dicte ville apposuerunt. Datum apud Lenn die Lune proximo post festum Sancti Tiburtii martiris anno domini MCCCLII et anno regni Regis Edwardi tercii post conquestum vicesimo sexto.

33

[fo.13] INDENTURA[41] COMPOSICIONIS FACTE SUPER CREATIONE MAIORIS LENN.[42] Hec indentura testatur quod cum orta fuisset pridem materia contencionis et discordie inter reverendum in Christo patrem dominum Willelmum de Norwico dei gratia Norwicensem episcopum dominum burgi seu ville Lenn ex parte una, et burgenses ac communitatem dicte ville sue Lenn ex altera super creatione maioris dicte ville, prefato domino episcopo pro se et ecclesia sua Norwicensi asserente quod nullus debet creari in maiorem dicte ville per electionem burgensium dicte ville set quod ad dictum dominum episcopum tanquam ad dominum dicte ville et predecessores suos episcopos Norwicenses ut dominos dicte ville pro temporibus iure ecclesie Norwicensis pertinuit et pertinet libere ordinare ponere et constituere unum prepositum quem duxerit eligendum qui regimen habere debet dicte ville et excercitium iusticie et iurisdictionis in dicta villa ac omnia excercere que ad maioratus officium haberent de consuetudine pertinere, burgensibus et communitate contrarium asserentibus; tandem annuente pacis auctore est inter eos taliter compositum consensum et unanimiter concordatum, videlicet quod dictus episcopus cum consensu capituli sui concessit de sua gratia speciali pro se et successoribus suis burgensibus et communitati ville sue Lenn predicte quod exnunc imperpetuum possunt burgenses dicte ville singulis annis eligere aliquem de suis comburgensibus in maiorem loco prepositi dicte ville; ita tamen quod quilibet maior singulis annis ut premittitur electus in dicta villa et iuratus presentetur apud Geywode per aliquos comburgenses domino episcopo

---

[40] MS. *poterunt*
[41] Followed by *FACTA*, cancelled.
[42] There is also a marginal heading *Lenn*.

Norwicensi qui pro tempore fuerit tanquam domino dicti burgi seu ville prima vice qua ipsum contigerit ad manerium suum de Geywode iuxta Lenniam declinare, vel eo absente presentetur apud Geywode senescallo suo maiori [fo.13^v] baronie seu senescallo suo Lenn aut officialem Lenn specialem ad hoc potestatem habenti infra tres dies a tempore quo prefatus maior electus et iuratus qui pro tempore fuerit verbo vel litteris per aliquem dictorum senescallorum aut officialis premunitus, quodque maior quiscumque electus iuratus et presentatus ut premittitur domino episcopo qui pro tempore fuerit seu alteri ut premittitur deputato promittet in manu prefati episcopi seu alicuius deputatorum predictorum fide media quod omnia et singula que ad officium maioratus pertinent diligenter faciet et fideliter observabit et quod omnia iura et libertates ecclesie Norwicensis quantum in eo fuerit illesa integraliter conservabit. In cuius rei testimonium huic parti indenture penes dictum dominum episcopum remanenti dicti maior et communitas sigillum commune dicte ville apposuerunt. Datum apud Lenn die Lune proximo post festum Sancti Tyburtii martiris anno domini MCCCLII et anno regni Regis Edwardi tercii post conquestum vicesimo sexto.

59

[fo.41^v] SOUTHELMHAM SANCTI PETRI. Secundo die mensis Martii anno domini MCCCXLIII London in hospicio domini .. episcopi[43] Johannes Bynch presbiter institutus fuit canonice per predictum dominum .. electum confirmatum in ecclesia parochiali Sancti Petri de Southelmham Norwicensis diocesis per liberam resignacionem domini Ricardi de Usflet ultimi rectoris eiusdem ex causa permutacionis per eundem Ricardum de dicta ecclesia cum prefato Johanne de vicaria ecclesie parochialis de Gayselee dicte diocesis, cuius vicarius extiterat, certis et legitimis ex causis per prefatum dominum .. electum examinatis discussis et approbatis rite et legitime factam vacante, ad presentacionem excellentissimi principis domini Edwardi dei gratia regis Anglie et Francie illustris hac vice patroni dicte ecclesie, ratione temporalium episcopatus Norwicensis nuper vacantis per obitum bone memorie domini Antonii quondam episcopi Norwicensis in manu dicti domini regis pro tunc existentium.

60

[fo.41^v] VICARIA DE GAYSELEE. Eisdem vero die mense anno et loco predictus Ricardus de Usflet presbiter institutus fuit canonice per predictum dominum .. electum confirmatum in dicta vicaria ecclesie parochialis de Gayselee per liberam resignacionem predicti Johannis Bynch ultimi vicarii eiusdem ex causa permutacionis predicte facte vacante, prestito per ipsum Ricardum iuramento de residencia facienda in eadem vicaria iuxta formam constitucionum Otonis et Ottoboni quondam in Anglia .. legatorum in hac parte editarum, ad presentacionem dicti domini .. regis hac vice patroni dicte

---

[43] Followed by a blank about nine letters in length.

vicarie ratione temporalium prioratus de Stok iuxta Clare occasione guerre mote inter ipsum dominum regem et illos de Francia in manu sua existentium.

61

[fo.41^v] POTESTAS .. PRIORIS NORWIC' .. VICARII GENERALIS. Tenor commissionis facte .. Priori ecclesie Norwicensis sequitur in hec verba: Willelmus permissione divina electus Norwicensis ecclesie confirmatus dilecto in Christo religioso viro Fratri Willelmo ecclesie nostre predicte .. priori salutem in salutis auctore. Quia cure et solicitudini in nostra diocesi Norwicensi excercendis arduis ac variis negotiis occupati personaliter vacare non possumus de presenti, vos de cuius legalitate ab experto confidimus vicarium nostrum generalem in spiritualibus et temporalibus constituimus per presentes, vobis in hac parte vices nostras specialiter committentes, cum potestate corrigendi excessus crimina subditorum, omniaque cetera jurisdictionis capitula excercenda ac cum cuiuscumque canonice cohercionis potestate.

Damus etiam vobis et concedimus potestatem generalem et mandatum speciale .. officiales .. commissarios clericos seneschallos ballivos et ministros quoscumque, tam in temporalibus quam in spiritualibus nobis necessarios, ponendi creandi et preficiendi, et ipsos et eorum singulos quotiens et quando vobis videbitur expediens removendi, et alios loco ipsorum subrogandi; proviso quod omnes et singuli .. officiales .. commissarii clerici seneschalli ballivi et ministri prefecti et preficiendi, tactis sacrosanctis evangeliis, corporale in ipsorum prefectione prestent in manibus vestris iuramentum quod nichil ad eorum vel suorum utilitatem seu comodum a quocumque occasione seu causa officii eorum ultra stipendia seu salaria taxanda seu consueta recipiant vel admittent, esculentis et poculentis parvi seu moderati valoris iuxta personarum qualitatem dumtaxat exceptis. Datum London sub sigillo quo utimur in presenti quarto idus Marcii anno domini MCCCXLIII.

62

[fo.41^v] SUBYR' SANCTI GREGORII CUM CAPELLA SANCTI PETRI. Die [......] mensis Martii anno domini MCCCXLIII Norwic' Henricus de Caumpeden presbiter institutus fuit canonice per venerabilem et religiosum virum Fratrem Willelmum de Claxton .. priorem ecclesie cathedralis Sancte Trinitatis Norwic' predicti domini .. electi vicarium ut premittitur generalem in ecclesia parochiali Sancti Gregorii cum capella Sancti Petri de Subyria vacante, ad presentacionem religiosarum mulierum .. priorisse et conventus de Nunne Eton ordinis Fontis Ebraudi Conventrensis et Lichfeldensis diocesis patronarum eiusdem ecclesie, ad nominacionem excellentissimi principis domini Edwardi dei gratia regis Anglie et Francie illustris, ratione temporalium episcopatus Norwicensis pridem vacantis et in manu dicti domini regis pro tunc existentium, quam quidem nominacionem predictus dominus .. electus confirmatus secundo die mensis Martii anno domini supradicto London ex certa scientia ratificavit et approbavit eo quod nominacio ad dictam ecclesiam in singulis vacacionibus eiusdem ad .. episcopum Norwicensem qui pro tempore fuerit dinoscitur pertinere.

63

[fo. 42] SISELOND. Die vicesimo tercio mensis Martii anno domini MCCCXLIII apud Norwicum Johannes Cavel acolitus institutus fuit canonice per predictum dominum vicarium generalem in ecclesia parochiali de Siselond vacante, ad presentacionem Walteri Cavel veri patroni eiusdem.

64

[fo. 42] MEDIETAS ECCLESIE DE RYNGESTEDE PARVA. Die xxvii mensis Martii anno domini MCCCXLIIII Norwic' Robertus de Caldewelle presbiter institutus fuit canonice per dictum dominum vicarium generalem in medietate ecclesie de Ryngestede Parva, per liberam resignacionem domini Thome Forester ultimi rectoris eiusdem ex causa permutacionis per eundem Thomam de dicta medietate ecclesie prefate, cum predicto Roberto de ecclesia parochiali de Thorp Parva, cuius rector extiterat, certis et legitimis ex causis per ipsum dominum vicarium generalem examinatis discussis et approbatis, rite et legitime facte vacante, ad presentacionem domine Elizabeth de Burgo domine de Clare patrone eiusdem medietatis ecclesie supradicte.

65

[fo. 42] THORP PARVA. Eisdem vero mense die anno et loco prefatus Thomas Forester presbiter institutus fuit canonice per dictum dominum vicarium generalem in predicta ecclesia de Thorp Parva per liberam resignacionem predicti Roberti de Caldewelle ultimi rectoris eiusdem ex causa permutacionis predicte facte vacante, ad presentacionem Kateryne de Neketon patrone eiusdem.

66

[fo. 42] WALSOKNE. Venerabili in Christo patri domino Willelmo dei gratia electo Norwicensis ecclesie confirmato Simon eiusdem permissione Eliensis episcopus salutem et fraternam in domino caritatem. Paternitatis vestre litteras recepimus in hec verba.

Venerabili in Christo patri domino .. dei gratia episcopo Eliensi Willelmus permissione divina electus Norwicensis ecclesie confirmatus salutem et mutuam in domino caritatem. Ad recipiendum resignacionem discreti viri domini Bartholomei de Bourne rectoris ecclesie de Walsokne nostre diocesis de ecclesia sua predicta quam permutare intendit ut asserit cum ecclesia de Hadenham vestre diocesis, quam obtinet de presenti venerabilis vir dominus Thomas de Hatfeld et ad consentiendum permutacioni huiusmodi, si ea ex causis legitimis vobis videbitur facienda ac etiam instituendum dictum dominum Thomam in ecclesia de Walsokne predicta, et omnia alia et singula facienda que in huiusmodi permutacionis negocio necessaria fuerint vel etiam oportuna quantum ad nos pertinet, salva nobis vel vicariis nostris inductione corporali, vobis committimus vices nostras. Datum apud Dovorr' undecimo die mensis Martii anno domini MCCCXLIII.

Nos igitur commissionem vestram predictam mutua vicissitudine amplectentes, auditis examinatis et discussis causis nobis expositis dicte permutacionis quas veras et legitimas comperimus ad permutacionem huiusmodi faciendam et etiam approbavimus iustitia suadente, examinata inquisitione per .. officialem domini archidiaconi Norwicensis nobis in hac parte directa, concurrentibus etiam omnibus et singulis que in hac parte requiruntur de iure, auctoritate vestri predicta dominum Thomam predictum ad ecclesiam de Walsokne predicta vestre diocesis resignacione domini Bartholomei de Bourne nuper rectoris eiusdem ratione permutacionis huiusmodi et dicte commissionis obtentu per nos legitime acceptata in forma iuris admisimus, et virtute permutacionis predicte rectorem canonice instituimus in eadem, reservatis vobis omnibus que in eisdem commissionis vestre litteris reservantur. Ad ecclesie sue sancte regimen vitam vestram conservare dignetur incolumem misericordia redemptoris. Datum apud Dounham tercio die mensis Aprilis, anno domini MCCCXLIIII^{to}.

MEMORANDUM DE OBEDIENCIA PREFECTA PRO EADEM. Postmodum vero iiii^{to} die mensis Aprilis anno domini MCCCXLIIII^{to} apud Norwicum predictus dominus vicarius generalis scripsit .. archidiacono Norwicensi vel eius .. officiali ad inducendum ipsum dominum Thomam vel procuratorem suum in corporalem possessionem dicte ecclesie de Walsokne, et ad recipiendum ab eo canonicam obedienciam. Et Thomas Attefen procurator dicti domini Thomas ad hoc legitime deputatus promisit obedienciam canonicam dicto domino electo confirmato et successoribus suis, prout in litteris patentibus sigillo officialis dicti domini .. archidiaconi signatis penes registrum residentibus continetur.

67

[fo.42] VICARIA DE BRANDESTON'. Terciodecimo die mensis Aprilis anno domini MCCCXLIIII Norwic' Edmundus Wymark de Burnedissh presbiter institutus fuit canonice per dictum dominum vicarium generalem in vicaria ecclesie de Brandeston vacante, ad presentacionem religiosorum virorum .. prioris et confratrum de Wodebrigg [fo.42^{v}] verorum eiusdem vicarie patronorum; recepto primitus ab eodem corporali iuramento de personaliter residencia in dicta vicaria facienda iuxta formam constitucionum Ottonis et Ottoboni quondam in Anglia legatorum in hac parte editarum.

69

[fo.42^{v}] HAVERHULL'. Eisdem anno mense die et loco Thomas Byman de Freton institutus fuit canonice in ecclesia parochiali de Haverill et capella eidem

annexa per dictum vicarium generalem per liberam resignacionem domini
Edmundi de Kettelbergh ultimi rectoris eiusdem ex causa permutacionis per
eundem dominum Edmundum de dicta ecclesia de Haverhull et capella eidem
annexa cum ecclesia parochiali de Drencheston predicta cuius prefatus Thomas
rector exstiterat, certis et legitimis ex causis per dictum dominum vicarium
generalem examinatis discussis et approbatis rite et legitime facte vacante, ad
presentacionem nobilis viri domini Johannis comitis Warenn veri ecclesie de
Haverhull et capelle predictarum hac vice patroni ratione advocacionum
ecclesiarum vacancium spectantium ad priorem et conventum de Castelacre
in manu eiusdem comitis hac vice existent, ex concessione domini regis Anglie
illustris, et iuravit obedienciam.

70

[fo.42^v] ESTON BAVENT. Vicesimoseptimo die dicti mensis Aprilis anno et
loco predictis per dictum vicarium generalem Symon Deneys presbiter canonice
institutus fuit in ecclesia parochiali de Eston Bavent vacante ad presentacionem
Willelmi Bavent veri eiusdem ecclesie patroni et iuravit obedienciam.

96

[fo.45] PREFECTIO PRIORIS DE BROMHIL'. Die viii dicti mensis Augusti
anno domini MCCCXLIIII in ecclesia parochiali de Methelwold Frater
Thomas de Saham canonicus regularis [prioratus] de Bromhil per mortem
Fratris Johannis de Welle ultimi prioris eiusdem vacantis ad regimen dicte
domus concorditer electus et in ipsa domo ordinem regularem Sancti Augustini
professus et presbiter, observato iuris ordine qua requiritur in hac parte,
confirmataque electione de ipso Fratre Thoma de Saham ut premittitur facta
per venerabilem et discretum dominum Magistrum Thomam de Methelwolde
iuris civilis professorem rectorem ecclesie Omnium Sanctorum de Wetingg
Norwicensis diocesis (per venerabilem et religiosum virum Fratrem Willelmum
de Claxton priorem ecclesie cathedralis Norwicensis venerabilis patris domini
Willelmi dei gratia Norwicensis episcopi vicarium in spiritualibus generalis
commissarium in hac parte specialiter deputatum) in priorem dicte domus
canonice fuit prefectus. Idemque Magister Thomas curam et administracionem
spiritualium et temporalium eiusdem prioratus ibidem sibi commisit et iuravit
obedienciam canonicam eidem patri et successoribus suis ut est moris. Et
scriptum fuit ad installandum eum archidiacono Norffolc vel eius officiali.
Tenor commissionis de qua superius fit mentio sequitur in hec verba.

102

[fo.45^v] PREFECTIO PRIORIS NORWICENS'. Die xxv^{to} mensis Augusti
anno domini MCCCXLIIII in capella palacii episcopalis apud Norwicum
Frater Symon Bozoun monachus ecclesie cathedralis Sancte Trinitatis
Norwic' presbiter in dicta ecclesia ordinem regularem Sancti Benedicti expresse

professus in priorem dicte ecclesie cathedralis per mortem bone memorie Fratris Willelmi de Claxton ultimi prioris eiusdem prioris solacio destitute per .. suppriorem et capitulum dicte ecclesie concorditer electus, confirmata electione de ipso facta, concurrentibusque omnibus et singulis que in ea parte requirebantur canonice prefectus fuit in priorem dicte ecclesie per prefatum Magistrum Hamonem vicarium generalem predictum, et commisit eidem curam et administracionem spiritualium et temporalium eiusdem prioratus cum suis iuribus et pertinentiis universis ac de gratia sua speciali ea vice commisit vices suas Fratri Rogero de Eston monacho dicte ecclesie ad installandum dictum priorem in prioratu predicto prout moris est, per suas certi tenoris litteras quarum tenor in certificatorio dicti Fratris Rogeri de Eston de verbo ad verba continetur. Prefatus[44] quoque prior sic prefectus iuravit obedienciam canonicam dicto domino .. episcopo et successoribus suis canonice intrantibus ac ministris eorumdem.

Tenor vero certificatorii de quo superius fit mentio talis est. Reverendo discrecionis viro Magistro Hamoni Belers canonico ecclesie Lincolniensis reverendi patris domini Willelmi dei gratia Norwicensis episcopi in remotis agentis vicario in spiritualibus et temporalibus generalis suus humilis et devotus Frater Rogerus de Eston monachus ecclesie cathedralis Norwicensis obedienciam reverenciam pariter et honorem. Mandatum vestrum in hec verba recepi:

Hamo[45] Belers canonicus ecclesie Lincolniensis reverendi patris domini Willelmi dei gratia Norwicensis episcopi in remotis agentis vicarius in spiritualibus et temporalibus generalis dilecto nobis in Christo Fratri Rogero de Eston monacho ecclesie Norwicensis salutem in amplexibus salvatoris. Quia nos religiosum virum Fratrem Symonem Bozoun confratrem et conmonachum dicte ecclesie presbiterum in dicta ecclesia ordinem regularem Sancti Benedicti expresse professum per suppriorem et capitulum dicte ecclesie in priorem prioratus eiusdem ecclesie per mortem bone memorie Fratris Willelmi de Claxton ultimi prioris eiusdem vacantis electum, confirmata per nos electione de ipso Fratre Symone rite facta, observato iuris ordine qui requiritur in hac parte, auctoritate dicti patris in priorem dicte ecclesie prefecimus iustitia suadente, administracionem spiritualium et temporalium eiusdem prioratus eidem plenarie committentes; vobis hac vice de gratia nostra speciali committimus et mandamus quatinus dictum Fratrem Simonem in dicta ecclesia iuxta iuris exigenciam vice et auctoritate dicti patris canonice installetis et faciatis in omnibus quod incumbat. Ita tamen quod occasione istius commissionis seu cuiuscumque alterius preterite pro tempore preterito seu futuro capitulum Norwicense nullatenus in huiusmodi installacione in futurum facienda [fo.46] possit vindicare,[46] sed liceat dicto domino .. episcopo et cuicumque .. episcopo futuro officium installandi priorem pro tempore cuicumque voluerit pro sue libito voluntatis. Et quid feceritis in premissis nos citra festum Sancti Egidii abbatis proximo futurum distincte et aperte certificetis per litteras vestras patentes harum seriem continentes sigillo communi dicti capituli consignatas.

---

[44] In the margin here the scribe (S8) noted, *Memorandum de obediencie prestacione*
[45] In the margin here the scribe (S8) noted, *Memorandum de installacione eiusdem in* [indecipherable] *forma*
[46] MS. *vendicare*

Datum Norwic' sub sigillo quo in huiusmodi vicariatus officio utimur xxv^{to} die mensis Augusti anno domini MCCCXLIIII.

Cuius[47] auctoritate mandati prefatum Fratrem Symonem priorem prioratus predicti in dicta ecclesia vice et auctoritate dicti patris canonice installavi et feci in omnibus quod in ea parte fieri incumbebat. Et sic mandatum vestrum secundum omnem sui formam et tenorem in omnibus reverenter sum executus. In cuius rei testimonium has litteras meas sigillo communi dicti capituli consignatas vobis transmitto patentes. Datum Norwic' xxvii die dicti mensis Augusti anno domini supradicto.

107

[fo.46^{v}] TUNSTED CUM CAPELLA DE RYSTON AB EADEM DEPEN-DENTE. Eisdem vero mense die anno et loco Magister Symon de Brusele clericus institutus fuit canonice per dictum dominum vicarium generalem in ecclesia parochiali de Tunsted *cum capella de Riston ab eadem dependente*[48] per liberam resignacionem Roberti Parsone ultimi rectoris eiusdem vacante, ad presentacionem domini Johannis Stroth militis veri eiusdem ecclesie cum capella patroni.

113

[fo.47] PREBENDA PRECENTORIE IN CAPELLA COLLEGIATA BEATE MARIE IN CAMPIS IN NORWICO. Die xix mensis Octobris anno domini supradicto apud Norwicum prefatus vicarius generalis contulit prebendam precentorie in capella collegiata Beate Marie in Campis in Norwico per liberam resignacionem Magistri Stephani de Catton clerici procuratoris Walteri de Pappeworth ultimi prebendarii eiusdem sufficientem potestatem in ea parte a dicto Waltero optinentis vacantem et ad dicti domini Norwicensis episcopi collacione pleno iure spectantem cum omnibus suis iuribus et pertinentiis universis Roberto de Redegrave presbitero intuitu caritatis, et scriptum fuit decano dicte capelle ad installandum prout moris est.

127

[fo.48] DECANATUS DE HENGHAM. Die xviii mensis Novembris Anno domini supradicto apud Norwicum prefatus dominus vicarius generalis vice et auctoritate domini Norwicensis episcopi contulit decanatum de Hengham vacantem ad dicti patris collacionem pleno iure spectantem cum omnibus suis iuribus et pertinenciis universis Henrico filio Willelmi de Wynterton clerico intuitu caritatis, et scriptum fuit universis abbatibus prioribus rectoribus vicariis

---

[47] In the margin here the scribe (S8) noted, *Memorandum de communi Sigillo Capituli apposito certificatorio installationis*

[48] The clause in italics was written at the end of the entry by the scribe (S8), and marked for insertion here.

et capellanis parochianis per dictum decanatum constitutis ad inducendum et intendendum prout moris est.

169

[fo.50ᵛ] COLLACIO CAPELLE SANCTI EDMUNDI GIPPEWIC'. Willelmus permissione divina Norwicensis episcopus dilecto filio Ricardo le Clerc' de Lexham presbitero salutem gratiam et benedictionem. Capellam Sancti Edmundi de Gippewic' nostre diocesis vacantem et ad nostram collacionem pleno iure spectantem cum omnibus suis iuribus et pertinenciis universis tibi conferimus intuitu caritatis et te capellanum perpetuum cum onere quod eidem incumbit canonice instituimus in eadem, salvis et cetera. Datum apud Baketon xvii die mensis Julii anno domini MCCCXLV et consecracionis nostre secundo.

174

[fo.51] VICARIA DE RUGHTON'. Die xvj mensis Augusti anno domini MCCCXLV apud Terlyngg, Richardus Wade de Norton presbiter institutus fuit canonice per dictum patrem in vicaria ecclesie de Rughton vacante, salvo iure cuiuscumque provisoris apostolici, si quod in dicta vicaria quis habuerit vel ad eam, recepto ab ipso iuramento[1] de personali residencia in dicta vicaria continue facienda iuxta formam constitucionum legatorum in Anglia in hac parte editarum, ad presentacionem priorisse et conventus de Bungeye verarum eiusdem vicarie patronarum.

175

[fo.51] HOSPITALE BEATE MARIE MAGDALEN' IUXTA NORWICUM. Die xxxj mensis Augusti Anno supradicto apud Hoxne dominus episcopus contulit Hospitale Sancte Marie Magdalene iuxta Norwicum per liberam resignacionem Johannis de Bromholm ultimi custodis eiusdem ex causa permutacionis per eundem Johannem de dicto hospitali cum Rogero de Naffreton de ecclesia de Framingham Comitis, cuius rector extiterat, certis et legitimis ex causis per ipsum patrem examinatis discussis et approbatis rite et legitime facte vacans et ad dicti patris collacionem pleno iure spectans prefato Rogero de Naffreton presbitero ex causa dicte permutacionis cum omnibus suis iuribus et pertinenciis universis una cum gubernacione eiusdem et adminis- tracione spiritualium et temporalium eiusdem iuxta tenorem constitucionis Clementis pape quinti que incipit, Quia contingit, et recepto ab ipso Rogero iuramento in hac parte de iure debito et consueto, ipsum in dicti hospitalis custodem canonice prefecit.

---

[1] MS. repeats *iuramento*

187

[fo.51ᵛ] PRIORATUS DE ALNESBOURN. Die vero mense et anno predictis in domo capitulari prioratus de Alnesburn per mortem Johannis de Stok ultimi prioris eiusdem tunc vacantis dominus episcopus[2] suplevit omnem defectum[3] electionis de Fratre Johanne de Fynyngham per concanonicos dicte domus facte que peccavit in materia et in forma, et iure suo providit dicto Johanni de Fynyngham de dicto prioratu et ipsum in priorem eiusdem canonice prefecit, et commisit ei administracionem spiritualium et temporalium eiusdem domus et ipsum per venerabilem virum Magistrum Hamonem Belers cancellarium suum ibidem presentem in dicto prioratu fecit prout moris est installari.

205

[fo.53] VICARIA DE HELGHETON'. [*Royal letter of presentation to Helhoughton vicarage, contained within this entry.*] TENOR PRESENTACIONIS DOMINI REGIS SUPER EADEM. Edwardus dei gratia rex Anglie et Francie et dominus Hibernie venerabili in Christo patri .W. eadem gratia episcopo Norwicen' salutem. Ad vicariam ecclesie de Helgheton vestre diocesis vacantem, ad quam habetis nobis ut dicitur nominare personam per nos vobis ulterius ratione temporalium prioratus Sancte Fidis de Horsham in manu nostra occasione guerre inter nos et adversarios nostros Francie mote existencium [iurem] presentandi, Johannem de Bodeneye capellanum nobis per vos ad vicariam predictam ex causa predicta nominatum vobis presentamus intuitu caritatis, rogantes quatinus ipsum Johannem ad vicariam illam admittatis et vicarium instituatis in eadem. In cuius rei testimonium has litteras nostras fieri fecimus patentes. Teste meipso apud Westmonasterium xii die Martii anno regni nostri Anglie vicesimo regni vero nostri Francie septimo.

300

[f.61ᵛ] COLLACIO ARCHIDIACONATUS SUFF'. Die tercio mensis Maii anno et loco predictis prefatus dominus .. episcopus contulit archidiaconatum Suff' vacantem cum omnibus suis iuribus et pertinentiis universis Magistro Ricardo de Lyng' rectori ecclesie de Redham sacre pagine professori intuitu caritatis et ipsum per birreti sui tradicionem canonice vestivit de eodem.

---

[2] Interlined by the scribe of this entry.
[3] Interlined by the scribe of this entry.

309

[Interleaved between ff.61ᵛ–62] UNIO PORCIONUM IN ECCLESIA DE BIKERESTON.[4] Nos Willelmus permissione divina Norwicensis episcopus, duas porciones in ecclesia parochiali de Bykereston nostre diocesis propter earum exilitatem et ex aliis causis coram nobis plene discussis et compertis, decernentes illas duas porciones unicum beneficium fore et decetero reputari et per unicum rectorem amodo cedente vel decendente altero rectorum porcionariorum regi volumus et gubernari, volumus tamen quod cuilibet rectori dum vixerit in forma qua prius liceat suam ecclesiam retinere et fructus libere percipere de eadem. Actis quintadecima die Aprilis anno domini MCCCXLVII in prioratu Norwicensi.

355

[fo.66] PRIORATUS DE ROMBURGH'. [*Closed letter from the abbot of St Mary's Abbey, York, contained within this entry.*] PRESENTACIO PRO EODEM. Venerabili in Christo patri et domino domino Willelmo dei gratia Norwicen' episcopo suus humilis et devotus Thomas permissione divina abbas monasterii Beate Marie Eboracensis salutem et reverenciam tanto patri debitas cum honore. Cum nos Fratrem Allexium de Wath nuper priorem celle nostre de Romeburgh vestre diocesis ex causis certis et honestis domu duxerimus revocandum ac Fratrem Ricardum de Burton comonachum nostrum regimini[5] dicti prioratus quem ad hoc utilem et idoneum reputamus loco dicti Fratris Alexi prefecerimus in priorem, ipsum Fratrem Ricardum priorem vestre paternitati presentamus humiliter supplicantes quatenus eundem Fratrem Ricardum ex affectu paterno dignemini sic fovere ut a deo premium et a nobis exinde vobis impendatur debita solucio gracia. Valeat vestra reverenda paternitas per tempora longiora. Datum apud Eboracum in monasterio nostro predicto vicesimo octavo die mensis Decembris anno domini MCCCXLVII.

378

[fo.67ᵛ] Die xxii mensis Marcii anno domini MCCCXLVII apud Norwic', vacantibus vicariis ecclesie de[6] Holkham per liberas puras et simplices[7] resignaciones dominorum . . .[8] et Stephani Heryng ultimorum vicariorum earumdem in sacras manus dicti venerabilis patris simpliciter factas, idem dominus et venerabilis pater dictas resignaciones admisit et alteram vicariarum

---

[4] This entry is found on a slip of parchment which measures 26.9 cm wide and 8.5 cm high, bound into the gathering between ff.61ᵛ and 62, facing f.62. The heading is centered.

[5] MS. *regiminn*

[6] *Vacantibus vicariis ecclesie de* written over an erasure.

[7] Interlined from *puras*

[8] Left blank.

predictarum alteri annexuit[9] et univit, ita ut decetero unica vicaria habeantur, et per unicum vicarium gubernetur. Et subsequenter prefato[10] domino Stephano[11] vicariam antedictam contulit et ipsum nominavit ad eandem et in eadem instituit, recepto ab eo iuramento de corporali residencia in eadem facienda iuxta formam constitucionum Othonis et Ottoboni in Anglia legatorum in hac parte editarum.

379

[fo.68] PETRESTR'. Die xviii mensis Marcii anno domini MCCCXLVII apud Norwicum Robertus Edrich presbiter institutus fuit canonice per dictum patrem in ecclesia parochiali de Petrestre vacante ad presentacionem domini Edwardi regis Anglie veri eiusdem ecclesie ratione minoris etatis filii et heredis Rogeri de Huntyngfeld militis defuncti in custodia dicti domini existentis hac vice patroni. Tenor vero revocacionis regie domino .W. episcopo Norwicensi in hac parte directe sequitur in hec verba.

[Letter of Edward III revoking an earlier presentation of his clerk, Roger de Chestrefeld (incomplete).]

413

[fo.70ᵛ] COMMISSIO FACTA PER DICTUM PATREM MAGISTRO PETRO DE NORMANDEBY AD EXCERCENDUM JURISDICTIONEM ARCHIDIACONALEM IN ARCHIDIACONATU NORWICI. Willelmus permissione divina Norwicensis .. episcopus dilecto filio Magistro Petro de Normandeby rectori ecclesie de Burghcastr' nostre diocesis salutem gratiam et benedictionem. Licet ad nos, tam ex commisso nobis presulatus officio quam a sacrorum canonum tradicionibus, quorumcumque subditorum nostrorum nostre diocesis immediate pertineant cura et regimen animarum, de et pro quibus etiam in extremo tenemur examine respondere, fuerintque et sint archidiaconi in partem sollicitudinis pontificibus subrogati,[12] qui velud eorum occuli et vicarii loca suorum archidiaconatuum circuire debeant et ecclesias ac capellas visitare, populumque errantem corrigere et punire et fructum boni operis seminare. Fama tamen per archidiaconatum Norwicensem diu et noviter pululante fidedignisque relacionibus nobis constat quod Magister Hamo Belers archidiaconus eiusdem archidiaconatus curam et regimen eiusdem longius retro temporibus neglexit et negligit de presenti propter quamdam controversiam de dicto archidiaconatu motam, ac de dicto archidiaconatu[13] eiusque iuribus et pertinentiis se nullatenus intromisit nec curat intromittere hiis diebus, propter quod dicti archidiaconatus iura depereunt ac insolencie et vicia in eodem plus solito committuntur.

---

[9] Written over an erasure.
[10] Written over an erasure.
[11] *Ad* has been scraped out between *Stephano* and *vicariam*
[12] Corrected from *subrogari*
[13] MS. *motam ac de dicto Archidiaconatu* written over an erasure.

Nos vero premissa debite intuentes et ipsius Magistri Hamonis negligenciam suplentes, ad visitandum omnes et singulas parochias ecclesias et capellas dicti archidiaconatus quas archidiaconus dicti loci visitare consueverat de consuetudine vel de iure et in eis visitacionis archidiaconalis officium libere excercendum, necnon ad inquirendum prout hactenus inquiri consuevit de et super excessibus criminibus et delictis quorumcumque infra dictum archidiaconatum delinquencium, eosque et eorum excessus crimina et delicta huiusmodi corrigenda punienda et canonice reformanda, testamenta quoque sive ultimas voluntates quorumcumque decedencium infra archidiaconatum predictum, quorum probacio et approbacio ad eiusdem loci archidiaconum pertinent de consuetudine vel de iure probande approbande et infirmande, administraciones bonorum committendas et administratores bonorum quitantes et absolvendos, fructus redditus proventus et iura dicti archidiaconatus ratione visitacionis et alia qualitercumque dicto archidiaconatui debita petenda exigenda colligenda levanda et recipienda ac iuxta disposicionem nostram salvo custodienda, ceteraque omnia et singula facienda gerenda exequenda excercenda et expedienda que in premissis et circa ea necessaria fuerint seu oportuna et que ad iurisdictionem archidiaconalem pertinent seu pertinere debent quovismodo, ita tamen quod in preiudicium iurisdictionis nostre ordinarie nichil attemptes, tibi de cuius industria et fidelitate plenam fiduciam obtinemus tenore presentium committimus vices nostras cum cuiuslibet cohercionis canonice potestate donec eas ad nos duxerimus revocandas.

Volumus autem quod sigillo officialitatis dicti archdiaconatus quod tibi tradidimus in officio commissariatus predicti utaris. Protestamur nichilominus quod per premissa non intendimus preiudicare iuribus alicuius, immo volumus fructus redditus proventus et iura predictos ad usus illius ad quem pertinent seu pertinere debent integre conservare. Datum apud South Elmham xii die mensis Augusti anno domini MCCCXLVIII et consecracionis nostre quinto.

419

[fo.71] ANNECTIO VICARIORUM DE HOLKHAM'. Universis sancte matris ecclesie filiis ad quos presentes littere pervenerint Willelmus permissione divina Norwicensis episcopus salutem in domino sempiternam. Nos nuper auctoritate nostra ordinaria ex causis veris utilibus necessariis atque iustis, servatoque iuris ordine qui requiritur in hac parte, redintegravimus et univimus medietatem ecclesie de Holkham nostre diocesis religiosis viris abbati et conventui monasterii de Westderham ordinis Premonstratensis dicte nostre diocesis, qui a tempore redintegracionis et unionis prefatarum totam ecclesiam ut iuste et canonice eisdem unitam et appropriatam integre tenuerunt, salvis duabus porcionibus duarum vicariarum quas vicarias ut duo beneficia divisa duo vicarii divisim tenebant temporibus quibus medietatis ecclesie predicte per diversas personas divisim teneri consueverant et haberi vacante insuper altera vicariarum ecclesie predicte, videlicet pro porcione illa quam dictis abbati et conventui redintegravimus et univimus prout vacat etiam de presenti.

Nos considerantes porciones dictarum vicariarum adeo tenues et exiles quod habite et possesse divisim per duos vicarios beneficiatos non sufficerent prout nec sufficere consueverunt[14] quod debitam sustentacionem duorum vicariorum et supportacionem onerum incumbencium duobus divisim vicariis ut prefertur prout per informacionem legitimam nobis factam invenimus luculenter, considera[n]tes insuper unitate ecclesie et beneficii rectorie unici que rectoris eiusdem cui de iure convenientius fore dinoscitur unicum in dicta ecclesia habere vicarium quam plures habere vicarios in unice ecclesie ac unici rectoris cura unica concurrentes, dictam porcionem vicarie iam vacantis porcioni vicarie alterius per dominum Stephanum Heryng' vicarium superstitem iam possesse unimus et annectimus dictasque duas vicarias unimus et eas unam decetero haberi ac reputari decernimus, ac per dictum vicarium ex nunc toto vite sue tempore ut unicum beneficium et extunc dictam vicariam ex dictis duabus porcionibus sit unitam ut unicum beneficium per unicam personam ydoneam in ea canonice instituendam perpetuis temporibus possidendum decernimus per presentes.

Salva[15] et reservata nobis et successoribus nostris nominacione vicarie antedicte sub forma [fo.71^v] quem redintegracionis litteris continetur. Salva etiam nobis taxa dicte vicarie pro ista vacacione nobis integre persolvenda ac primis fructibus dicte vicarie pro singulis vacacionibus in futurum. In quorum omnium testimonium sigillum nostrum presentibus duximus apponendum. Datum Norwic' xxi die mensis Marcii anno domini MCCCXLVII et consecracionis nostre quarto.

424

[fo.72] VICARIA DE SCOTHOWE. Die viii mensis Octobris anno domini supradicto apud Norwicum dominus Willelmus de Berneye presbiter institutus fuit canonice per Magistrum Thomam de Methelwold vicarium dicti patris in spiritualibus[16] generalem in vicaria ecclesie parochialis de Scothowe auctoritate dicti patris noviter creata, recepto ab ipso iuramento de corporali residencia in dicta vicaria continue facienda iuxta formam constitucionum Othonis et Ottoboni quondam apostolice sedis in Anglia legatorum, ad presentacionem abbatis et conventus monasterii Sancti Benedicti de Hulmo iuxta nominacionem dicti patris eisdem .. abbati et conventui primitus[17] factam in hac parte prout moris est, qui quidem dominus Willelmus incontinenti obedienciam canonicam dicto patri iuravit.

462

[fo.75^v] VICARIA DE GORLESTON'. Die vicesima tercia mensis Februarii anno domini supradicto apud Flicham Hugo de la More de Carleton Lincolniensis diocesis presbiter institutus fuit canonice per dictum patrem in vicaria ecclesie parochiali de Gorleston vacante ad presentacionem religio-

---

[14] The MS. reads *consueuerut*.
[15] Corrected from *Saluis*
[16] Interlined from *dicti*
[17] Interlined.

sorum virorum prioris et conventus Sancti Bartholomei de Smethefeld London' eiusdem vicarie patronorum, recepto ab eo iuramento de corporali residencia in dicta vicaria facienda iuxta formam constitucionum dominorum Othonis et Ottoboni quondam apostolice sedis in Anglia legatorum in hac parte editarum.

Willelmus permissione divina Norwicensis episcopus dilecto filio Hugoni de la More de Carleton Lincolniensis diocesis presbitero salutem gratiam et benedictionem. Ad vicariam ecclesie parochiali de Gorleston nostre diocesis vacantem ad quam per religiosos viros priorem et conventum Sancti Bartholomei de Smethefeld London nobis presentatus existis [licet]¹⁸ ad nos pertineat predicte nominacio vicarie, salvo nobis et successoribus nostris iure nominacionis predicte, de gratia nostra speciali te admittimus et te perpetuum vicarium canonice instituimus in eadem, recepto a te iuramento de corporali residencia in eadem facienda iuxta formam constitucionum dominorum Othonis et Ottoboni quondam apostolice sedis in Anglia legatorum in hac parte editarum, salvis in omnibus consuetudinibus episcopalibus et ecclesie nostre Norwicensis iure et dignitate. In cuius rei testimonium has litteras nostras tibi fieri fecimus patentes. Datum apud Flycham xxiii die Februarii anno domini MCCCXLVIII et consecracionis nostre quinto.

734

[fo.91^v] PREFECTIO PRIORISSE DE CARHOWE. Die iiii mensis Julii Anno et loco predictis domina Alicia de Hedersete ecclesie conventualis de Carhowe ordinis Sancti Benedicti monialis expresse professa mulier provida et discreta prefecta fuit canonice per dictum reverendum patrem de gratia sua speciali iuxta electionem de ea canonice factam, et commissa est eadem administracio bonorum spiritualium et temporalium eiusdem quatenus ad dictum patrem atinuit, iure episcopali in omnibus semper salva. Et scripta fuit ad installandam domino Simoni de Babbyngle auctoritate dicti patris.

893

[fo.99^v] VICARIA DE BUNGEYE TRINITATIS. Die xxviii mensis Julii anno et loco predictis dominus contulit vicariam ecclesie parochialis Sancte Trinitatis de Bungeye vacantem et ad collacionem dicti patris pleno iure hac vice spectantam, pro eo quod abbas et conventus de Barlyngges ad dictam vicariam presentare recusarunt iuxta nominacionem eis factam, cum omnibus suis iuribus et pertinenciis universis Rogero Rose de Elyngham capellano intuitu caritatis, recepto ab eo iuramento de corporali residencia in dicta vicaria facienda iuxta formam constitucionum in ea parte editarum.

---

¹⁸ Illegible.

1004

[fo.104ᵛ] PREFECTIO PRIORIS DE LETHERYNGHAM. Die xvi mensis Augusti anno domini supradicto apud Southelmham Frater Rogerus de Huntyngfeld ecclesie conventualis Sancti Petri Gyppewico canonicus regularis professus presbiter prefectus fuit canonice per dictum reverendum patrem in priorem prioratus de Letheryngham per cessionem Fratris Radulphi de Framelyngham ultimi prioris eiusdem vacantis iuxta electionem de eodem ad regimen prioratus predicti unanimiter factam, et comissa fuit eidem administracio bonorum spiritualium et temporalium eiusdem quatenus ad dictum patrem pertinuit, iure et consuetudine episcopalibus in omnibus semper salvis.

1005

[fo.104ᵛ] PREFECTIO PRIORIS DE PENTENEYE. Die xvi mensis Augusti anno et loco predictis Frater Radulphus de Framelyngham ecclesie conventualis Sancti Petri de Gyppewico ordinis Sancti Augustini[19] canonicus regularis professus presbiter dictique prioratus de Letheringham nuper prior translatus fuit per dictum reverendum patrem ad prioratum de Penteneye eiusdem ordinis priore et canonicis ad prioris statum digne eligendis totaliter destitutum, et prefectus fuit per[20] ipsum reverendum patrem in priorem prioratus de Penteneye ex officio debito dicti patris, et comissa fuit ei administracio bonorum spiritualium et temporalium eiusdem quatenus ad dictum patrem pertinuit.

1155

[fo.111ᵛ] COLLACIO SCOLARUM GRAMMATICALIUM NORWICO. Die octava mensis Octobris anno et loco predictis dominus contulit custodiam scolarum grammaticalium Norwico vacantem et ad collacionem dicti patris pleno iure spectantem Magistro Petro Petyt de Herlyngflet intuitu caritatis.

1256

[fo.116] (i) PORINGLOND MAGNA. Die xxvi mensis Novembris anno et loco predictis dominus dispensavit cum Thoma de Mor de Saham diacono super defectu etatis auctoritate sedis apostolice dicto patri pro sexagintis clericis sue diocesis concessa, qui quidem Thomas nondum erat xxiii annorum maior tamen. viginti, deindeque institutus fuit canonice per dictum reverendum patrem in ecclesia parochiali de Poringlond Magna vacante ad presentacionem domine Marie comitisse Norffolc et marescalle Anglie vere eiusdem patrone.

[19] Interlined from *ordinis*
[20] Interlined.

(ii) INSTITUCIO EIUSDEM.[21] Willelmus permissione divina Norwicensis episcopus dilecto filio Thome de Mor de Saham nostre diocesis diacono salutem gratiam et benedictionem. Ad ecclesiam parochialem de Poringlond Magna nostre diocesis vacantem ad quam per dominam Mariam comitissam Norff' et marescallum Anglie nobis presentatus existis, licet nondum viginti trium annorum maior tamen viginti existas iuxta comissam nobis a sede apostolica potestatem sub certa forma prout in litteris nostris inde confectis plenius[22] continetur tecum favorabiliter primitus dispensantes, te admittimus et te rectorem canonice institutimus in eadem, salvis et cetera. Datum apud Thorp xxvi die Novembris anno domini MCCCXLIX et consecracionis nostris sexto.

1267

[fo.116ᵛ] (ii) DISPENSACIO.[23] Ut tu Roberte de Walton accolite qui viginti annorum etatem et ultra habere diceris ad beneficium ecclesiasticum curam etiam animarum habens necnon ad omnes sacros ordines non obstante etatis defectu licite valeas promoveri, nos Willelmus etc. tecum auctoritate apostolica dispensamus, ac ecclesiam parochialem de Thorneg' nostre diocesis vacantem et ad nostram collacionem pleno iure spectantem tibi cum omnibus suis iuribus et pertinenciis universis conferimus intuitu caritatis, salvis etc.

1296

[fo.118ᵛ] BULLA SUPER DISPENSACIONE ETATIS PRO LX CLERICIS CONCESSE. Clemens episcopus servus servorum dei venerabili fratri Willelmo episcopo Norwicensi salutem et apostolicam benedictionem. Ne propter ministrorum carenciam cultus minuatur divinus seu animarum cura vel regimen negligatur eiusdem, libenter apostolici favoris presidium quantum cum deo possumus impartimur. Sane peticionis tue series nobis exhibite continebat quod propter epidimiam et mortalitatis pestem que proximis temporibus in illis partibus ingruit nonnulle parochiales ecclesie tue diocesis suis rectoribus et presbiteris destitute existant.

Nos itaque qui huiusmodi divini cultus augmentum ac animarum salutem ferventer appetimus in premissis congruum adhibere[24] remedium cupientes, tuis in hac parte supplicacionibus inclinati fraternitati tue de qua plenam in domino fiduciam gerimus dispensandi hac vice auctoritate apostolica cum sexaginta clericis dumtaxat alias ydoneas tuarum civitatis et diocesis Norwicensis patientibus in etate defectum, quos ad hoc duxeris eligendos dumtamen eorum quilibet vicesimum primum etatis sue annum attigerit et supra, super quo tuam conscientiam oneramus quod huiusmodi defectu ac Vienensis concilii et quibuslibet constitucionibus apostolicis et statutis et consuetudinibus contrariis nequamquam obstantibus, quilibet eorum in presbiterum promoveri et

---

[21] In the inner margin is a contemporary note, *primus in gratia*
[22] Corrected from *plenis*
[23] Contemporary note in inner margin: *tertius in gratia*
[24] Interlined over *appone*, cancelled.

beneficium ecclesiasticum curatum si eis canonice conferatur libere recipere et licite retinere valeat auctoritate apostolica de speciali gratia tenore presencium licentiam elargimur.

Nulli ergo omnino hominum liceat hanc paginam nostre concessionis infringere vel ei ausu temerario contraire. Siquis autem hoc attemptare presumpserit indignacionem omnipotentis dei et beatorum Petri et Pauli apostolorum eius se noverit incursurum. Datum Avinon' iii idus Octobris pontificatus nostri anno octavo.

1338

[fo.120ᵛ] RESIGNACO EIUSDEM. In dei nomine amen. Ego Willelmus de Motton rector ecclesie de Bryston Norwicensis diocesis volens certis de causis a cura et regimine ecclesie mee de Bryston predicte exonerari dictam ecclesiam meam in sacras manus venerabilis patris domini Willelmi dei gratia Norwicensis episcopi resigno.

1358

[fo.121ᵛ] BLOFELD. Die penultima Aprilis anno domini supradicto London' dominus contulit Roberto de Stratton bacalario in iure civili primam tonsuram clericalem habenti ecclesiam parochialem de Blofeld per liberam et simplicem resignacionem dicti reverendi patris, quam nuper idem pater obtinuit tanquam mense sue unitam auctoritate apostolica, sibi facta vacantem et ad collacionem ipsius reverendi patris pleno iure spectantem cum omnibus suis iuribus et pertinenciis universis intuitu caritatis. Et scripta fuit cuidam capellano ad inducendum.

1391

[fo.124] RESIGNACIO PRIORIS DE ALNESBORNE. Die penultima Julii anno domini supradicto apud Thorneg Frater Robertus Dwyt prior de Alnesborn statum suum et officium prioris certis de causis per dictum patrem tunc approbatis in ipsius patris manus sacras pure sponte et simpliciter resignavit et eidem cessit, et iuravit ad sancta dei evangelia restituere omnia per ipsum ablata seu distracta tempore suo sique fuerint si de eis poterit constare in futurum.

1399

[fo.125] HEMENHALE. Et memorandum quod licet in antiquo registro de taxacione ecclesiarum vicaria de Hemenhale inter vicarias ad nominacionem episcopi Norwicensis qui pro tempore fuerit pertinentes sit scripta; compertum est tamen per registra videlicet bone memorie domini Johannis episcopi Norwicensis quod v. nonas Julii anno domini MCCCIII apud Eccles pontificatus dicti patris quarto Robertus de Nuccole presbiter institutus fuit canonice per dictum .J. episcopum in vicaria de Hemenhale predicta cum ceteris clausis debitis et consuetis. Et tempore bone memorie domini W. episcopi Norwicensis videlicet iiii kalendas Junii anno domini MCCCXXVIII apud Thorp Thomas Seward presbiter institutus fuit canonice per dictum W. episcopum in vicaria ecclesie de Hemenhale predicta. Item tempore bone memorie domini Antonii episcopi Norwicensis videlicet iii die Maii anno domini MCCCXLII apud Thorneg Thomas atte Thorn de Coulyng presbiter institutus fuit canonice per dictum patrem in vicaria ecclesie de Hemenhale memorata ad presentacionem dictorum prioris et conventus de Donemowe dumtaxat absque nominacione episcopi Norwicensis pro tempore existentis.

1408

[fo.125ᵛ] BRUNSTEDE. Die xxiii Augusti anno domini supradicto apud Thorneg Adam Charles presbiter institutus fuit canonice per dictum reverendum patrem in ecclesia parochiali de Brunstede vacante per liberam resignacionem Baldewini de Merwode ad presentacionem domini Johannis Hakeluyt veri[25] eiusdem patroni. Et memorandum quod dominus Henricus de Plumpstede cui dictus reverendus pater contulit ecclesiam de Brunstede supradictam renunciavit iuri suo quod habuit in [fo.126] dicta ecclesia pro ea quod dictus pater contulit illam ecclesiam incumbenti dicto domino Baldewyno de Merwode.

1465

[fo.129ᵛ] COLLACIO HOSPITALIS BEATE MARIE MAGDALENE IUXTA NORWICUM. Die ultimo Januarii anno domini supradicto apud Hoxn dictus pater contulit custodiam hospitalis Beate Marie Magdalene iuxta Norwicum vacantem et ad collacionem dicti patris pleno iure spectantem cum omnibus suis iuribus et pertinenciis universis et onere eidem incumbente domino Thome de Claxton presbitero intuitu caritatis, reservata dicto patri et suis successoribus libera potestate dictum Thomam ad compotum seu ratiocinium super administracione sua in dicto officio facta reddendum annuis singulis compellendum, salvis in omnibus consuetudinibus episcopalibus etc.

1466

[between ff.129ᵛ–130] R[ex] dilecto sibi in Christo Fratri Michaeli Reynard, priori de Eye salutem.[26] Cum commiserimus vobis custodiam prioratus predicti ac omnium terrarum tenementorum et possessionum ad prioratum predictum spectantium que inter cetera prioratus terras tenementa possessiones et

---

[25] Interlined from *ad*

[26] This entry is on parchment measuring 26.2 cm wide and 11 cm high, folded at the left margin and sewn into the gathering. In the top margin *recto* is Blomefield's mark. It is blank *verso*.

beneficia religiosorum alienigenarum occasione guerre inter nos et adversarios nostros Francie mote capta fuerant in manum nostram habendam sub certa forma in litteris nostris patentibus inde confectis contenta, reddendo inde nobis per annum centum et quadraginta libras; et nos postmodum intelligentes quod venerabilis pater .W. episcopus Norwicensis pretendens primos fructus sive taxam ecclesie de Laxfeld quam vos in proprios usus tenetis et que parcella firme nostre predicte existit in qualibet vacacione prioratus predicti per mortem sive cessionem prioris eiusdem ad ipsum episcopum pertinere, fructus eiusdem ecclesie racione ultime vacacionis prioratus predicti per mortem tunc prioris ibidem pro primis fructibus sive taxa eiusdem ecclesie inde ad opus suum levandis sequestrari et sub sequestro huiusmodi custodiri fecerit, eidem episcopo per brevem nostrum prohibuerimus ne quicquam in hac parte quod in preiudic[i]um seu firme nostre predicte dimunicionem sive retardacionem cedere posset attemptaret seu per ministros suos attemptari faceret.

Et quia dicto negocio coram nobis et consilio nostro deducto, visum est consilio quod predictus episcopus ius habet ad primos fructus sive taxam quarumcumque ecclesiarum vacantium in episcopatu suo predicto obtinendos, nolentes ipsum episcopum super iure suo in hac parte preiudicari, vobis mandamus quod eidem episcopo primos fructus sive taxam dicte ecclesie de Laxfeld racione ultime vacacionis supradicte solvi et haberi[27] faciatis, recipientes a prefato episcopo literas suas acquietancie solucionem predictam testificantes, et nos vobis inde in firma vestra predicta ad scaccarium nostrum debitam allocacionem habere faciemus.

Teste meipso apud Westmonasterium xvi die Maii anno regni nostri Anglie vicesimo quinto, regni vero nostri Francie duodecimo.

1535

[fo.133] MASSYNGHAM MAGNA SANCTE MARIE. Die xxvi Junii anno domini supradicto London' Magister Laurencius de Lyttelton acolitus institutus fuit canonice per dictum patrem in ecclesia parochiali de Massingham Magna Sancte Marie vacante ad presentacionem domini Edwardi dei gratia Anglie et Francie regis illustris racione temporalium episcopatus Norwicensis nuper in manu sua existentium eiusdem hac vice patroni.

1538

[fo.133ᵛ] VICARIA ECCLESIE DE NEUTON' IUXTA CASTELACR'. Die xxvii Septembris anno domini supradicto apud Geywode[28] dominus contulit vicariam ecclesie de Neuton iuxta Castelacr' vacantem et ad collacionem dicti patris iure devoluto hac vice spectantem cum omnibus suis iuribus et pertinenciis universis dilecto filio Willelmo Gray presbitero intuitu caritatis, recepto ab eo iuramento de corporali residencia in dicta vicaria iuxta formam constitucionum in hac parte editarum.

---

[27] MS. *habere*
[28] Interlined from *apud* by S10.

1553

[fo.134] COLLACIO HOSPITALIS SANCTI JACOBI DE GYPPEWICO. Die xiiii Octobris anno et loco predictis dictus pater contulit custodiam hospitalis Sancti Jacobi [fo.134ᵛ] de Gyppewico Willelmo Olde de Debenham presbitero cum omnibus suis iuribus et pertinenciis universis et gubernacione ac administracione bonorum spiritualium et temporalium de hospitale iuxta formam constitucionis felicis recordacionis domini Clementis pape²⁹ quinti que incipit, Quia contingit, et ipsum prefecit in custodem, prestito per eum iuramento de iure debito et consueto.

1558

[fo.134ᵛ] SPECTESSAL'. Die xvi Novembris anno domini supradicto apud Hoxn' Robertus de Isingwold presbiter institutus fuit canonice per dictum patrem in ecclesia de Specteshale per liberam resignacionem Willelmi de Welleton ultimi rectoris eiusdem vacante ad presentacionem abbatis et conventus Beate Marie Eboracensis. Et iuravit prefatus Robertus ad sacra dei evangelia quod ad dictam ecclesiam rediret circa festum Sancti Mathei Apostoli exnunc proximo sequentem et extunc personaliter ministraret eidem ecclesie.

1559

[fo.134ᵛ] PREFECTIO CUSTODIS CANTARIE DE RUSSHEWORTH'. Die xvii Novembris anno domini supradicto apud Hoxn' Hugo Herbert capellanus et confrater collegii sive domus Sancti Johannis Evangeliste de Russheworth per confratres dicti collegii unanimiter electus, prefectus fuit per dictum reverendum patrem canonice in custodem dicti collegii per liberam resignacionem domini Nicholai de Wrotham ultimi custodis eiusdem vacantem obtentu electionis prefate ad presentacionem domini Johannis de Gonevill rectoris ecclesie de Estharlyng et Edmundi fratris eius dicti collegii patronorum.

1572

[fo.136] VICARIA DE POTTERE HEGHAM.³⁰ Die ix Januarii anno domini supradicto apud Hoxn' dictus pater contulit Johanni Colyn de Cranewyz presbitero vicariam ecclesie parochialis de Pottere Hegham vacantem et ad collacionem dicti patris hac vice spectantem, pro eo quod abbas et conventus Sancti Benedicti de Hulmo recusarunt presentare personam eis per dictum patrem nominatam iuxta huiusmodi nominacionem ac iuxta composicionem

---

²⁹ In a slightly darker ink than the text, *pape* is stricken out and *Episcopi* written above the line; this is not likely to have been done earlier than the 16th century.
³⁰ A contemporary hand, probably the same which wrote this marginal heading, added *prima institutio*.

initam[31] inter eos cum omnibus suis iuribus et pertinenciis universis intuitu caritatis, recepto ab eo iuramento de corporali residencia in dicta vicaria facienda iuxta formam constitucionum Othonis et Ottoboni quondam apostolice sedis in Anglia legatorum in hac parte editarum.

1586

[fo.136ᵛ] LOPHAM. Die iiii Marcii anno et loco predictis Egidius de Wyngreworth prime tonsure institutus fuit canonice per dictum patrem in ecclesia parochiali de Lopham vacante ad presentacionem Edwardi regis Anglie racione terrarum et tenementorum domini Johannis de Segrave militis nuper in manu dicti domini regis existentium veri eiusdem ecclesie hac vice patroni et per recuperacionem judicii in curia domini regis et per dimissionem in Curia de Arcibus. Willelmus de Atterton possesioni dicte ecclesie ultimo incumbebat.

1587

[between fo.136ᵛ–137] Willelmus[32] permissione divina Norwicensis episcopus dilecto filio Willelmo de Blyclyngg nostre diocesis presbitero salutem gratiam et benedictionem. Ad unam de tribus Cantariis in capella palacii nostri Norwicensis per bone memorie dominum Willelmum de Ayremynne nuper episcopum Norwicensem ordinatis celebrandam iam vacantem et ad nostram assignacionem spectantem te iuxta formam ordinacionis inde facte tenore presencium assignamus, et recepto a te iuramento de fideliter administrando in cantaria predicta te capellanum perpetuum deputamus in eadem, salvis in omnibus consuetudinibus episcopalibus et ecclesie nostre Norwicensis iure ac etiam dignitate. In cuius rei testimonium [unfinished].

1630

[fo.139] FRETONE. Die xviii Maii anno domini supradicto apud Terlyngg' Robertus Colston prime tonsure institutus fuit canonice per dictum patrem in ecclesia parochiali de Freton' per ammocionem Thome Ryvet per consideracionem curie regie, eo quod dominus noster rex Anglie recuperavit presentacionem ad ecclesiam predictam, vacante ad presentacionem dicti domini nostri regis racione terrarum et tenementorum domini Johannis de Segrave militis nuper in manu dicti domini regis existentium veri eiusdem hac vice patroni.

---

[31] MS. *inhitam*
[32] This entry is on a strip of parchment, 24.9 cm wide and 5.4 cm high, sewn together with four other such pieces (see **1588–91**). A filing hole was pierced in the left end (*recto*), about 1.5 cm from the edge. Blomefield's mark appears in the lower margin. The hand is contemporary, but cannot be identified as belonging to any of the register's scribes.

1640

[fo.140] WESTBRADENHAM. Die xxiii Junii apud Terlyngg Rogerus filius Willelmi de Wylby presbiter institutus fuit canonice per dictum patrem in persona domini Simonis rectoris ecclesie de Rollesby procuratoris sui sufficienter constituti in ecclesia parochiali de Westbradenham pro eo quod Magister Johannes de Brynkele ultimus eiusdem rector possessionem archidiaconatus de Notyngham pacificam est adeptus vacante, ad presentacionem Roberti de Rokelond, Roberti Bysshop, Willelmi Hulle et Laurencii Mendeware de Bokenham verorum eiusdem patronorum iure adquisicionis.

1647

[fo.140 in margin] Memorandum de vicaria de Parva Jernemuth que vacavit tempore pestilencie et non registrata.

1649

[fo.140ᵛ] TENOR PRESENTACIONIS PRO EODEM. Reverendo in Christo patri ac domino domino dei gratia Norwicensi episcopo Robertus eiusdem permissione humilis abbas monasterii Beate Marie de Becco Helluyni ordinis Sancti Benedicti Rothomagensis diocesis salutem et reverenciam tanto patri debitam cum honore. Ad prioratum de Stokes vestre diocesis per priorem solitum gubernari de monasterio nostro assumendum per liberam cessionem dilecti in Christo filii Fratris Johannis de Aqua Partita alias Goullafr' commonachi[33] nostri ultimi prioris eiusdem vacantem et ad nostram presentacionem spectantem dilectum in Christo filium Fratrem Guillelmum de Bello[34] Monte commonachum nostrum dicti monasterii nostri presbiterum expresse professum reverende paternitati vestre presentamus, eidem humiliter supplicantes quatenus dicti Fratris Johannis cessionem huiusmodi recipere velitis et dictum Fratrem Guillelmum ad dictum prioratum ac curam et regimen dicti prioratus virtute presentacionis nostre predicte admittere et ipsum ibidem perficere in priorem, ceteraque peragere que vestro incumbit[35] officio in hac parte. In cuius rei testimonium sigillum nostrum presentibus duximus apponendi. Datum Becci anno domini MCCCLI xvii die mensis Marcii.

1676

[fo.142] PREFECTIO CUSTODIS CANTARIE DE CAMPESSE. Die xxiiii Septembris anno domini supradicto apud Massyngham Johannes de Aston presbiter prefectus fuit canonice per dictum patrem in custodem officii custodie

---

[33] MS. *commanachi*
[34] Interlined by S10.
[35] MS. *incumbut*

cantarie Annunciacionis Beate Marie de Campesse per liberam resignacionem sive cessionem Johannis de Caketon ultimi custodis eiusdem vacantem cum onere eidem incumbente ad presentacionem priorisse et conventus de Campesse eiusdem patronarum.

1707

[fo.144] INSTITUCIO EIUSDEM. Willelmus permissione divina Norwicensis episcopus dilecto filio Roberto de Borewode de[36] Aylesham nostre diocesis presbitero salutem gratiam et benedictionem. Ad vicariam ecclesie parochialis de Stalham dicte nostre diocesis vacantem ad quam per discretos viros custodem et collegium Aule Sancte Trinitatis in Universitate Cantebriggiensi una cum alia persona ydonea iuxta composicionem inter nos initam atque factam nobis presentatus existis, te de dictis duabus personis nobis ut premittitur presentatis eligimus et admittimus ac perpetuum vicarium canonice instituimus in eadem, recepto a te iuramento de corporali residencia etc. In cuius etc.

1714

[fo.144ᵛ] CERTIFICATORIUM DOMINI WYGORN' EPISCOPI SUPER ECCLESIA DE TRUNCH'. Reverendo in Christo patri ac domino domino Willelmo dei gratia Norwicensi episcopo Johannes eiusdem permissione Wygorniensis episcopus salutem et sincere caritatis in domino continuum incrementum. Literas vestras nuper recepimus tenorem qui sequitur continentes:

Reverendo in Christo patri ac domino domino Johanni dei gratia Wygorniensi episcopo Willelmus permissione divina Norwicensis episcopus salutem cum reverentia et honore debitis tanto patri. Presentarunt nobis prior et conventus de Castelacr' Johannem Edward de Fresyngfeld nostre diocesis ad ecclesiam parochialem de Trunch dicte nostre diocesis vacantem. Verum quia per inquisicionem auctoritate nostra super articulis dictam presentacionem concernentibus factam, de omnibus circumstanciis excepta literatura presentati plenarie nobis constat, nos per partem dicti Johannis presentati plurimum excitati, ad instituendum eundem Johannem in ecclesia supradicta si per debitam examinacionem eum inveneritis in literatura ydoneum, iuramento obediencie et inductione eiusdem in casu quo eundem duxeritis instituendi nobis specialiter reservatis, vestre reverentie committimus vices nostras, eidem attencius supplicantes quatinus expedito negocio supradicto nos de toto eo quod feceritis in premissis certificare velitis per literas vestras patentes harum seriem continentes. Paternitatem vestram reverendam conservet in prosperis Christus feliciter atque diu ad ecclesie sue regimen et munimen. Datum London' ultima die Novembris anno domini MCCCLII et consecracionis nostre nono.

Quarum auctoritate literarum predictum Johannem super literatura per nos diligenter examinatum et in ea competenter ydoneum repertum, ad ecclesiam

---

[36] MS. *nostre de* (*nostre* cancelled).

de Trunch vestre Norwicensis diocesis predictam admisimus et rectorem instituimus canonice in eadem, inductione ipsius Johannis in corporalem possessionem prefate ecclesie et iuramento obediencie vobis per eundem prestandi vobis specialiter reservatis. Paternitatem vestram reverendam diu conservet incolumen clementia redemptoris. Datum London' viii die Decembris anno domini MCCCLII et nostre translacionis quarto.

1732

[fo.145ᵛ] COMMISSIO VICARIORUM GENERALIUM. Willelmus permissione divina Norwicensis episcopus dilectis filiis religioso viro Fratri Laurencio priori ecclesie nostre cathedralis Norwicensis et Magistro Ricardo de Lyng archidiacono nostro Norwicensi salutem gratiam et benedictionem. Cum ad partes Calesii extra regnum Anglie pro tractatu pacis inter nobilem principem dominum nostrum regem ex parte una et adversarium suum Francie ex altera utinam faciende iam arripuerimus iter nostrum, de vestris literarum scientia ac legalitate merito commendandis ab experto fiducialiter confidentes, vos tam coniunctim quam divisim exnunc usque quoad civitatem London' duxerimus per dei gratiam redeundi vicarios nostros in spiritualibus generales facimus et constituimus per presentes, collacione nominacione et provisione dignitatum personatuum officiorum ac aliorum quorumcumque beneficiorum ecclesiasticorum quorum collacio nominacio seu provisio ad nos de iure ecclesie nostre Norwicensis et episcopatus nostri pertinet seu pertinere poterit quovismodo necnon potestate dispensandi ac permutationes beneficiorum acceptandi seu admittendi ac absolvendi quoscumque super et ab excessibus in preiudicium nostrum seu ecclesie nostre Norwicensis prefate commissis vel inposterum committendis nobis specialiter reservatis. Datum apud Dortforde Roffensis diocesis undecimo die Februarii anno domini MCCCLII et consecrationis nostre nono.

1736

[fo.146] CRANESFORDE VICARIA. Die[37] xxix Marcii anno domini supradicto apud Terlyngg dictus reverendus pater contulit vicariam ecclesie parochialis de Cranesforde vacantem pro eo quod Adam Shene ultimus eiusdem vicarius dictam vicariam reliquit desolatam per menses plurimos et ad collationem dicti patris pleno iure spectantem cum omnibus suis iuribus et pertinenciis universis Willelmo Tuffin presbitero[38] intuitu caritatis, recepto ab eo iuramento de corporali residencia in dicta vicaria facienda iuxta formam constitutionum Othonis et Ottoboni in hac parte editarum.

[Margin] xl. s'. Mich' & Pas. coll'

---

[37] Entry written by S10.
[38] Interlined from *Willelmo*

1779

[fo.148ᵛ] SHELTON' MEDIETAS. Die xxi Septembris anno domini supradicto apud Novum Mercatum Nicholas le Millere de Honyng presbiter institutus fuit canonice per dictum patrem in ecclesia parochiali de Schelton pro medietate per liberam resignationem Johannis de Kentforde ultimi rectoris eiusdem sub certa protestationem factam et per dictum patrem admissam (videlicet si idem Johannes ecclesiam parochialem de Naringg Magna pacifice non haberet quod dictam medietatem ecclesie tanquam de ipso plenam et consultam valeret reingredi et eam ut prius pacifice possidere) vacante, ad presentationem abbatis et conventus de Langele eiusdem patronorum, salva semper protestatione predicta que est inserta in litteris dicti Nicholai.

1834

[fo.151ᵛ] HOSPITALIS DE BEK' IN BILLINGFORDE. Die xvi Maii anno et loco proximis supradictis idem pater contulit custodiam hospitalis Beati Thome de Bek' vacantem et ad collationem dicti patris sive dispositionem pleno iure spectantem cum omnibus suis iuribus et pertinenciis universis ac onere quod eidem iminet et incumbit Roberto Markant presbitero intuitu caritatis, recepto ab eo iuramento de fideli compoto annis singulis de bonis dicti hospitalis reddendo, iuxta formam constitutionis [fo.152] novelle que incipit, Quia contigit, edite in hac parte ac de omnibus aliis observandis que in dicto capitulo continentur.

1844

[fo.152ᵛ] SNORYNG MAGNA. Die primo Junii anno domini supradicto apud Geywode Thomas Rous presbiter institutus fuit canonice per dictum patrem in ecclesia parochiali de Snoryng Magna, pro eo quod excellentissimus princeps dominus Edwardus rex Anglie recuperavit in curia sua presentationem eiusdem versus dominum Radulphum de Shelton militem, vacante ad presentationem dicti domini regis et per breve de iudicio, et per consultationem super prohibitionibus[39] porrectis an placito pendente inter dictum dominum Radulphum et Radulphum filium suum, ut patet per dicta brevia.

1873

[fo.153ᵛ] COMMISSIO VICARIORUM GENERALIUM. Willelmus permissione divina Norwicensis episcopus dilectis filiis Magistro Ricardo de Lyng archidiacono nostro Norwicensi et Magistro Waltero de Elveden precentori ecclesie Herefordensis salutem gratiam et benedictionem.[40] De vestris litterarum

---

[39] MS. *prohibitiones*
[40] MS. repeats *et benedictionem*

scientia morum honestate ac legalitate merito commendandis ab experto fiducialiter confidentes, vos in toto episcopatu nostro Norwicensi tam in spiritualibus quam in temporalibus coniunctim et divisim [fo.154] nostros vicarios generales constituimus per presentes. Volentes insuper personas vestras amplius honorare, damus et concedimus vobis et utrique vestrum in solidum specialem et plenariam potestatem conferendi per vos seu alterum vestrum omnia et singula beneficia ecclesiastica tam curata quam non curata dignitates personatus et officia in ecclesia nostra cathedrali vel extra quorum collatio provisio nominatio presentatio vel quecumque alia dispositio ad nos iure et ratione episcopatus nostri et ecclesie nostre Norwicensis, seu iure hereditario vel alio quovismodo pertinent vel poterunt pertinere. Datum Dovorr' Cantuariensis diocesis vi die Octobris anno domini MCCCLIIII et consecrationis nostre undecimo.

1874

[fo.154] COMMISSIO FACTA VICARIIS GENERALIBUS AD FACIEN-DUM PROCESSUS GRACIARUM APOSTOLICARUM IN FORMA PAU-PERUM. Willelmus permissione divina Norwicensis episcopus dilectis in Christo filiis Magistro Ricardo de Lyng archidiacono nostro Norwicensi et Magistro Waltero de Elveden legum doctori precentori ecclesie Herefordensis salutem gratiam et benedictionem. Ad inquirendum de vita moribus conversatione et conditionibus quorumcumque pauperum clericorum quibus per sedem apostolicam in forma dicta vel alia infra nostram diocesim providetur vel etiam nobis hac vice in remotis agentibus contigerit quomodolicet provideri, huiusmodique provisionum gratias iuxta omnem earum exigentiam purificandum et iuxta inquisitionem premissam pronunciandum et decernendum, beneficia eisdem provisis apostolicis auctoritate gratiarum huiusmodi debita conferenda eosque in corporalem possessionem huiusmodi beneficiorum auctoritate premissa inducendum, ac processus quoscumque in premissis vel circa ea debitos faciendos necnon gratias supradictas usque ad finalem earum expeditionem ulterius exequendas, omniaque alia et singula expedienda et excercenda cum suis emergentibus dependentibus et connexis, quem litteris huiusmodi videbuntur apostolicis contineri et que circa expeditionem et executionem premissorum necessaria fuerint seu etiam oportuna, vobis et utrique vestrum quos vicarios nostros constituimus generales vices nostras committimus cum cohercionis canonice potestate. Datum Dovorr' Cant' diocesi vi die Octobris anno domini MCCCLIIII et consecrationis nostre undecimo.

APPENDIX II

Institutions, Collations and Appointments
which are not found in the register

Usually not included in this list are cases in which the last known beneficiary could have been replaced during the vacancy which preceded Bateman's provision; the Canterbury registers which would have included such *sede vacante* activity do not survive.

Badley [S]. On 11 Nov. 1339 Dns Roger de Norton was instituted to this rectory, on the presentation of Vincent de Norton, John de Foxlee, and William de Wichyngham, the attorneys-general of the patron, Sir John Noioun (Reg. Bek ff.31–31ᵛ). On 28 June 1351 John de Dobaknay resigned the vicarage [*sic*] of Badley in an exchange with Roger Whitlok (**1517**). Dobaknay may have been instituted *sede vacante*; Whitlok's institution is not recorded.

Burnham deanery [N]. On 18 July 1349, Thomas de Walton received this deanery (**837**); on or before 6 Feb. 1352, William de Hales resigned the deanery (**1578**). His collation was unregistered, but probably took place around 25 Dec. 1349, when the bishop dispensed Thomas de Walton for defect of age and conferred on him the rectory of St James, South Elmham [S] (**1282**).

Coston [N]. This rectory was annexed to the archdeaconry of Norfolk between 1291 and 1335 (*Taxatio* 85, Reg. Ayremynne fo.73). The parish was served by stipendiary chaplains.

Cranwich deanery [N]. On 10 June 1347, the bishop collated the deanery to M. Laurence de Maners (**317**); on 7 Aug. 1349, Robert de Walton was identified as dean of Cranwich in a witness list (**19**). His collation was not registered.

Dereham, East [N]. On 10 Oct. 1351, M. John Barnet was instituted to the rectory on the presentation of the bishop of Ely (**1546**); this was confirmed by the king three months later (*CPR 1350–1354*, p. 210). Barnet had a papal dispensation to hold several benefices (**1544**). According to Emden (*BRUO* 3, p. 2218), this benefice turned over again on 31 Mar. 1352, when M. Simon de Sudbury was provided to East Dereham by the pope. There is no record of his institution in this register.

Earlham [N]. On 19 July 1349, William atte Cherche of Blickling was instituted to Earlham vicarage (**842**); on 17 April 1352, William de Worstede resigned it (**1613**). If he was not the same man (Blickling and Worstead are seven miles apart), the intervening institution was unregistered.

Edgmere [N]. On 21 Jan. 1340, Ralph Drye of Edgmere was instituted to a moiety of Edgmere at the presentation of Dns John le Leche of Edgmere (Reg. Bek fo.32ᵛ). On 4 June 1349, John Leche was noted as rector of a moiety of Edgmere (**577**). On 11 July 1349, John Leche was instituted to the rectory of Wood Dalling [N] (**782**), but the next institution to Edgmere is not recorded until 13 Dec. 1350 (**1450**, with four patrons). On 9 December 1354, the same moiety as in **1450** turned over again, this time with Dns John Leche and John de Eggemere as patrons (**1902**). There could well have been two men in the diocese named John Leche; or one man might have been patron of a moiety of Edgmere and rector of the other moiety; or other explanations may be constructed. It seems probable that at least one institution to one moiety of Edgmere was not registered.

Elmham, North [N]. On 2 Nov. 1344, Edmund de Chevele received this vicarage in the bishop's advowson (**123**); on 8 Oct. 1354, John de Cressingham exchanged this vicarage for another benefice (**1875–6**). His collation was not registered.

Elmham, South [S], **St Margaret**. On 29 Apr. 1349, John de Brymthampton, *alias* de Stanlak, was collated to St Margaret's in South Elmham (**517**); in early Sept. 1349, John de Stanlak was collated to Bacton [S] (**1077, 1644**). There is no sign of a new rector at South Elmham St Margaret in the rest of the register. It is possible that these are two different men, or perhaps the bishop allowed one man to hold two rectories under a dispensation or license which is not recorded. It is also possible that the collation of a new rector to St Margaret's is unregistered.

Eye Priory [S]. In 1347, Prior Robert de Mornay of Eye died (Dugdale, *Monasticon* 3, p. 402); a royal writ of 16 May 1351 shows the new prior was Michael Reynard (**1466***). The election was not registered.

Feltwell [N], **St Mary**. On 7 Feb. 1339, Robert de Stanhowe was instituted to this rectory (Reg. Bek fo.20); on 16 June 1350 the king presented Thomas de Lexham, his clerk, to the rectory "by provision of the apostolic see" (*CPR 1348–1350*, 536). His institution was not registered.

Framlingham Pigot [N]. On 7 June 1349, John son of Richard de Hemplond was instituted as rector (**591**); on 12 June 1352, John de Stethenache resigned the rectory (**1643**). No intervening institution was recorded.

Haverhill [S]. On 11 May 1348, John Devennys was instituted to this rectory (**386**). On 12 Nov. 1350 the king presented his clerk, John de Tyngewyk of *Brehull*, then rector of Haverhill, to Meppershall, Beds. (*CPR 1350–1354*, 10); by 9 Dec. 1350, John de Tyngwyk had resigned Haverhill (**1447**). His institution was not registered.

Horsford [N]. In carly July 1349, John Ingelond (*alias* Hengelone) was instituted to Horsford (**723, 746**). On 14 March 1350 the king presented Richard de Sancta Fide to this vicarage (*CPR 1348–1350*, 481). On 7 Dec.

1353, Richard le Cook resigned this vicarage (**1804**). The Richards may be the same or different, but at least one institution to Horsford was not registered.

Lynn [N]. St Margaret priory, the cathedral's dependent house at Lynn, had parochial jurisdiction over the entire town; the appointment of men to exercise cure of souls in the town is therefore not registered, since it was at the discretion of the prior of the cathedral. There were a number of chapels-of-ease in Lynn, attached to St Margaret priory.

Melles [S], **St Margaret free chapel**. On 24 July 1349, Harvey (*Herveus*) de Threston was instituted to this chapel (**871**); on 27 June 1354, Henry (*Henrici*) Man resigned it (**1859**). His institution was not registered.

Norwich [N], **St Michael at Plea**. In 1349 John de Heydon was instituted to this rectory (**649**). In 1354 John Baxtere is identified as the rector (**1858**). This may be the same man; no intervening institution was registered.

Norwich archdeaconry. Hamo de Belers was provided to the archdeaconry of Norwich by the pope, at Bateman's request, on 17 Jan. 1347 (*CPP* 1, 105), which is confirmed by the provision document of 9 Mar. 1347 (*CPL* 3, 236). The institution was not registered at Norwich.

Sudbury archdeaconry. On 20 Nov. 1349, Thomas de Wynchester was collated to this office in exchange for a Hereford benefice; the collation is not found here, but in Reg. Trillek (*Registrum Johannis de Trillek*, ed. J. H. Parry, Canterbury & York Society 8, London 1912, p. 406). Wynchester resigned on or before 8 Dec. 1349 (**1263**).

Suffolk archdeaconry. On 27 May 1347, Michael de Northborough received the archdeaconry by royal grant (*CPR 1345–1348*, 293), and there is no mention of it in the register; he resigned on 29 June 1353 in exchange for a prebend in York (**1759**).

Tunstead [N]. On 4 Oct. 1344, Sir John Stroth was the patron of Tunstead rectory with Sco Ruston chapel (**107***). On 23 June 1350 the king gave licences to Henry, earl of Lancaster, for alienation in mortmain of the advowson of this rectory to the nuns of Campsey Ash, and to the nuns for the appropriation of the rectory (*CPR 1348–1350*, 560). On 20 Mar. 1352, the priory presented to the vicarage of Tunstead (**1599**). The appropriation was not registered at Norwich.

Walton [S]. The marginal note on **1708** states that 'J. de Gersingdon [John le Somenour of Garsington] was instituted in this benefice around the feast of the Lord's Assumption 1351', i.e., around 26 May 1351. His institution was not otherwise registered.

Witton in Waxham deanery [N]. On 22 Jan. 1350, John Jay was instituted to the vicarage of Witton (**1302**) and on 5 Feb. 1351 he was instituted to the rectory of Merton (**1467**). On 31 Mar. 1352, Hugh Wodeherde resigned Witton (**1604**); his institution had not been registered.

Yarmouth, Great [N]. St Nicholas priory, the cathedral's dependent house here, had parochial jurisdiction in the town, and the same conditions applied as for Lynn.

Donatives

At least 99 benefices were donatives: preferment was made to these by the patrons, without presentation to the bishop. In addition to the sources given in volume I, viii–ix, this list was compiled with the help of the excellent series of Suffolk Charters published by the Suffolk Record Society since 1979, and *Religious Women in Medieval East Anglia*, by Roberta Gilchrist and Marilyn Oliva (Norwich 1993). The donative benefices and their patrons which I have identified for William Bateman's episcopate were:

Aldeby [N], St Mary (cathedral priory)
Aldringham [S], St Andrew (Leiston abbey)
Ashfield Magna [S], All Saints (Ixworth priory)
Aspall [S], St Mary (Butley priory)
Badwell Ash, Ashfield Parva [S], St Mary (Ixworth priory)
Blythburgh [S], Holy Trinity (Blythburgh priory)
Blythford, Blyford [S], All Saints (Blythburgh priory)
Bricett, Great [S], St Mary and St Laurence (Great Bricett priory)
Buckenham, Old [N], All Saints (Buckenham priory)
Buckenham, New [N], St Martin (Buckenham priory)
Bungay [S], Holy Cross and St Mary (Bungay priory)
   St Thomas (Bungay priory)
Bury St Edmunds [S], St James (Bury St Edmunds abbey)
   St Margaret (Bury St Edmunds abbey)
   St Mary (Bury St Edmunds abbey)
Butley [S], St John (Butley priory)
Bylaugh [N], Virgin Mary (Butley priory)
Capel St Andrew [S], (Butley priory)
Costessy [N], St Edmund (Savigny abbey)
Cringleford [N], St Peter (St Giles hospital, Norwich)
Culpho [S], St Botulph (Leiston abbey)
Denston [S], St Nicholas (Tonbridge priory)
Dereham, West [N], St Andrew (Dereham abbey)
Farnham [S], St Mary (Butley priory)
Finborough, Little [S], St Mary (Great Bricett priory)
Gedgrave [S], St Mary and St George (Butley priory)
Glemham, Great or North [S], All Saints (Butley priory)
Glemham, Little or South [S], St Andrew, one-fourth part (Butley priory)
Herringfleet [S], St Margaret (Herringfleet St Olave priory)
Horsham [N], St Faith (Horsham St Faith priory)
Hunston, Hunterstone [S], St Michael (Ixworth priory)
Ipswich [S], St Clement (Ipswich Ss Peter and Paul priory)
   St Helen (Ipswich, Ss Mary Magdalene and James hospital)
   St John the Baptist at Caldwell (Ipswich Holy Trinity priory)
   St Laurence (Ipswich Holy Trinity priory)
   St Margaret (Ipswich Holy Trinity priory)

St Mary at Elms (Ipswich Holy Trinity priory)
St Mary le Tower (Ipswich Holy Trinity priory)
St Nicholas (Ipswich Ss Peter and Paul priory)
St Peter (Ipswich Ss Peter and Paul priory)
Ixworth [S], St Mary (Ixworth priory)
Ixworth Thorpe [S], All Saints (Ixworth priory)
Kersey [S], St Mary (Kersey priory)
Kesgrave [S], All Saints (Butley priory)
Knoddishall [S], St Laurence (Butley priory)
Langley [N], St Michael (Langley abbey)
Leiston [S], St Margaret (Leiston abbey)
Letheringham [S], St Mary (Letheringham priory)
Lindsey [S], St Peter (Kersey priory)
Middleton [S], St Mary (Leiston abbey)
Norwich [N], All Saints at Fye Bridge (cathedral priory)
    Castle free chapel (king)
    Holy Cross or St Crowche (cathedral priory)
    St Benedict (Buckenham priory)
    St Cuthbert (cathedral priory)
    St Etheldreda (cathedral priory)
    St George of Colegate (cathedral priory)
    St Giles (cathedral priory)
    St Gregory (cathedral priory)
    St Helen[1] (cathedral priory)
    St James[2] (cathedral priory)
    St John Baptist & Holy Sepulchre (cathedral priory)
    St John Baptist of Timberhill or Berstreet (cathedral priory)
    St Martin at Oak of Coslany (cathedral priory)
    St Martin at the Palace Gates (cathedral priory)
    St Mary the Less (cathedral priory)
    St Michael at Thorn, Berstreet, and St Martin in the Bailey (Horsham St
        Faith priory)
    St Paul (cathedral priory)
    St Saviour (cathedral priory)
    St Vedast (cathedral priory)
Ramsholt [S], All Saints (Butley priory)
Redisham Magna [S], St Peter (Butley priory)
Redlingfield [S], St Andrew (Redlingfield priory)
Rumburgh [S], St Michael (Rumburgh priory)
Rushworth, Rushford [N], St John the Evangelist (Rushworth college)
Shelley [S], All Saints (Butley priory)
Sheringham [N], All Saints (Notley abbey)
Shouldham [N], All Saints and St Margaret (Shouldham priory)
Shouldham Thorpe [N], St Mary (Shouldham priory)

---

[1] St Helen's church was taken down in the 13th century and the cure consolidated with the church of St Giles hospital (Tanner, *Church in Norwich*, 122; White, *Norfolk*, 111).
[2] St James was later united with St Paul, attached to the hospital of the same name, and the two served by one chaplain (Tanner, *Church in Norwich*, 133, 174, 177; White, *Norfolk*, 111)

Snarehill, Little [N], (Thetford St Mary priory)
Stoke [S], St Augustine (Stoke-by-Clare priory)
Stoke Ferry [N], All Saints (Shouldham priory)
Thetford [N & S], St Cuthbert (Thetford Holy Sepulchre priory)
 St Edmund (Thetford Holy Sepulchre priory)
 St Giles (Thetford Holy Sepulchre priory)
 St Mary the Less (Thetford St Mary priory)
 St Nicholas (Thetford St Mary priory)
Walsham le Willows [S], St Mary (Ixworth priory)
Walsingham, Great [N], St Peter (Walsingham priory)
Walsingham, Little [N], St Mary (Walsingham priory)
Wangford, near Southwold [S], St Peter (Wangford priory)
Wantisden [S], St John (Butley priory)
Wattisham [S], St Nicholas (Great Bricett priory)
Wendling [N], Ss Peter and Paul (Wendling abbey)
Weybourne [N], All Saints (Weybourne priory)
Wisset [S], St Andrew, annexed to Rumburgh, *q.v.*
Woodbridge [S], St Mary (Woodbridge priory)
Worlingham Parva [S], St Peter (Butley priory)
Wormegay [N], St Michael (Wormegay priory)

Another 28 benefices were probably donatives during this time, although the evidence for them is less clear:

Acre, West [N], All Saints (West Acre priory)
Campsea Ash [S], St John the Baptist (Campsey Ash priory)
Denham (near Bury), West [S], St Mary (St Osyth abbey)
Dunwich [S], All Saints (Eye priory)
Foxhall [S], All Saints (Ipswich Trinity priory)
Hardley [N], St Margaret (St Giles hospital, Norwich)
Higham [S], St Mary (Ipswich Trinity priory)
Linstead Magna [S], St Peter (Mendham priory)
Linstead Parva [S], St Margaret (Mendham priory)
Norwich [N], St Catherine or St Winewaloy (Carrow priory)
 St Margaret at Fye Bridge (cathedral priory)
 St Margaret at Newbridge (cathedral priory?)
 St Olave of Colegate (cathedral priory)
Pentney [N], St Mary Magdalene (Pentney priory)
Playford [S], St Mary (Eye priory)
Repps with Bastwick [N], St Peter (St Giles hospital, Norwich)
Sturston [N], Holy Cross (Dunmow priory)
Sustead [N], Ss Peter & Paul (Thetford St Mary priory)
Thetford[3] [N & S], All Saints (?)[4]

[3] The population of Thetford was shrinking in the 14th century, and by the mid-16th century seven of the ten churches noted here as donatives or possible donatives had been abandoned (All Saints, St Andrew, St Edmund, St Giles, Holy Trinity, St Lawrence and St Michael).
[4] This and the following four churches were probably donatives of one of the Thetford priories.

Holy Trinity (?)
St Andrew (?)
St Lawrence (?)
St Michael (?)
Thorpland[5] [N], in Fincham deanery, St Thomas (West Acre priory)
Whitlingham [N], St Andrew (Herringfleet priory)
Wicken [Cambs.], (Spinney priory)
Willisham [S], St Mary (Ipswich Trinity priory)
Wretton, Stoke Wretton [N], All Saints (Dereham abbey)

Peculiars

Finally, there was no registration of institutions or collations to the few peculiar[6] jurisdictions within the diocese. Hadleigh [S], Monks Eleigh [S] and Moulton [S] were peculiars of the archbishop of Canterbury. Freckenham [S] was a peculiar of the bishop of Rochester. The cathedral priory had four peculiars:[7] Lakenham, Sedgford, Sprowston, and Trowse, all in Norfolk. The rector of Castle Rising [N] had one peculiar,[8] Roydon [N]. Emneth [N] was a peculiar of the bishop of Ely. Thorpe next Norwich [N] was a peculiar of the bishop of Norwich.[9]

[5] The other Thorpland in the county was just north of Fakenham in Burnham deanery, on the south side of the Stiffkey River, and was not a parish; Batcock appears to confuse the two in his index (*Ruined Churches*, 197).
[6] The maps of Norfolk and Suffolk by the Institute of Heraldic and Genealogical Studies (Canterbury 1964) show a number of peculiars which were not so in the first half of the fourteenth century. For instance, Great Cressingham [N] is listed as a peculiar of the king, but was in the bishop's advowson at this period (Reg. Ayremynne fo.72, Reg. Bek fo.25, and **710**); and see below.
[7] Arminghall (**298, 428, 448, 1233**), East Beckham (**45, 1412**), West Beckham (**1198, 1342**), Eaton (**629**), Hindolveston (**500**), Martham (**662**), and Great Plumstead (**490, 1435**), listed as peculiars of the cathedral on the Institute map of Norfolk, were merely in cathedral advowson in Bateman's time.
[8] Castle Rising itself was not a peculiar (**870, 1415**), nor were North (**1840**) or South Wootton (**729, 1298, 1865**) in this period.
[9] Institutions to this rectory were usually registered (Reg. Bek ff.29, 59, 64[v]–65, **1423**, e.g.).

APPENDIX III

Administrators and Office-Holders of Norwich Diocese, 1299–1369

Details of the careers of most of these men can be found in 'the new LeNeve' (*Fasti*) and Emden (*BRUO* and *BRUC*), but this list occasionally corrects or augments their sources. For Bateman's contemporaries, see also the Index of Persons and Places. Academic degrees and titles mentioned are the highest known to have been obtained, where there is a record, and otherwise as given in the registers.

Archdeacon of Norwich[1]

——,[2] ca. June 1291–before 4 February 1302.

M. William de Knapton (Cnapeton), DCnCL, 1302–1324.
Collated 4 Feb. 1302, resigned before 16 April 1324 (Reg. Salmon ff.7^v, 106^v). See also archdeacon of Suffolk, below, and *BRUC* 340.

M. Roger de Snetesham, 1324–1328.
Collated 16 April 1324, resigned before 8 Sept. 1328 (Reg. Salmon fo.106^v, Reg. Ayremynne fo.24^v). See also archdeacon of Sudbury, below, and *BRUC* 538f.

M. William Bateman (de Norwico), DCL, 1328–1340.
Collated 8 Sept. 1328, resigned soon after 21 Aug. 1340 (Reg. Ayremynne fo.24^v, *CPL* 2, 547). See *BRUC* 44.

M. Thomas Fastolf, DCL, 1340–1347.
Reservation by the pope on 21 Aug. 1340, promised obedience to the bishop by proxy 6 Jan. 1341, resigned before 17 Jan. 1347 (*CPL* 2, 547, Reg. Bek fo.42^v, *CPP* 1, 105). See *BRUO* 3, 2147f.

[1] In 1302 the rectory of Eccles Episcopi [N] was annexed to this benefice (Reg. Salmon fo.7^v), but the annexation did not last (Reg. Bek ff. 13^v, 41 and **739**). In 1335, when Bateman was archdeacon, he petitioned the pope for a benefice with adequate incomes, as he said he reaped no profit from his archdeaconry (*CPL* 2, 525). In 1351, Lyng acquired a residence for the archdeacon in Norwich, possibly the first (*CPR 1350–1354*, 178).
[2] B. Jones (*Fasti* 4, 26) lists M. Thomas de Skerning as archdeacon of Norwich '1274 – ?', but Skerning is last mentioned as Norwich archdeacon on 20 October 1289, and reappears in May x June 1291 as archdeacon of Suffolk. He was transferred to the archdeaconry of Surrey in November 1296, and died before 12 March 1301 (*Fasti ecclesiae Anglicanae, 1066–1300*, 3 vols., rev. by Diana E. Greenway, 1968–1977, vol. 2, pp. 64, 68f, 95).

M. Hamo Belers, DCnCL, 1347–1349.

M. Thomas de Bradwardine, STD, 1347.

M. John Berenger, 1349.

Papal provision of Belers at Bishop Bateman's request on 17 Jan. 1347, confirmed by provision document 9 March 1347 (*CPP* 1, 105, *CPL* 3, 236). Royal grant to Bradwardine 8 Feb. 1347, another to Berenger on 8 May 1347 (*CPR 1345–1348*, 251, 280). Belers may have abandoned the archdeaconry by 12 Aug. 1348 (**413***), as Berenger was called archdeacon on 12 Feb. 1349 (*CPL* 3, 304) and died in this office before 27 Aug. 1349 (*CPP* 1, 189 and **1051**). For Belers see also bishop's chancellor, below; he died 1 May 1370 (*BRUO* 3, 2150f).

M. Richard de Lyng, STD, 1349–1355.

Collated 27 Aug. 1349, papal confirmation 10 Dec. 1349 (**1051**, *CPP* 1, 189, *CPL* 3, 335). Died 10 March x 7 April 1355 (Reg. Islip, Lambeth Palace Library, ff.337–337ᵛ). See archdeacon of Sudbury and archdeacon of Suffolk, below, as well as *BRUC* 381.

Richard de Norwico, 1355–1361.

Royal grant 9 April 1355, admitted 18 April 1355, died before 17 Oct. 1361 (*CPR 1354–1358*, 199, Reg. Percy ff.9, 53ᵛ). See *BRUO* 2, 1375f.

William de Swyneflet, BCL, 1361–1387.

Collated 17 Oct. 1361, resigned in exchange 27 March 1387 (Reg. Percy fo.53ᵛ, Reg. Depsenser, NRO Reg/3/6, fo.121). See *BRUC* 572.

Archdeacon of Norfolk[3]

Thomas de Kerdeston, ?–1326.[4]

Occurs 25 Jan. 1313, possibly incapacitated by 24 June 1326, died before 26 July 1326 (Reg. Salmon fo.50, Reg. Ayremynne ff.81ᵛ, 82).

William de Herlaston, 1326–1327.

Royal grant 25 July 1326, resigned before 2 Feb. 1327 (*CPR 1324–1327*, 278, *CPR 1327–1330*, 3).

M. Adam de Ayremynne, 1327–1335.

Collated 4 Jan. x 2 Feb. 1327, papal confirmation 2 Feb. 1327, probably died before 16 April 1335 (Reg. Ayremynne ff.12, 15, 72; *CPR 1327–1330*, 3, *CPL* 2, 247). See *BRUC* 25.

---

[3] United to the rectory of Coston [N] in Hingham deanery sometime after 1291 (*Taxatio* 85, Reg. Ayremynne fo.73).

[4] Kerdeston was archdeacon of Norfolk in 1313 and in 1326; it is possible that the 'M. R. de S.' whom B. Jones (*Fasti* 4, 28) lists as archdeacon of Norfolk in July 1325 is M. Roger de Snetesham, archdeacon of Norwich at that time.

John de Neuland, 1335.
Collated 16 April 1335, resigned[5] before 25 June 1335 (Reg. Ayremynne ff.72, 73).

M. Robert de Usflet (Ouseflet), 1335–1359.
Collated 25 June 1335, collation ratified by the king on 27 June 1335 (Reg. Ayremynne fo.73, *CPR 1334–1338*, 133); royal grant to M. John de Harewell, BCL, 4 March 1351 was revoked when Usflet was shown still to be in possession on 22 June 1351 (*CPR 1350–1354*, 52, 107). Died before 22 May 1359 (Reg. Percy fo.32). See *BRUC* 603, s.v. 'Ufflete'.

M. William de Blythe, MA, 1359–1374.
Collated 22 May 1359 (Reg. Percy fo.32); royal grant to Richard de Ravenser 20 June 1359, but the estate of Blythe was ratified 14 Sept. (*CPR 1358–1361*, 231, 290), and confirmed by the pope 14 Oct. 1359 ('the said bishop being then excommunicate and the archdeaconry reserved to the pope' (*CPL* 3, 608, *CPP* 1, 345). Died before 13 March 1374 (Reg. Despenser, NRO Reg/3/6, fo.24^v). See *BRUO* 1, 207.

Archdeacon of Sudbury[6]

M. Ralph of York.
Occurs 29 Aug. 1285, chancellor of Salisbury by 17 Sept. 1294, still alive 17 Feb. 1299 but may not have been archdeacon (*Fasti 1066–1300*, 2, 71; *CPR 1292–1301*, 87, 395). Unnamed archdeacon of Sudbury occurs 6 Jan. 1300 (Reg. Salmon fo.6).

Henry de Bradenham, ? –1308.
Occurs 20 June 1307, died before 1 April 1308 (*CPL* 2, 24, Reg. Salmon fo.27).

Alan de Ely, 1308–1324.
Collated 1 April 1308, resigned before 28 March 1324 (Reg. Salmon ff.27, 105^v). See also archdeacon of Suffolk, below.

M. Roger de Snetesham, 1324.
Collated 3 April 1324, resigned before 16 April 1324 (Reg. Salmon ff.105^v, 106^v). See also archdeacon of Norwich, above, and *BRUC*, 538–9.

M. Simon de Creake (Creyk), DCL, 1324–1330.
Collated 16 April 1324, died or resigned before 17 Jan. 1330 (Reg. Salmon fo.106^v, Reg. Ayremynne fo.33). See *BRUO* 3, 2166.

---

[5] That he had not died is shown by his institution as rector of Great Massingham, and receipt of license to be absent for one year (Reg. Ayremynne ff.73^v, 96).
[6] This archdeaconry was of small value, and had no manor or church annexed to it (*CPL* 4, 33).

M. Firmin de Lavenham, 1330–1346.
   Collated 17 Jan. 1330, died before 31 Aug. 1346 (Reg. Ayremynne fo.33, **237**).
   See also diocesan corrector, below, and *BRUC*, 355–6.

M. Gilbert de Yarewell, 1346–1348.
   Collated 31 Aug. 1346, died before 24 Sept. 1348 (**237**, *CPP* 1, 141, *CPL* 3,
   273). See also diocesan corrector, below, and *BRUC*, 664, 687.

M. Richard de Lyng, STD, 1348–1349.
   Collated 13 Oct. 1348, resigned before 27 Aug. 1349 (**441**, **1050**). See also
   archdeacon of Norwich, above, archdeacon of Suffolk, below, and *BRUC*,
   381.

M. Walter de Elveden (de Stanes), DCnCL, 1349.
   Collated 27 Aug. 1349, resigned in exchange 20 Nov. 1349 (**1050**, *Registrum
   Johannis de Trillek*, ed. J. H. Parry, CYS 8 (1912), 406). See also bishop's
   official-principal, below, and *BRUC* 210.

M. Thomas de Winchester (Wynchester),[7] 1349.
   Collated 20 Nov. 1349, resigned before 8 Dec. 1349 (*Registrum Johannis de
   Trillek*, op. cit., 406, and **1263**).

M. Thomas de Methelwolde, DCnCL, 1349–1351.
   Collated 8 Dec. 1349, resigned before 3 Jan. 1351 (**1263**, **1460**). See also
   bishop's official-principal, below.

M. Henry de la Zouche, 1351–1361.
   Papal reservation of the archdeaconry to him 24 Sept. 1348, admitted by the
   bishop on 3 Jan. 1351, died before 11 Aug. 1361 (*CPP* 1, 141, 320, 374, *CPL* 3,
   273; **1460**).

M. William Graa de Trusthope, BCnCL, 1362–1363.
   Collated 7 Jan. 1362, resigned before 15 July 1363 (Reg. Percy fo.58, *CPL* 4,
   33).[8] See also archdeacon of Suffolk, below.

John de Hambleton (Hembletone, Ouleton), 1363–1384?
   Occurs 15 July 1363, 15 April 1366 (*CPL* 4, 33, *CPP* 1, 444, 525); the benefice
   was not filled again until 1384 (*CPR 1381–1385*, 408, 458).

---

[7] Bateman's nephew; in 1343 he had obtained a papal dispensation to be absent from his
English benefice for five years while studying civil law at Bologna (*CPP* 1, 73).
[8] Material for June 1362 through July 1364 is not included in the institution section of
Bishop Percy's register, and Jones is mistaken in citing an entry for July 1363 on fo.65ᵛ of
that register (*Fasti* 4, 31).

Archdeacon of Suffolk

M. Sayerus[9] (Saer, Saerus), occurs 1298?
Occurs 3 February 1298 (*Fasti* 4, 32). Unnamed archdeacon of Suffolk mentioned 1 Oct. 1306 (Reg. Salmon fo.21).

Simon de Ely, 1312–1324.
Collated 10 Jan. 1312, resigned before 28 March 1324 (Reg. Salmon ff.45, 106^v).

Alan de Ely, 1324.
Collated 28 March 1324, resigned before 16 April 1324 (Reg. Salmon ff.105^v, 106^v). See also archdeacon of Sudbury, above.

M. William de Cnapeton (Knapton), DCnCL, 1324–1331.
Collated 16 April 1324, resigned before 31 March 1331 (Reg. Salmon fo.106^v, Reg. Ayremynne fo.40^v). See also archdeacon of Norwich, above, and *BRUC* 340.

M. John de Fenton, DCL, 1331–1347.
Collated 31 March 1331, died before 3 May 1347 (Reg. Ayremynne f.40^v, **300***). See *BRUO* 2, 677.

M. Richard de Lyng, STD, 1347.
Collated 3 May 1347, deprived 27 May 1347 by the royal grant made to Northburgh (next), as the temporalities of the see of Norwich were then in the king's hand (**300***, *CPR 1345–1348*, 293, *CPL* 3, 335). See archdeacon of Sudbury and archdeacon of Norwich, above, as well as *BRUC* 381.

M. Michael de Northburgh (Northborough), DCL, 1347–1353.
Royal grant 27 May 1347, resigned in exchange 29 June 1353 (*CPR 1345–1348*, 293, and **1759**). See *BRUO* 2, 1368–70.

William de Flisco (Fieschi), 1353–1357.
Collated 29 June 1353, deprived when the exchange was declared invalid by the pope 28 Feb. 1357 (**1759–60**, *CPP* 1, 294).

M. Francis de Sancto Maximo, 1357.
Papal provision 28 Feb. 1357, died before 28 Nov. 1357 (*CPP* 1, 294, 303).

Elias, Cardinal Talleyrand de Perigord, 1357–1359.
Papal provision 28 Nov. 1357, resigned before 5 June 1359 (*CPP* 1, 303, Reg. Percy fo.32).

---

[9] Possibly M. Saierus de Ros: *BRUC* 488.

M. John de Carleton, DCnCL, 1359–1363?

Collated 5 June 1359, vacated at a date unknown (before 24 May 1365, possibly before 15 July 1363, when Graa vacated the archdeaconry of Sudbury) (Reg. Percy fo.32, *CPR 1364–1367*, 122, *CPL* 4, 33).[10] See the next two items.

M. William Graa de Trusthope, BCnCL, 1363?–1365.

Royal grant of 18 July 1365 indicates that the king had recovered the right of presentation to the archdeaconry of Suffolk, by reason of the vacancy of the see of Norwich in 1355, in a case in which the defendants were Bishop Percy and William Graa de Trusthope (*CPR 1364–1367*, 134). Graa resigned the archdeaconry on 21 July 1365, in an exchange with Carleton (Reg. Percy fo.65ᵛ). See also archdeacon of Sudbury, above.

M. John de Carleton, DCnCL, 1365–1367.

Royal grant 24 May 1365, second royal grant 18 July 1365, indicating that the king had won his suit in the royal court against Bishop Percy and Graa, recovering his right to fill the archdeaconry of Suffolk by reason of the 1355 vacancy of the see of Norwich (*CPR 1364–1367*, 122, 134); Carleton then received Suffolk in exchange from Graa on 21 July 1365, and died in office before 16 Jan. 1367 (Reg. Percy ff.65ᵛ, 73). See also bishop's official-principal, below.

M. John de Ufford, 1367–1368.

Collated 16 Jan. 1367, deprived on or before 20 Jan. 1368 by papal provision of Aleyn (Reg. Percy fo.73, *CPL* 4, 71). See also *BRUC* 603.

John Aleyn, 1368–1373.

Provided by the pope 20 Jan. 1368, admitted 29 March 1368, died before 10 Dec. 1373 (*CPL* 4, 71, Reg. Percy fo.80ᵛ, Reg. Despenser fo.23ᵛ).

Bishop's Official-Principal

for Salmon:

M. Nicholas de Whitechurche (Witechirche), occurs from January 1306 through 3 July 1309 (Reg. Salmon ff.19, 25ᵛ, 31, 32ᵛ). See *BRUC* 634.

M. Hamo de Gatele, occurs 8 September 1310 through March 1311 (Reg. Salmon f.37ᵛ).

M. Thomas de Foxtone, DCnCL, occurs 29 December 1316 through July 1320 (Reg. Salmon ff.67ᵛ, 85ᵛ). See also *BRUC* 241.[11]

---

[10] If Carleton vacated this archdeaconry between June 1362 and July 1364, this would explain the absence of any record of the change, which Jones (*Fasti* 4, 33) remarks upon, since material for this period is missing from Percy's register (the citation of Reg. Percy fo.65ᵛ is a mistake).

[11] Emden (*BRUC*, 241) mistakenly cites Reg. Salmon fo.67ᵛ for Foxtone's appointment as official; the letters on fo.67ᵛ appoint him vicar-general with special authority for benefices in the bishop's advowson in Salmon's absence.

M. John de Brecham, occurs sometime in 1322–1323 (Reg. Salmon ff.99^v–100). See also *BRUO* 3, 2155.

Robert de Houtone, occurs February 1325 (Reg. Salmon fo.114^v) See also official of the archdeacon of Norfolk, below.

official of spiritualities sede vacante on Salmon's death:

M. Ralph de Palgrave (Pagrave), appointed 11 July 1325 (Reg. Reynolds, Lambeth Palace Library, fo.276).[12] He received notice to release the spiritualities to Robert de Baldok[13] on 14 Aug. 1325 (Reg. Reynolds, Lambeth Palace Library, fo.276).[14] See bishop's chancellor, below, and *BRUC* 440.

for Ayremynne:

M. John de Skyrenne, occurs 14 Oct. 1326 through June 1328 ((Reg. Ayremynne ff.10^v, 23). See also *BRUC*, 533.

M. Robert de Strattone, occurs 29 May 1335 and 11 Aug. 1335 (Reg. Ayremynne ff.74^v, 76^v). See also *BRUC*, 562.

for Bateman:

M. Thomas de Methelwolde, DCnCL, occurs 20 Dec. 1347 *passim* to 9 March 1349; may have resigned before 8 Dec. 1349, when he was collated as archdeacon of Sudbury (**12***, **13**, **470**, **1263**), but there is no evidence.[15]

sede vacante on Bateman's death:

M. Walter de Elveden, DCnCL, appointed 28 Jan. 1355 (Reg. Islip, Lambeth Palace Library, fo.333).[16] See archdeacon of Sudbury, above, and next below, as well as *BRUC* 210–11.

---

[12] The commission is transcribed by Churchill, *Canterbury Administration* 2, 69.

[13] Bishop Salmon died 6 July 1325; on 13 July the cathedral priory received royal license to hold an election (*CPR 1324–1327*, 150). At the nomination of Edward II, they elected Robert de Baldok, archdeacon of Middlesex and the king's chancellor, on 23 July (*Fasti 1300–1541*, 4, 23). Edward confirmed the election on 28 July, and released the temporalities to Baldok on 12 August (*CPR 1324–1327*, 157, 159). Archbishop Reynolds assented to the election and released the spiritualities, and Baldok appointed a vicar-general (*Fasti* 4, 23, Reg. Salmon f.112^v). Within days, however, Baldok learned that Pope John XXII had provided William de Ayremynne to the see on 19 July 1325 (*CPL* 2, 245), and he resigned before the archbishop on 3 September. For the most balanced assessment of this papal provision see J.L. Grassi, 'William Airmin and the bishopric of Norwich', *English Historical Review* 70 (1955), 550–561.

[14] Churchill cites Reg. Reynolds, fo.278, and transcribes the letter (*Canterbury administration* 2, 69).

[15] The last notice of Methelwold is on 26 June 1350 (**1370**); Thompson suggests that after the disappearance of Methelwold, Elveden probably became official-principal ('William Bateman', 127), but there is no evidence of the official for the rest of Bateman's tenure.

[16] Churchill gives the letter of commission (*Canterbury Administration* 2, 70–72).

for Percy:

M. Walter de Elveden, DCL, occurs 26 July 1357 and 12 December 1357, resigned before 27 June 1359 (Reg. Percy ff.21, 23, 32^v). See archdeacon of Sudbury, above, and *BRUC* 210–11.

M. John de Carleton, DCnCL, occurs 27 June 1359 through October 1361, died before 16 January 1367 (Reg. Percy ff.32^v, 52^v, 73). He was archdeacon of Suffolk simultaneously (see above), and a royal clerk (*CPR 1364–1367*, 122, 134).

Official of Lynn

for Ayremynne:

Roger de Kymburle, rector of Drayton [N], appointed 17 February 1326 (Reg. Ayremynne fo.79).

Hugh de Langhale, occurs 19 August 1331 (Reg. Ayremynne fo.42^v).

Official of the Bishop's Manors

Not named. Office attested in **149, 194, 287, 516**, and Reg. Percy fo.26.

Diocesan Corrector

Sede vacante at Salmon's death:

Thomas de Stowe, appointed 9 July 1325 (Reg. Reynolds, Lambeth Palace Library, fo.275^v).[17]

for Ayremynne:

M. Firmin de Lavenham,[18] commissioned 16 December 1325, until before 17 April 1326; again in October 1328, resigned before 5 December 1330 (Reg. Ayremynne ff. 79, 80, 85, 95). See also archdeacon of Sudbury, above, and *BRUC* 355–6.

---

[17] The letter of commission is dated 9 April 1325, when Bishop Salmon was still alive, and Churchill considers this to be a mistake for 9 July 1325 (*Canterbury Administration* 1, 195*n*.; the letter is transcribed *ibid.*, 2, 70).

[18] Lavenham, who had been Bishop Salmon's clerk (Reg. Salmon fo.90^v), served Ayremynne as corrector of the bishop's manors and special commissary for probate of testaments during his term as diocesan corrector, and also as corrector of the bishop's manors, auditor of executors' accounts, and diocesan collector of the first fruits from before 2 Oct. 1328 until after 28 Nov. 1329 (Reg. Ayremynne ff.79, 85–85^v, 94^v).

M. Ralph de Hakeford,[19] commissioned 17 April 1326, until after 12 February 1328 (Reg. Ayremynne ff.80, 91^v).

M. Gilbert de Yarewell, occurs 5 December 1330 through 25 January 1334, resigned before 28 June 1334 (Reg. Ayremynne ff.95, 96). See also archdeacon of Sudbury, above, and *BRUC* 664, 687.

M. Thomas de Lenn, occurs 28 June 1334, 21 Oct. 1335 (Reg. Ayremynne ff.96, 76^v). He may be the same man as in *BRUO* 2, 1131.

for Percy:

M. Thomas de Morle, BCnCL, occurs 18–20 Dec. 1357 (Reg. Percy ff.23^v–24). See also official of the archdeacon of Norwich, below, and *BRUC* 411–12.

Bishop's Chancellor

for Salmon:

M. Ralph de Palgrave (Pagrave), occurs 16 Nov. 1311, until sometime before Oct. 1315 (Reg. Salmon ff.43^v, 63). See also bishop's official-principal *sede vacante*, above, and *BRUC* 440.

for Bateman:

M. Hamo de Belers, DCL, occurs 9 Nov. 1345 (**187**). See also archdeacon of Norwich, above, and *BRUO* 3, 2150–1.

Bishop's Chamberlain

for Bateman:

Ralph de Longham, occurs 13 Apr. 1351 (**39**).

M. Thomas de Lexham (later DCnCL), occurs Jan. 1355, at Bateman's death (*CPP* 1, 276). See *BRUC* 366.

Official of the Archdeacon of Norwich

M. Thomas de Morle, MA, BCnCL, occurs 3 Nov. 1340 (Reg. Bek fo. 41^v). See also diocesan corrector, above, and *BRUC* 411–12.

---

[19] Like Lavenham before and after him, Hakeford was also commissioned as corrector of the bishop's manors and assigned to hear the accounts of the executors of testaments (Reg. Ayremynne fo.80).

⟨M. Peter de Normandeby,[20] commissioned 12 Aug. 1348 (**413***)⟩

Official of the Archdeacon of Norfolk

M. Richard de Ringgested, occurs 1315.[21] See also *BRUC* 482.

Robert de Houtone (Howton), occurs 1316.[22] See also bishop's official-principal, above.

M. Simon de Cleye, appointed 24 June 1326 (Reg. Ayremynne fo.81ᵛ).[23]

Official of the Archdeacon of Sudbury

M. John Mauneseyn, occurs 8 Dec. 1333 (Reg. Ayremynne fo.62).

M. Adam de Blofeld, took oath of obedience and received office 3 Feb. 1343 (Reg. Bek fo.66).

⟨John de Tomeston.[24]⟩

Official of the Archdeacon of Suffolk

M. John de Knapton (Cnapeton), occurs 4 Sept. 1327 through 21 July 1333 (Reg. Ayremynne ff.16, 95*bis*ᵛ).[25]

M. Robert Spenser, occurs 10 Feb. 1366 (*CPR 1364–1367*, 134).

[20] He was Bateman's commissary in the place of the archdeacon's official (and see Belers' term as archdeacon of Norwich, above). Normandeby had earlier been made keeper of 'tabelliones' (notary) by papal permission (Reg. Bek ff.73ᵛ–74).
[21] According to Francis Blomefield (*An Essay Towards a Topographical History of the County of Norfolk*, 5 vols., Fersfield 1739–1775, vol.2, 477); Ringgested was also dean of the College of St Mary in the Fields at Norwich from 25 Jan. 1305 (Reg. Salmon ff.15, 62).
[22] On Blomefield's authority (*ibid.*).
[23] Ayremynne appointed Cleye, then dean of the College of St. Mary in the Fields, since the archdeaconry of Norfolk was 'in our hand and custody for certain and legitimate reasons'; these reasons may have included illness of the archdeacon, Kerdeston, who died before 25 July 1326 (Reg. Ayremynne ff.81ᵛ–82).
[24] Blomefield (*Essay* 2, 477), lists this man, said to be rector of Hepworth [S], but gives no date for his service.
[25] Cnapeton served Archdeacon William de Cnapeton and his successor, John de Fenton.

APPENDIX IV

Religious Houses, Colleges, Friaries and Hospitals in Norwich Diocese, 1299–1500

This list of religious houses, colleges, friaries and hospitals does not include those which had ceased to exist before the fourteenth century or were not founded until the sixteenth century. Dates of foundation or dissolution are given only if they fall within these limits. Hospitals are listed separately, after the list of religious houses, colleges and friaries. In addition to the episcopal registers, the sources listed on pp. viii–ix in volume 1 (especially Knowles & Hadcock), and those cited in the notes, the following were consulted:

Gilchrist, Roberta and Marilyn Oliva. *Religious Women in Medieval East Anglia.* Norwich 1993.

Morgan (Chibnall), Marjorie M. 'The Suppression of the Alien Priories', *History* 26 (1942), 204–12.

Page, William, editor. *The Victoria History of the County of Norfolk.* 1901–6.

——. *The Victoria History of the County of Suffolk.* 1907–11.

Power, Eileen. *Medieval English Nunneries c.1275 to 1535.* 1922.

Prescott, Elizabeth. *The English Medieval Hospital, 1050–1640.* 1992.

Tanner, Thomas. *Notitia Monastica.* 1744.

Finally, for religious houses in Suffolk, the excellent volumes of Suffolk Charters published by Boydell are invaluable.

Religious Houses, Colleges and Friaries

Acre, Castle [N]. St Mary and Ss Peter and Paul priory of Cluniac monks. Alien dependency of Lewes [Susx.] until 1351 × 74, then independent.

Acre, West [N]. St Mary and All Saints priory of Augustinian canons. Maintained a school.

Aldeby [N]. St Mary priory of Benedictine monks. Small cell of Norwich cathedral priory.

Alnesbourn [S]. Blessed Virgin Mary priory of Augustinian canons. Appropriated to Woodbridge priory (*q.v.*) ca. 1466.

Attleborough [N]. Secular college of the Holy Cross in the church of St Mary, founded 1405 for a master and four chaplains.

Babwell, *see* Bury St Edmunds

Bacton, *see* Bromholm

Battisford [S]. Knights Hospitallers preceptory.

Beck College, *see* Norwich

Beeston Regis [N]. St Mary (of Mt Carmel) priory of Augustinian canons. May have maintained a school.

Binham [N]. St Mary priory of Benedictine monks, cell of St Alban's [Herts.].

Blackborough [N]. St Mary and St Katherine priory of Benedictine nuns.

Blakeney [N] (*alias* Snitterly). Carmelite friary founded 1304 × 16.

Blakenham, Great [S]. Grange of the Benedictine monks of Bec-Hellouin, associated with Ogbourne St George [Wilts.]. Dissolved ca. 1415, granted to Eton College in 1441.

Blythburgh [S]. Blessed Virgin Mary priory of Augustinian canons, dependency of St Osyth [Esx.].

Bricett, Great [S]. St Leonard priory, cell of the Augustinian canons of St Léonard de Noblat, France. Dissolved ca. 1444 and granted to King's College, Cambridge.

Bromehill (Broomhill) [N]. Blessed Virgin Mary and St Thomas the Martyr priory of Augustinian canons.

Bromholm (Broomholm or Bacton) [N]. St Andrew priory of Cluniac monks, dependency of Cluny until after 1390, then denizen.

Bruisyard [S].

    Annunciation abbey[1] of Poor Clare nuns, founded 1364–7.

    Annunciation college of five secular clerks, moved from Campsey Ash in 1354. Dissolved 1366 and granted to the Poor Clare abbey.

Buckenham, Old [N]. St Mary, St James and All Saints priory of Augustinian canons. May have maintaned a school.

Bungay [S]. St Mary and Holy Cross priory of Benedictine nuns.

Burnham Norton [N]. Carmelite friary.

Burnham Overy, *see* Peterstone

Bury St Edmunds [S].

    Jesus College for seven secular priests, founded 1480–1.

    Franciscan friary, north of town at Babwell (or Babberwell).

    St Edmund abbey of Benedictine monks.

Butley [S]. Blessed Virgin Mary priory of Augustinian canons. Maintained a school.

Campsey Ash [S].

    Annunciation College.[2] Secular college founded 1347, attached to the priory (next); moved to Bruisyard (*q.v.*) 1354.

    Annunciation of the Blessed Virgin Mary priory of Augustinian nuns.

    Secular college founded 1390 for the chaplains of the priory.

Carbrooke [N]. Knights Hospitallers preceptory. Maintained a hospital.

Carrow [N]. St Mary and St John the Baptist priory of Benedictine nuns. Maintained a school.

Cavenham (*alias* Togrynd) [S]. Knights Templars Preceptory, suppressed 1308 × 12.

Chipley [S]. Blessed Virgin Mary priory of (three or four) Augustinian canons until 1468, when it was probably dissolved and granted to the college at Stoke-by-Clare (*q.v.*).

Chippenham [Cambs.]. Knights Hospitallers preceptory. Infirmary for members of the order, annexed to Carbrooke (*q.v.*) by 1489.

---

[1] For this foundation and its relationship to the secular college it succeeded, see A. F. C. Bourdillon, *The Order of Minoresses in England* (Manchester 1926), 22ff.

[2] *Ibid.*

Clare [S].
  Augustinian friary.
  See also Stoke-by-Clare
⟨Coddenham [S]. St Mary rectory was appropriated to Royston priory [Herts.];
  sometimes identified as a cell of Royston, but it was served by vicars and
  there is no sign of canons here.⟩
Coxford [N]. St Mary priory of Augustinian canons, founded in East Rudham
  [N] and moved in the 13th century several miles east of the village.
  Maintained a hospital at Boycodeswade.
Crabhouse [N]. Blessed Virgin Mary and St John the Evangelist priory of
  Augustinian nuns at Wiggenhall [N].
Creake, North [N]. St Mary de Pratis abbey of Augustinian canons.
Creeting [S].
  St Mary priory, a grange of the Benedictine monks of Bernay, France. Shared
  a prior with Everdon [Northants.] from 1327. Dissolved 1414, granted to
  Eton College 1462.
  St Olave priory, a grange of the Benedictine monks of Grestein, France.
  Dissolved 1347 × 1348 and the lands sold privately.[3]
Dalling, Field [N]. Grange of Cistercian monks of La Trinité, Savigny, France;
  dissolved in 1414.
Dammesende, *see* Hempton
Dereham, West [N]. Blessed Virgin Mary abbey of Premonstratensian canons.
Docking [N]. Grange of Benedictine monks of Ivry, France; dissolved in 1415
  and granted to Eton College.
Dodnash [S]. St Mary the Virgin priory of Augustinian canons in Bentley [S].
Dunwich [S].
  Franciscan friary.
  Dominican priory.
  Knights Templars preceptory, suppressed 1308 × 12 and granted to the
  Knights Hospitallers, who kept only a chaplain there.
  Priory or cell of Eye priory, lost to the sea *temp.* Edward I.
Eye [S]. St Peter priory of Benedictine monks. Alien cell of Bernay until 1385,
  then independent.
Fakenhamdam, *see* Hempton
Felixstowe, Walton St Felix [S]. Ss Peter and Paul priory, a cell of the
  Benedictine monks of Rochester.
Flitcham [N]. St Mary ad Fontes priory of Augustinian canons.
Flixton [S]. St Mary and St Katherine priory of Augustinian nuns.
Fordham [Cambs.]. St Peter and St Mary Magdalene priory of Gilbertine
  canons. Maintained a hospital for poor persons.
Gislingham [S]. Knights Templars, suppressed 1308 × 1312.
Gorleston [S]. Augustinian friary.
Haddiscoe [N]. Knights Templars, suppressed 1308 × 1312.
Haveringland, *see* Mountjoy
Heacham [N]. Grange of the Cluniac monks of Lewes.

---

[3] White identifies Sir Edmund de la Pole as the buyer (*Suffolk*, 232); Matthew shows that
the sale was part of an attempt to ransom the patron of Grestein, captured at Crécy
(*Norman Monasteries and their English Possessions*, 142n.).

Hempton (*alias* Fakenhamdam, Damnesende) [N]. St Stephen priory of Augustinian canons; founded as a hospital and maintained that ministry after becoming a priory.

Herringby [N]. St Ethelbert secular college founded 1447 for four priests; maintained a hospital for poor men.

Herringfleet [S]. St Olave and St Mary priory of Augustinian canons.

Hickling [N]. St Mary, St Augustine and All Saints priory of Augustinian canons.

Holy Sepulchre, *see* Thetford

Horsham St Faith [N]. St Mary the Virgin priory of Benedictine monks. Alien dependency of Conches until 1390, then independent.

Horstead [N]. Grange of the Benedictine nuns of La Trinité, Caen; dissolved in 1414 and granted to King's College, Cambridge.

Hoxne [N]. St Edmund priory, a cell of the Benedictine monks of Norwich cathedral priory. Maintained a school.

Hulme, *see* St Benet's, Hulme

Ingham [N]. House or college of the Holy Trinity and All Saints, of Trinitarian canons, founded 1355–60 in the parish church.

Ipswich [S].
  Carmelite friary.
  Dominican priory.
  Franciscan friary.
  Holy Trinity priory of Augustinian canons.
  Ss Peter and Paul priory of Augustinian canons.

Ixworth [S]. Blessed Mary priory of Augustinian canons.

Kersey [S]. St Mary the Virgin and St Anthony priory of Augustinian canons. Dissolved before 1444 and granted to King's College, Cambridge.

Kirkscroft [N]. St Mary the Virgin priory, moved to Horsham, *q.v.*

Langley [N]. Blessed Virgin Mary abbey of Premonstratensian canons.

Leiston [S]. Blessed Virgin Mary abbey of Premonstratensian canons. Moved inland to new site ca. 1365, and the old site was treated as a cell.

Lessingham [N]. Called a priory, actually a grange of the Benedictine monks of Bec-Hellouin, associated with Ogbourne Priory. Dissolved 1415 and granted to King's College, Cambridge.

Letheringham [S]. Blessed Virgin Mary priory, three or four Augustinian canons. Dependency of Ss Peter and Paul priory at Ipswich.

Lyng [N]. Priory, moved to Thetford St George, *q.v.*

Lynn [N].
  Augustinian friary.
  Carmelite friary.
  Dominican priory.
  Franciscan friary.
  Friars of the Sack friary, dissolved 1307 × 1314.
  St Margaret's priory, a cell of the Benedictine monks of Norwich cathedral priory.

Marham [N]. St Mary, St Barbara and St Edmund abbey of Cistercian nuns, incorporated with Waverley abbey [Surrey].

Massingham, Great [N]. St Mary and St Nicholas priory of Augustinian canons. Also a hospital; became a cell of West Acre priory in 1476.

Mendham [S]. St Mary priory of Cluniac monks, dependency of Castle Acre
until 1351 × 74, then independent.
Mettingham [S], Mettingham Castle. St Mary, St Andrew and All Saints secular
college, moved in 1394 from Norton Subcourse, *q.v.* Maintained a school.
Modney, Modeney [N], in Hilgay parish. Cell of the Benedictine monks of
Ramsey abbey [Hunts.].
Molycourt, Mullicourt [N], in Outwell parish. St Mary de Bello Loco priory of
Benedictine monks. Became a cell of Ely cathedral in 1449.
Mountjoy [N], in Haveringland parish. St Mary, St Michael and St Laurence
priory of Augustinian canons.
Narford [N]. Cell of Augustinian canons of nearby West Acre, maintaining a
chapel of St Thomas à Becket.
Normansburgh, Norman's Burrow, Norman's Barrow [N]. St Mary the Virgin
and St John the Evangelist priory in South Raynham parish. Founded for
Augustinian canons but became a cell of Cluniac monks of Castle Acre.
Became independent 1351 × 74.
Norton Subcourse [N]. St Mary, St Andrew and All Saints secular college,
moved from Raveningham (*q.v.*) in 1387, then moved again to Mettingham
Castle (*supra*) in 1394. Maintained a school.
Norwich [N][4]
Colleges
⟨Beck or St Thomas Martyr secular college.⟩[5]
Carnary college of St John Evangelist, secular college founded in 1316,
adjoining the charnel chapel. May have maintained a school.
Chantry college at the bishop's palace, subject to the cathedral priory;
dissolved in 1449.
St Mary in the Fields secular college of prebends, chaplains and choristers.
Friaries
Augustinian friary. Maintained a school of philsophy.
Carmelite friary.
Dominican priory.
Franciscan friary.
Friary of the Pied Friars of Blessed Mary, probably dissolved 1307.
Friary of the Friars of the Sack, dissolved 1307.
Monastic houses
Holy Trinity cathedral priory of Benedictine monks.
St Giles priory, founded 1310 when the hospital brothers became Augus-
tinian canons.
St Leonard's priory of Benedictine monks, a cell of the cathedral priory.
Orford [S]. Augustinian friary.
Pentney [N]. Holy Trinity, St Mary the Virgin and St Mary Magdalene (*alias* St
Mary de Insula) priory of Augustinian canons. Maintained a school for
poor boys.

[4] For the religious houses of Norwich, see particularly N. Tanner, *Church in Norwich*, and
White, *Norfolk*, 108–120.
[5] Knowles and Hadcock state that a secular college of as many as 24 priests was founded
here ca. 1350 by the master of Beck hospital (249, 433); but N. Tanner points out that the
only source for this is Blomefield (*Church in Norwich*, 18n.), and it seems unlikely that no
medieval references to so large a community would have survived.

Peterstone [N]. St Peter priory of Augustinian canons in Burham Overy. Also a hospital until annexed to Walsingham priory in 1449.

Raveningham [N]. St Andrew secular college, founded 1337 × 1344,[6] moved to Norton Subcourse (*q.v.*) in 1387.

Raynham, *see* Normansburgh

Redlingfield [S]. Blessed Virgin Mary and St Andrew priory of Benedictine nuns. Maintained a school.

Reydon [S], *see* Wangford

Rudham, East [N], *see* Coxford

Rumburgh [S]. St Michael priory, a cell of the Benedictine monks of St Mary abbey, York.

Rushworth, Rushford [N]. St John the Evangelist secular college founded 1341–2. Grammar school was added in 1490.

St Benet's, Hulme [N]. St Benet's abbey of Benedictine monks.

St Edmund, *see* Bury St Edmunds

St Faith, *see* Horsham

St Laurence, *see* Mountjoy

St Olave, *see* Herringfleet

St Sepulchre, *see* Thetford Holy Sepulchre

St Winwaloe, *see* Wereham

Sheringham [N]. All Saints priory, a cell of the Augustinian canons of Notley abbey [Bucks.]; destitute in 1345, canons withdrawn by 1500.

Shouldham [N]. Holy Cross and the Blessed Virgin Mary priory of Gilbertine canons and nuns. Maintained a school.

Sibton [S]. Blessed Virgin Mary abbey of Cistercian monks. Maintained a hospital.

Slevesholm [N], in Methwold parish. St Mary priory, a cell of the Cluniac monks of Castle Acre.

Snape [S]. St Mary priory, a dependency of the Benedictine monks of St John's, Colchester.

Spinney [Cambs.], in Wicken parish. St Mary and the Holy Cross priory, of Augustinian canons until 1449, then a cell of the Benedictine monks of Ely.

Sporle [N]. St Mary priory, a cell or grange of the Benedictine monks of St Florent-sur-Saumer. Dissolved 1414 × 24, granted to Eton College in 1440.

Stoke-by-Clare [S]. St John the Baptist priory, alien dependency of the Benedictine monks of Bec-Hellouin until 1395, then denizen. Converted to a secular college in 1415; the college maintained a school.

Stow, Stow Hill, Stove [N], in Paston parish. Grange of the Cluniac monks of Castle Acre.

Sudbury [S].
Dominican priory.
St Bartholomew priory, a cell of the Benedictine monks of Westminster.
St Gregory secular college, founded 1375.

Thetford [N & S].
Augustinian friary, assumed care of hospital of St John in 1387.[7]
Dominican priory, received the hospital called Domus Dei in 1347.

[6] See **23**; Knowles and Hadcock place the foundation in 1350.
[7] Or perhaps 1413: see Knowles and Hadcock, 244, 398.

Holy Sepulchre priory of Augustinian canons.

St George priory of Benedictine nuns, allied to Bury St Edmunds.

St Mary alien priory of Cluniac monks.

St Mary secular college at Bailey End, founded *temp.* Edward I.

Thirling [Cambs.], in Upwell parish. Cell or (probably) grange of Ixworth priory.

Thompson, Thomeston [N]. Blessed Virgin Mary and All Saints secular college, in the church of St Martin, founded 1349.[8]

Toft Monks [N]. St Margaret priory or cell of the Benedictine monks of St-Pierre, Préaux, Lisieux diocese. Dissolved in 1415, granted to Witham priory [Som.], then in 1462 to King's College, Cambridge.

Togrynd, *see* Cavenham

Walsingham, Little [N].

Franciscan friary, maintained a hospice for pilgrims.

St Mary priory of Augustinian canons.

Walton St Felix, *see* Felixstowe

Wangford [S]. St Mary (and Ss Peter and Paul) priory of Cluniac monks, moved here from Reydon. Dependency of Thetford St Mary.

Well Hall, Welle in Gayton [N]. Cell in Gayton parish, of the Benedictine monks of St Etienne abbey, Caen. Associated with their cell at Panfield [Esx.]. Dissolved in 1415, granted to St Stephen at Westminster in 1469.

Welnetham, *see* Whelnetham

Wendling [N]. Blessed Virgin Mary abbey of Premonstratensian canons.

Wereham [N]. St Winwaloe priory, a cell of the Benedictine monks of Montreuil, France. Sold in 1321, granted to Dereham abbey in 1336.

Weybourne [N]. St Mary and All Saints priory, a cell of the Augustinian canons of West Acre until 1314, independent thereafter.

Weybridge [N], in Acle parish. St Mary priory of Augustinian canons.

Whelnetham, Great [S]. Priory of the Crosiers, or Crutched Friars, in the chapel of St Thomas the Martyr. Dependency of their London convent.

Wiggenhall, *see* Crabhouse

Wingfield [S]. St Mary, St John the Baptist and St Andrew secular college, in the parish church of St Andrew, founded 1362.

Witchingham, Great [N]. Grange of the Cluniac monks of Longueville, associated to Newton Longville [Bucks.]; dissolved ca. 1414, granted to New College, Oxford, in 1460.

Woodbridge [S]. Blessed Virgin Mary priory of Augustinian canons.

Wormegay [N]. Blessed Virgin Mary, Holy Cross and St John the Evangelist priory of Augustinian canons; became a cell of Pentney 1468.

Wretham, West [N]. Grange of the Benedictine monks of Conches, associated with Wooten Wawen [Warw.]; probably dissolved or sold in the 15th century.

Wymondham [N]. St Mary the Virgin priory, a cell of the Benedictine monks of St Alban [Herts.], until 1449, then independent.

Yarmouth [N].

Cell of Augustinian friars?[9]

[8] See **16**.

[9] Uncertain: see Knowles and Hadcock, 245.

Carmelite friary.

Franciscan friary.

Dominican priory.

St Nicholas priory, a cell of the Benedictine monks of Norwich cathedral priory, with parochial jurisdiction over the town.

Hospitals

Medieval hospitals provided temporary hospitality for travellers, long-term shelter for the sick and aged, and charitable refuge for the (deserving) poor. They were often founded to secure the prayers of their residents for the souls of the founder and other benefactors; many were apparently informally organized and inadequately endowed, and thus soon disappeared. Hospitals in the 14th and 15th centuries were less well-documented than other religious establishments, so that it is not certain when some of the following ceased to exist or were incorporated to other nearby hospitals, almshouses, or religious communities.

Beccles [S]. St Mary Magdalene, for lepers.

Beck [N] in Billingford parish. St Thomas the Martyr, for poor pilgrims and wayfarers. Said to have founded Beck College in Norwich, q.v.

Boycodeswade [N]. St Andrew. Attached to Coxford Priory.

Bungay [S]. Ss John and Mary (possibly Magdalene).

Bury St Edmunds[10] [S].

St John the Evangelist, alias Domus Dei, for the poor, aged and infirm. Dependency of the abbey, with three or more chantry priests.

St Nicholas, originally for lepers, later for poor men. Dependency of the abbey, but the brothers had the right to elect their master.

St Peter, primarily for old, sick, or leprous priests, but admitted other infirm poor. Dependency of the abbey.

St Petronilla, alias St Parnel, originally for leprous women, later for the poor. Dependency of the abbey.

St Saviour, primarily for old and sick priests. Dependency of the abbey.

St Stephen. Dependency of the abbey.

Almshouse, founded around 1480 by College of Jesus.

Carbrooke [N]. St John the Baptist. Attached to the Preceptory.

Castle Rising [N]. Lepers.

Choseley [N]. St Lazarus, for lepers. Dependency of Burton Lazars [Leics.], gone by 1428.

Clare [S]. Almshouse, founded 1462.

Croxton [N], in Rockland deanery. Domus Dei, dependency of Thetford Domus Dei.

Dunwich [S].

St James, originally for lepers, later for the poor sick. Staffed by sisters.

Maison Dieu or Holy Trinity.

[10] For these foundations see *Charters of the Medieval Hospitals of Bury St Edmunds*, ed. C. Harper-Bill, Suffolk Charters 14 (Woodbridge 1994).

Eye [S]. St Mary Magdalene, originally for lepers, later for the poor sick. Not attached to the priory.

Fordham [Cambs.]. St Peter and St Mary Magdalene, for poor persons. Attached to the priory.

Gaywood[11] [N].

Lazar-house, for lepers.

St Mary Magdalene, for a prior and 12 brothers and sisters, to include lepers and the sick.

Gorleston [S].

Ss Mary and Nicholas (later St James?), originally for lepers, then for the sick poor.

St John the Baptist.

Hadleigh [S]. Almshouse, founded 1497.

Hardwick [N]. St Laurence, for lepers. Last reference was in 1339, dissolved before 1350.

Hautbois, Great [N]. St Mary or Domus Dei, for wayfarers and the poor. Dependency of Horning, *infra*.

Heacham [N]. Leper hospital. Possibly attached to Heacham grange.

Hempton [N]. St Stephen. Attached to the priory.

Herringby [N]. God's House, for poor men. Founded 1447, dependency of the college.

Hingham [N]. Almshouse, founded 1483.

Horning [N]. St James, for the poor and wayfarers. Dependency of St Benet's, Hulme.

Horsham [N]. Attached to Horsham St Faith Priory.

Ickburgh [N], in the part of the parish called Newbridge. Ss Mary and Laurence, originally for lepers, later for wayfarers. In the care of Augustinian friars by 1449.

Ipswich [S].

St James, for lepers. Administratively united to St Mary Magdalene in the 14th century.

St Leonard, for lepers and the sick.

St Mary Magdalene, for lepers. Administratively united to St James in the 14th century.

Langwade [N]. Lepers. Dissolved after 1380.

Lynn [N], *see* also Gaywood; Setchey.

Almshouses by St James chapel, founded before 1415.

Cowgate. Lepers. Founded by 1352, dissolved after 1432.

St John the Baptist, for poor men and women. Dependency of the priory.[12]

West Lynn. Lepers. Dissolved sometime after 1432.

Massingham, Great [N]. Ss Mary and Nicholas. Attached to the priory.

Newbridge, *see* Ickburgh

Norwich [N], *see* also Sprowston.

Danyel's or St Stephen's Almshouses. Founded 1418 in St Stephen parish.

Garzon's Almshouse. In St Benedict parish.

[11] Knowles & Hadcock *s.v.* 'King's Lynn'.
[12] But in the bishop's advowson (Reg. Ayremynne ff.40ᵛ, 42ᵛ).

God's House outside St Giles's Gate, or Newport Gate, originally for lepers, then the sick poor.

God's House in St Giles parish. Almshouse.

God's House, St Margaret, in the parish of St Margaret Westwick, for the poor.

Hildebrand's, or Hildebrand Lemercer's, or St Mary, or Ivy Hall, for a master, brothers and homeless poor.

St Benedict, outside Westwick and St Benet's gate, originally for lepers, later the poor.

St Giles, or Holy Trinity, the Glorious Virgin, Blessed Anne and Blessed Giles, near Bishopsgate, for poor and infirm clerks and laymen. After 1310 the brothers became Augustinian canons.

St Leonard, outside Fyebridge or Magdalene gate, for lepers. Founded by 1335.

Ss Mary and Clement, outside St Augustine's gate, originally for lepers, later for the sick.

St Paul, or Norman's, or Normanspitel, in St Paul parish, for poor aged men and women; after ca. 1429, only women. Founded by a monk of the cathedral priory; later staffed by sisters.

St Saviour in Coslany. Last reference may be in 1305.

St Stephen, outside Needham gate, for lepers. Dependency of Horsham St Faith priory.

Orford [S].

St John the Baptist, founded before 1390.

St Leonard, for lepers; disappeared after 1320.

Peterstone [N]. St Peter, in Burnham Overy parish. Probably in the priory until 1449.

Racheness, Rackness [N]. St Bartholomew in South Acre,[13] for lepers. Dependency of Castle Acre priory, dissolved by 1350.

Ringstead, *see* Choseley

Rushworth, Rushford [N]. St John the Baptist, for wayfarers and guests of the college, founded 1492.

Setchey [N], on Hardwick Dam (now in South Lynn). Lepers. Dissolved after 1432.

Sibton [S]. For wayfarers and the poor. At the abbey gate, attached to the abbey.

Snoring, Little [N]. Lepers. Dissolved after 1380.

Somerton, West [N]. St Leonard, for lepers. Dependency of Butley Priory [S], probably dissolved in or before 1399.

Sprowston [N]. St Mary Magdalene, outside Magdalene Gate or Fyebridge, Norwich, originally for a master, brother and lepers.

Sudbury [S].

Jesus Christ and the Blessed Virgin Mary.

St Leonard, originally for lepers, later the sick or aged. Founded 1372.

St Sepulchre.[14] Dependency of Stoke-by-Clare priory. Possibly dissolved before 1383, becoming a free chapel.

---

[13] The site is now known as Bartholomew's Hills (cf. Faden, sheet 2, and White, *Norfolk*, 383, for earlier versions).

[14] See C. Harper-Bill and R. Mortimer, eds., *Stoke by Clare Cartulary, BL Cotton Appx. xxi* (Suffolk Charters 1982–84), I, **60–64**; III, 23.

Swaffham [N]. Hospice for travellers. Dependency of Sawtry abbey [Hunts.].

Thetford [N & S].

Domus Dei, for poor men. Refounded by the Dominican friars in 1347.

St John the Evangelist, originally for lepers, then the poor. Transferred to the Augustinian friars in 1387.[15]

St Margaret, for lepers and poor men.

Ss Mary and Julian, for poor pilgrims and wayfarers.

St Mary Magdalene, for lepers. Incorporated the earlier hospital of St John the Baptist.

Thurlow, Great [S]. St James. Alien dependency of the hospital of Hautpays, France. Dissolved in 1414.

Walsingham, Little [N].

Leper hospital, founded before 1486.

Hospice for poor pilgrims, founded before 1347 and attached to the Franciscan friary.

Walsoken [N]. Holy Trinity, almshouse for a master, chaplain, brothers and sisters.

Westwade, *see* Wymondham

Wicken [Cambs.]. St John, for poor men. Founded 1321, attached to Spinney priory until 1449, then to Ely cathedral.

Wymondham [N]. God and St Mary, for lepers. Dependency of Burton Lazars [Leics.]. At Westwade chapel, on a bridge east of the village, the brothers begged alms of travellers to support the hospital.

Yarmouth [N].

North Gate, two leper hospitals, probably one for men and one for women.

St Mary, Blessed Virgin for a warden, chaplains, brothers and sisters.

Town Hospital. Founded 1386.

[15] See Thetford Augustinian friary, above.

INDEX OF PERSONS AND PLACES

The numbers below are for entries in the calendar, with two exceptions. References to the Introduction are shown as pp. xi–xxxiv, and the numbers which follow 'App.' are pages in the appendices. *Addenda* are on p. viii of this volume.

A

Abdeyth, John, of South Cove, rector of Shipmeadow, 542
Aberforde, William de, rector of Syderstone, 1812
Abergwili collegiate church, Powys, 1622n.
Abingdon abbey, Berks., 292
Abingdon, Maynard de, vicar of Dersingham, 80–1
Abraham, John, rector of Brumstead, 1830
Acle [N], App. 165
Acre, Castle [N], 304, App. 159
  vicar, 1288
  priory [N] (alien), advowsons, 69*, 224, 386, 648, 713, 829, 835, 843, 898, 905, 1083, 1095, 1101, 1111, 1288n., 1334, 1351, 1418, 1447, 1538n., 1571, 1668, 1694, 1699, 1714*, 1799, 1805, 1882, 1899, App. 120, 159, 163–4, 168
Acre, South [N], hospital, App. 168
  rectors, 983, 1910
Acre, West [N]
  All Saints, App. 147
  priory, 308, 482, 484, 512, 866, 890, 925–6, 1027, 1058, 1078, 1084, 1098, 1128, 1250, 1275, 1489, 1506, 1633, 1671, 1827, App. 147–8, 159, 162–3, 165
  cells & dependencies, App. 164, 168
  prior elected, p. xxxi, 862
  school, App. 159
  See also Westacr'
Acre, John de, dean of Carlford, vicar of Coddenham, rector of South Elmham All Saints & of Gaywood, 17, 23, 225, 803, 839, 1749–50, 1815
Acton [S], 109
Acton Reygner, Richard de, vicar of Gazeley, 628
Acura, Akewra, John de, of Ingoldmels, prebendary in the College of St Mary in the Fields, 140
  John, rector of a moiety of Great Wreningham & of Framlingham Pigot, 1124, 1642–3
  Simon, chancellor of the College of St Mary in

the Fields & vicar of Wroxham, 847, 1482, 1550
Adderbury, Oxon., rector, 1667
Addington, Little, Nthn., 114, 405
Adyngton, John, *see* Houghton, John
Aisterby, Robert de, dean of Breckles, 1731n.
Akenham [N], rector, 1345
Akenham [S], 821, 1229, 1464
Akewra, *see* Acura
Akke, John, rector of Milden, 1480
Albot, Henry, rector of a moiety of Rockland Minor & vicar of Marham, 1633–4
Alburgh [N], rectors, 148, 549, 1254
Alby [N], rector, 1045
Alby, Robert de, vicar of Hanworth, 1172
Aldborough [N], rector, 258
Aldbury, Herts., rectors, 1521
Aldeburgh with Hazelewood chapel [S], vicar, 1556
Aldeby [N], App. 145, 159
Aldeby, Walter de, M., dean of Ipswich & fellow of Trinity Hall, 1436
  William de, rector of Felthorpe, vicar of Worstead & rector of Alderford, 251–2, 1738–9
Alderford [N], rectors, 1738–9
Aldham [S], rector, 557
Aldham, Nicholas de, rector of Hengrave & Whatfield, 1354–5, 1726
Aldhawe, John, of Toft Monks, rector of Windale, 863
Aldringham [S], App. 145
Alexander, Alexandr', William, *senior*, 1232, 1520
Aleyn, John, of Stanstead, rector of Wetheringsett, 260
  John, archdeacon of Suffolk, App. 154
  Peter, of Morningthorp, rector of Thwaite & a moiety of Taverham & Ashby, 1600–01, 1878, 1880
  William, of Weybourne, vicar of Binham, 950
Almot, Richard, vicar of Sibton 1525, 1881
Alnesbourn priory [S], acts dated from, 186–7
  prior, 1391*

Selsey, Suss., rector, 453

Seman, Bartholomew, of Halesworth, chaplain of Melles, 262

Semere, Richard de, vicar of Hindringham, 656

Sencler, Sancto Claro, Baldwin, of Wattisfield, 630

  Guy de, kt, 220, 1038, 1480

  Payne de, rector of Milden & Hargham, 219–20, 316

Serle, Robert, rector of Ilketshall St John, 1549

Setchey [N], chapel, 1094n.

  hospital, App. 168

Seton, John de, rector of Thwaite in Brooke deanery, 1600, 1906

Sewale, Roger, rector of Stratford St Mary, 341

Seward, Syward, John, of Middleton, rector of Hoo, 1374

  Thomas, vicar of Hempnall, 1399*

Seyer, Robert, rector of Stretham & Snailwell, 1542

Seyne, Richard, of Holkham, vicar of Watton, 1168

Sh- *see also* Sch-

Shadingfield [S], 393

  See also Schadnefeld

Shaftesbury, Dors., abbey, advowsons, 290

  St Rowaldus, rectors, 289–90

Shaftesbury, Shaftebury, John de, rector of Gaywood & South Elmham All Saints, 1562, 1749–50

Shanketon, Henry de, rector of Whittington, 566

Shardelow, Schardelowe, Agnes wife of John de, *senior*, 16

  Joan de, 16n.

  John de, *junior*, kt, 16, 1262, 1314n., 1617n., 1674, 1748

  John de, *senior*, kt, 16, 574, 822

  Thomas de, kt, 16, 1262, 1314n., 1617n., 1748, 1752

Sharp, Richard, of Fakenham, vicar of Hackford in Hingham deanery, 522, 1680

Sharrington [N], rector, 824

Shefford, Beds., 1839

Shelfanger [N] (*al.* Schelfangel)

  moiety of the Besewill family, rector, 345

  moiety of the Verdon family, rectors, 350, 436, 1204

Shelley [S], App. 146

Shelton [N]

  moiety of Langley abbey, rectors, 91–2, 374–5, 1779*

  moiety of Ralph de Hemenhale, rector, 850

Shelton, Schelton, Scheltone, Henry de, rector of a moiety of Brome, 1385n.

  John de, 191

  Ralph de, *junior*, 1844*, 1856

  Ralph de, *senior*, kt, 800, 945, 1752, 1755, 1844*, 1856–7

  Thomas de, 538, 1809, 1852

Shene, Adam, of Peasenham, vicar of Cransford, 1661, 1736*

Shenfield, Esx., rectors, 267

Shereford [N], 164–5, 531

  rector, 1076

  See also Schirford

Sheriff, *see* Shyrreve

Sheringham [N], App. 146

  priory, App. 164

Sherman, William, of Barton Bendish, chaplain of Hilborough St Margaret, 180

Shernborne [N], 288n.

  vicars, 632, 1046, 1636

  See also Scharneburn

Shimpling, unspecified, 341, 1735

Shimpling [N], rector, 838

  See also Schimpling

Shingham [N], 916n., 1319n.

  rectors, 99, 1316

Shipden [N] (*al.* Cromer)

  lawsuit concerning the advowson, 1788

  rectors, 1043, 1591, 1781

Shipeden, Shippeden, Schippeden, Geoffrey son of Alan de, 200, 1126

  Richard de, rector of Overstrand, 200

Shipmeadow [S], rectors, 74–5, 542

Shirlok, William, proctor, 214

Shirre, John, chaplain of Molton manor in Frampton & rector of West Lynn, 1745–6

Shortwode, John, vicar of a moiety of Scarning, 1414

Shotesham [N], 779, 1237, 1448, 1703n.

  All Saints, Low Shotesham, 981n.

    vicar, 989

  St Botulph, *see* St Mary

  St Martin, 981n.

    rectors, 1007, 1523

  St Mary and Saint Botulph, 981n.

    vicars, 981, 1703

  See also Chattisham; Shottisham

Shotesham, Simon de, rector of Little Hautbois, 1381

  See also Schatesham

Shott, Robert, of Blaxhall, vicar of Sudbourne-with-Orford, 1503

Shottisham [S], rectors, 616, 1794

  See also Chattisham; Shotesham

Shouldham [N], App. 146

  priory, App. 164

    advowsons, 166, 1363, 1499, 1641, App. 146

    appropriations to, p. xxv, 40, 42, 48, 1249n.

    school, App. 164

Shouldham Thorpe, Garbois-Thorpe [N], 429n., App. 146

  See also Schouldham

Shudecampes, Robert de, rector of Swanton Novers, 1803

Shyrreve, Nigel, rector of Wicklewood St Andrew, 1088

INDEX OF SUBJECTS

The numbers below are for entries in the calendar, with two exceptions: references to the Introduction are shown as pp. xi–xxxiv (of Volume I), and the numbers which follow 'App.' are pages in the appendices (in Volume II). Cross-references to persons and places are to those names in the preceding index.

A

Abbesses and Abbots, *see* Religious Superiors

Acolytes
  incompetent to hold vicarages, 263n.
  instituted to rectories, 63*, 90, 163, 240, 257, 264, 325, *et passim*

Accounts, 15, 18, 44

Advowsons, *see* Benefices; Bishop; Chantries; Churches; Hospitals; Knights; Licences; Nobles; Religious Houses; Women

Agriculture, p. xiii
  buildings, *see* Barns; Granges; Outbuildings; Stables

Alien priories, *see* Religious Houses

Alms, 11

Almshouses, p. xxvii, *and see* Hospitals, *below*

Altars
  cathedral, 1, 2, 4, 6–7, 12*–13, 53, 55
  portable, p. xxviii, 1754

Alteragium, 1, 14–15, 18, 20*, 42, 50, 420

Animals, 1, 15, 18, 20*, 42

Appeals, *see* Pope

Apples, *see* Fruit

Appropriations, *see* Benefices

Archbishop, *see* Canterbury

Archdeaconries, pp. xi, xiv, 413*, 1640*, App. 142, 144, 149–54, 158n.

Archdeacons, pp. xiv, xxvii, xxix, xxxi, xxxiin., 66*, 72, 76–77, 96*, 105, 209, 216, 233, 254, 256, 268, 276, 277n., 293, 367, 389, 408, 413*, 444, 454, 472–6, 478, 481, 483–9, 498, 518, 521, 592, 605, 640, 653, 678, 767, 816, 828, 862, 1290, 1346, 1365/6, 1377–8, 1396, 1452, 1557, 1577, 1579, 1592, 1639, 1715, 1732*, 1747, 1748, 1759–60, 1767, 1796, 1872–3*, 1879, 1894, App. 144, 149–58
  collations of, 237, 300*, 441, 1050–1, 1263, 1560, App. 144, 149–54
  commissary of, 413*
  house of, 1815, App. 149
  incomes and procurations of, 50, 53, 413*, App. 149, 151

oath of obedience of, 1760, App. 149
officials of, p. xxvii, 66*, 72, 75, 77, 81, 96*, 105, 108, 143, 209, 212, 216, 232–3, 236, 238–9, 246, 254, 267–8, 273, 284–5, 293, 321, 327, 336, 346, 377, 389, 407, 443, 456, 767, 828, 1378, 1430, 1579, 1592, 1638, 1817, 1871, App. 157–8
  commissary of, 1569, App. 158
  seal of, 413*
  procurations of, *see* incomes *above*
  resignations and removals of, 1050, 1263, App. 144, 149–54

Assessment, 17, 19, 21–2, 24, 28, 34, 36, 40–1, 43, 50–3, 57, 419*, 474–7, 1607, 1675, 1680, 1702–3, 1713
  See also Tenths, royal

Assise of darrein presentment, 248

Attorneys, p. xxv, 30*, 256, 1048, 1183, 1353, 1577, 1742, 1789, App. 142

B

Barns, 1, 14, 20*, 53, 131n., 709n., *and see* Outbuildings; Stables

Bees, Beehives and Beeswax, 18, 20*, 42

Benefices
  admission, *see* induction, *below*
  advowsons
    devolved to the bishop, 4, 6, 12*, 150, 307, 468, 893*, 923, 935, 1281, 1287–8, 1304, 1308, 1329, 1346, 1409, 1441, 1443–4, 1533–4, 1538*, 1554, 1572*, 1596, 1603, 1645–6, 1652, 1655, 1686, 1765
    disputed, 6, 12*–13, 248, 300*n., 341, 413*, 431, 433, 440n., 468, 630, 1231, 1277, 1445, 1588–90, 1630*, 1785, 1787–8, 1844*, 1855–7, App. 150–1, 153–4
    given as gift, 1617n., 1663n.
  appropriations of, pp. xiii, xxiv–xxv, xxvii–xxviii, 1–8, 12*–16, 27–9, 34–6, 41–2, 43, 45–57, 115, 308n., 419*, 867n., 1288n., 1707*, 1822n., 1823n.
    by papal authority, pp. xxv, xxvii, 17–24,

26, 40, 42, 50–51, 54, 57, 420, 1358*, 1744

collation, letters of, p. xiii, 169*, 237, 241, 244–5, 259, 283, 329

See also Archdeacons; Benefices, advowsons; Deaneries

cure of souls, p. xxvi, 1554*n.*, 1913*n.*, App. 144, 146*n.*

donatives, App. 145–8

exchanges of, inside diocese, p. xxxii, 59*–60*, 64*–65*, 68–69*, 78–9, 82–3, 85–6, 91–2, 116–19, 122–3, 125–6, 133–4, 145–6, 151–2, 157–8, 160–1, 164–5, 170–3, 175*–6, 191–2, 195–6, 213–14, 219–20, 222–3, 241–4, 249–52, 263–6, 275, 308, 310, 313–14, 318–19, 334–5, 351–4, 363–4, 370–1, 374–7, 380–1, 385–6, 396–7, 411–12, 415–16, 426–7, 432, 434, 446–7, 465–6, 478–9, 483–4, 507–8, 1354–5, 1360, 1362, 1382–3, 1419–20, 1423–4, 1491–2, 1547–8, 1633–4, 1642–3, 1659–60, 1670–1, 1693–8, 1701–2, 1704–5, 1708–13, 1717–18, 1723–4, 1738–9, 1742–3, 1749–50, 1762–3, 1773–4, 1786, 1789, 1797–1802, 1827–8, 1833–4*, 1836–7, 1840–1, 1845–6, 1854, 1858, 1862–3, 1875–6, 1882–3, 1885–6, 1889–90, 1897–1902, 1912–3, App. 142–3, 150, 154

exchanges of, outside diocese, pp. xxvii, xxxii, 414, 439, 467, 555, 1166–7, 1263, 1447, 1484, 1504, 1521, 1542, 1565, 1668–9, 1780, 1790–1, 1826, 1842–3, 1891–2, App. 144, 152–3

by commission of Bateman or his ministers, 66*, 71, 76, 108, 188, 193, 209, 232, 238, 267, 273, 284, 321, 327, 336, 346, 407, 443, 453, 1289, 1569, 1638, 1666, 1759, 1817, 1871

by commission of another, 74–5, 80–1, 104–5, 142–3, 207–8, 211–12, 217–18, 235–6, 255–6, 289–90, 332–3, 367–9, 377, 389, 402–4, 405, 449, 451, 455–6, 1349–50, 1371–2, 1394–5, 1429–30, 1580–3, 1594–5, 1622–4, 1626–7, 1684–5, 1689–92, 1745–6, 1809–10, 1813–14, 1820–1

farm of, 10*, 28–29, 34–36, 43, 360*n.*, 1466*

first fruits of, *see* Bishop

induction to, pp. xiii, xxvi, xxxi, 66*, 1358*, *et passim*

reserved to another bishop, 75, 333

institutions to, pp. xxvi, xxviii, 59*, *et passim*

letters of, 280, 462*, 1256*, 1470, 1618, 1707*, 1737, 1742, 1769, 1779*, 1858

not registered, 1604*n.*, 1647, 1708, 1807*n.*, 1822, 1859*n.*, App. 142–4, 148

sede vacante, pp. xxxi–xxxii, 1385*n.*, 1398*n.*, 1491*n.*, 1517*n.*, 1611*n.*, 1713*n.*, 1718*n.*, 1799*n.*, 1817*n.*, App. 142

nominations to, by bishop or his ministers, 4–

6, 8, 12*, 17, 19, 21–22, 24, 40, 57, 137, 150, 152, 155, 205*, 249, 307, 378*, 414, 416, 419*, 424*, 462*–3, 479, 617, 637, 660, 752, 755*n.*, 756, 769, 778, 803, 816, 860, 866, 886, 893*, 896, 904, 914, 923, 935, 961–2, 981, 1037, 1065, 1096, 1242, 1250, 1289, 1292, 1303, 1326, 1343–4, 1399*, 1406, 1499, 1543, 1572*, 1582, 1599, 1618, 1641, 1677, 1722, 1774, 1823, 1864, 1868, 1914

by king, 62*

by lay person, 846, 1161

peculiar, App. 148

pluralism, pp. xiv, xxviii, 1509, 1544, 1554, 1913–14, App. 142–3, *and see* Law, Canon; Popes, dispensation

presentations to, pp. xiii, xxxi, 4–6, 8, 12*, 462*, 487, 566, 617, 638*n.*

provisions, *see* Popes

removal from, 1630*, 1632, 1736*, 1785, 1844*n.*, 1866, 1887, 1906, App. 153–4

resignations of, pp. xiii, xxx, xxxii, 36*n.*, 39, 47, 66*, 89, 99, 107*, 1761, 1796, *et passim*; *and see* exchanges, *above*

conditional, 1410, 1779*

united, pp. xiii, xxv, xxvii–xxviii, 44, 82*n.*, 144, 172*n.*, 193*n.*, 263*n.*, 309*, 315*n.*, 358*n.*, 373, 378*, 414*n.*, 419*, 496*n.*, 520*n.*, 526*n.*, 561*n.*, 615*n.*, 687*n.*, 730*n.*, 779*n.*, 795*n.*, 801*n.*, 863*n.*, 876*n.*, 910*n.*, 916*n.*, 921*n.*, 926*n.*, 953*n.*, 972*n.*, 981*n.*, 984*n.*, 1036*n.*, 1037*n.*, 1058*n.*, 1061*n.*, 1080*n.*, 1088*n.*, 1120*n.*, 1202*n.*, 1218*n.*, 1237*n.*, 1269*n.*, 1304*n.*, 1308*n.*, 1319*n.*, 1330*n.*, 1339*n.*, 1356*n.*, 1498*n.*, 1551*n.*, 1633, 1652*n.*, 1655*n.*, 1678*n.*, 1771*n.*, 1782*n.*, 1817*n.*, App. 146*n.*, 150*n.*

vacant by death, 90, 93, 100, 1571, 1577, 1584, 1602, 1605, 1625, 1628, 1631, 1641, 1647*, 1657, 1662, 1665, 1673, 1674, 1678, 1681, 1721, 1731, 1733, 1735, 1740–1, 1751–2, 1753, 1755, 1757–8, 1764, 1775, 1781–2, 1808, 1812, 1829, 1832, 1835, 1850, 1884, 1908, *and see* Black Death

See also Chantries; Parishes; Vicarages

Birettas, 237, 300*

Bishop

advowson of, p. xxvi, *et passim*

collation by, *see* Benefices

consecration of, p. xv

death of, pp. xiv, xvii, xxix, xxi*n.*, 58, 59*, 1918/9, *and see* Vacancy

dispensations of, *see* Dispensations

dispute with Bury St Edmunds, p. xvi, 300*n.*, 1305–6, 1535*, App. 153

election of, by cathedral priory, p. xiv, 58

first fruits owed to, pp. xxiii–xxiv, 3–5, 7–8, 16, 19, 22–24, 28, 34, 40, 45–46, 50, 52–53, 194, 419*–20, 424*n.*, 437, 1466*,